THE 8TH MOUNTAIN

How the Mountain of the Lord
Transforms and Empowers
Leaders to Influence the
7 Mountains of Culture

DR. BRUCE COOK

THE 8TH MOUNTAIN

How the Mountain of the Lord Transforms and Empowers Leaders to Influence the 7 Mountains of Culture

First Printing August 2017. Printed in the United States of America.

ISBN (print media): 978-1-939944-39-9

ISBN (eBooks): 978-1-939944-40-5

LCCN: 2017951363

To Contact the Author:

Dr. Bruce Cook

c/o KCIA

PMB #242, 4810 Point Fosdick Dr. NW

Gig Harbor, WA 98335

brucecook77@gmail.com

bruce.cook@8thmountain.com

"Who may climb the mountain of the LORD? Who may stand in his holy place? Only those whose hands and hearts are pure, who do not worship idols and never tell lies. They will receive the LORD's blessing and have a right relationship with God their savior. Such people may seek you and worship in your presence, O God of Jacob."

PSALM 24:3-6, NLT

DEDICATION

To my fellow mountaineers and co-founding members of the 8thMountain® team – John Anderson, JoAn Risdon, Rick Weir, and Ruth Lum – you're the best! www.8thmountain.com

To my friends Drs. Berin and Lisa Gilfillan and their dedicated team of media professionals at Good Shepherd Ministries International (GSMI) dba International School of Ministry (ISOM) www.isom.org – blessings and thank you!

To my many other friends in the Seven Mountains of Culture, I invite you to "Come up higher!"

To all those who are leading, serving, innovating and making a difference in the world – either locally, regionally, nationally or globally – I invite you to take this journey with us and join the 8thMountain.com community as IdeaLeaders, or in any other capacity or role you choose.

And to the Chief Architect, Creator, Sustainer and Supreme Being of the Universe and the 8thMountain – God the Father, God the Son and God the Holy Spirit – and the myriad of holy angels, living creatures, cloud of witnesses, and 24 elders who attend them day and night, crying with a loud voice, *"Holy, Holy, Holy is the Lord, who was, and is, and is to come!"*

"But throughout the history of these kingdoms, the God of heaven will be building a kingdom that will never be destroyed, nor will this kingdom ever fall under the domination of another. In the end it will crush the other kingdoms and finish them off and come through it all standing strong and eternal. It will be like the stone cut from the mountain by the invisible hand that crushed the iron, the bronze, the ceramic, the silver, and the gold. The great God has let the king know what will happen in the years to come. This is an accurate telling of the dream, and the interpretation is also accurate."

DANIEL 2:44-46 (MSG)

ACKNOWLEDGEMENTS

Thank you to all of those who have helped me with this endeavor, which at times seemed beyond my reach. Special thanks for editorial contributions and recognition— John Anderson, who co-wrote Chapters 1 and 20; Ruth Lum, who co-wrote Chapter 6; Lynn Hare, who co-wrote Chapters 12 and 19; Sylvia Blair, who co-wrote Chapters 14, 20 and 21; Dr. A.L. (Papa) Gill, who wrote chapter 16; and Dan Dean, who co-wrote Chapter 17. Thanks also to John Anderson, Lynn Hare and Ruth Lum for providing helpful comments and suggestions on the manuscript.

Special thanks to my amazing, anointed and powerful intercessors, the Right Hand Team, who prayed this book through conception, birthing pains and into being – Alexis Alexander, John Anderson, Chuck & Diane Bartle, Sylvia Blair, Dr. James Brewton, Jim Campbell, Dan Dean, Jayne Ferriss, Lynn Hare, Ruth Lum, Purity Munyi, Paul Nesbitt, Coraleen Parris, JoAn Risdon, Grant & Lauri Russell.

Thanks to many others who have inspired me on this journey, and whom I have learned from, who shall remain nameless – including the members of KCIA.

Thanks to my friends Dr. Lance Wallnau and Johnny Enlow for their pioneering work in teaching, speaking and writing on the 7 Mountains of Culture over the last decade or two, and to Bill Bright, Loren Cunningham, and Francis Schaeffer for being the progenitors of the 7 Mountains vision and mandate from heaven in August 1975 — 42 years ago.

Thanks to Dave Hodgson and Paladin Corp. for their marketing support in helping us launch 8thMountain.com®. Please visit their three websites:

- ASP Movement—www.aspmovement.org,
- Kingdom Investors Ministry— www.kingdominvestors.com.au
- Paladin Corporation— www.paladincorp.com.au

Thanks to my wife Caroline for her love, support, encouragement, friendship and prayers.

And finally, thanks to Holy Spirit who gave me the inspiration, revelation and assignment to write this book in January 2017 while I was in Washington, D.C., as well as the strength, courage and resources to finish it.

CONTENTS

ENDORSEMENTS

Dr. Bruce Cook is a prolific writer and researcher on essential topics regarding the Kingdom of God. His insight into the 8th Mountain Is an eye opener for any person truly interested in impacting the world. The theory and practicality contained in *The 8th Mountain* make this a workbook for any World Changer.

Ambassador Clyde Rivers

Ambassador at Large - Republic of Burundi, Africa
Founder and President, I Change Nations
www.ichangenations.org

Dr. Bruce Cook has given us a great book to help us increase our influence and ensure that we live a life of intimacy with God to have an impact on culture. In *The 8th Mountain,* Bruce reveals the DNA of personal and cultural influence by allowing us to go deep into the understanding of what God has for every influencer if they will scale the 8th Mountain. I highly recommend this book to anyone who wants to go deeper into the things of God. Well done, Bruce!

Os Hillman

Author, TGIF, Today God Is First, The Joseph Calling, and 12 other books
President, Marketplace Leaders and Change Agent Network
www.marketplaceleaders.org
https://todaygodisfirst.com/
http://www.mychangeagentnetwork.com

The 7 Mountains of Culture are well known to many Christian leaders and most understand that God's goal is for His Church to reach and influence those high places for His Kingdom. Dr. Bruce, in this timely new book, introduces us to the 8th Mountain, the end-time Mountain of the Lord. Drawing on that 8th Mountain is what will enable us to be successful in all of our 7 Mountain assignments. This excellent book is about accessing that place in God that will release heavenly wisdom and revelation into your daily life. It is from the 8th Mountain that solutions to some of our world's most vexing problems are going to come. The world will seek the wisdom from this 8th Mountain through mature believers who will manifest the glory of that Mountain in their lives. This powerful, full of Scripture, book may well become the users' manual needed to navigate how to manifest that 8th Mountain glory to this emerging end time generation.

Dr. Berin Gilfillan
CEO, Good Shepherd Ministries International (GSMI) dba ISOM
www.isom.org

As the owner and CEO of the $800 million Paladin Corporation, the founder of Kingdom Investors ministry, and leader of the pioneering ASP Movement, which has established a national strategy to create the world's first Sheep Nation in Australia, I have firsthand experience of rising up out of the deepest valley to ascend what Dr. Cook has aptly named the 8th Mountain. In his brilliant book, *The 8th Mountain*, Bruce Cook has captured so much of what it means to attract the favor of God, so that we advance beyond the capabilities of our own DNA, and move into the realms of overflow and multiplication, leading to the influencing of the culture of our time and generation.

The 8th Mountain is a book that will compel its readers to plumb new levels of intimacy with the Lord, gain true wisdom and understanding, and in turn summon greater levels of faith in Him. It is only as we ascend this 8th Mountain, that grasshoppers will become Joshuas, who will receive revelation and strategy, and go on to win battles on the other 7 mountains, and achieve the peace of the Lord in their lands. I know this to be true, as I am speaking from direct, firsthand experience.

Dave Hodgson
CEO, Paladin Corporation
www.paladincorp.com.au
www.aspmovement.org
www.kingdominvestors.com.au

Finally – a pinnacle revelation from a seasoned apostle to both the marketplace and ecclesiastical world of ministry. The 8th Mountain revelation contained in this incredible book finally gives the 7 Mountain message its most sensible outflow and suitable outcome. In the 8th Mountain revelation, the reader quickly realizes that when men and women who are called to build the Kingdom of God in one of the 7 Mountains of Culture, actualize their Kingdom assignment to their specific Mountain, that Mountain will morph into the Mountain of the Lord's house. In other words, the 8th Mountain is the actualization of God's dream of transforming all of culture through His sons and daughters by the occupation, subjugation and assimilation of the 7 Mountains of Culture into the timeless and glorious culture of God's eternal Kingdom!

It's my sincere belief that the stone that was cut without human hands in the dream of King Nebuchadnezzar (Daniel 2) that became a great Mountain that covered the whole earth, is the Mountain of the Lord's house, or, as Dr. Bruce Cook calls it, "The 8th Mountain." It behooves every serious student of the Word of God to understand why King Nebuchadnezzar bowed down to Daniel after the interpretation of his famous dream. It was as though God was already giving us a foretaste of the incredible power of the Mountain of the Lord's house, when it's accurately applied, to transform the Marketplace. Dr. Bruce Cook, the apostolic scholar and scribe that he is, does a masterful job in explaining the revelation of the 8th Mountain and how to apply it to today's contemporary society for national transformation. I highly recommend this book. I believe God has raised Dr. Bruce Cook to become the apostle of this message.

Dr. Francis Myles

Bestselling Author: The Order of Melchizedek and many other books
Host: Kingdom Thinking Today TV Show (FaithUSA TV)
Senior Pastor: Royal Priesthood International Embassy (RPIE.TV)

Dr. Bruce Cook is well qualified to write on this subject and bring out the truth of the 8th Mountain or the "Mountain of the Lord" which is over all other mountains (Micah 4:1 and Isaiah 2:2). He has given a comprehensive study on the qualities of heart that prepare us to be like our Great Shepherd, combining tenderheartedness towards one another, with the strength that enables us to resist the proud in places of rulership today. The contributing writers are all people of influence in the world of today. The message of *The 8th Mountain* is one that has been strongly burning in my heart for my own nation of India. It is my prayer that this book will stir to action many in the nations of the West (of which America seems to be the natural leader) to provide Godly leadership and transformation to the whole world into the "Kingdom of our God and the power of His Christ" (Rev. 12:10).

Dr. Abraham Sekhar

Chairman
www.globalatm.net
www.spiritfilledchurches.net
www.globalmercyfoundation.in
www.indiahealingrooms.net

Literally and spiritually, I am very much a "mountain man". Raised in the mountains, and called to the mountains, I have tasted the glories of conquest, but often in the face of storms without and blisters and pangs within. The wise and persistent climber reminds himself at every point of weakness that breathless vistas await him at the summit, and so he trudges on. Bruce has whet our appetite for just such a view from the top of the 8th and Final Mountain, without holding back the vital and hard lessons that propel us upward. Some things are immutable: as in the natural, so with the spirit. There simply is no gain without pain.

One does not vanquish an enemy that he is not willing to engage. And, we will never reach our destiny at the heights of our cultures if we don't tread in the footsteps of 85 year old Caleb who looked up at the giant-held crags of Hebron and declared, "Give me this mountain of which the Lord spoke in that day ... the Lord will be with me, and I will drive them out." And so he did. And so shall we. The consummation of history awaits a people who will take on this final Hebron and prepare it for our King.

Kevin Graves
Apostle to the Chinese
President, Target Ministries
www.targetminisries.org

This book holds an incredible compilation of truths we all must know, understand and walk in. What a powerhouse resource for us all as we move in our divine assignments or are just learning what our assignment is! Either way, this book will expand your thinking and increase your wisdom and knowledge exponentially. There are wonderful nuggets of truth and revelation in each chapter to expand our faith, increase our knowledge, and build wisdom beyond measure. It's timely, it's revelatory, and it's a must read!

Wende Jones
CEO, Agile Business Services
Vice President, Kingdom Congressional International Alliance
Author and Speaker
www.agilenw.com

I absolutely recommend Dr. Bruce Cook's newest book, *The 8th Mountain.* I found this book to be both revelatory as well as practical. One of the chapters that I found very thought provoking was chapter 3, "Humility and Honor." It set the mood for me for how to operate in all 7 Mountains and in the Kingdom.

Humility does lead to honor. This book encouraged me to keep moving forward.

Mary Dorian
Prophet, Teacher and Assistant Pastor, Glorybound Ministries Center
www.gloryboundministries.com

My friend Dr. Bruce Cook really unearths biblical truths that are unique and refreshing. You will appreciate this work of the heart that Bruce has laid out in expert fashion. This is a real paradigm guide for all of us with real-world help. It demonstrates that we are not left alone on the mountains of culture, but empowered by a loving Father who transforms us for impact and miracle living. I found the writings on "Sonship and Identity" inspiring. But, then the truths of "Stewardship and Rest" knocked at my back door. This got personal for me. Thank you Bruce for once again allowing God to pour through you in an extraordinary way so that we can all get a closer glimpse of our Father's heart.

Doug Spada
CEO and Founder, WorkLife
www.WorkLife.org

Good books? There are thousands of good books. BUT, this is a great book! Good books can give you information and knowledge; great books give information, illumination, and revelation. Saul of Tarsus lived by information, until he caught the revelation of the true nature of his calling and identity, on his way to Damascus. Apostle Paul's transformative process was not complete until Ananias arrived to "open Saul's eyes" to who God was, and to God's true purpose and call wherein lay Saul's true greatness in his completed identity, his true purpose for being placed on earth. In *The 8th Mountain*, Dr. Bruce "Ananias" Cook, reveals and "removes the scales" of the often unknown, unspoken, unrecognized "blind" areas in even the greatest among us, to powerfully complete our identity and purpose, and propel us to the forefront of the now developing greatest outpouring in human history, the "mountain of the Lord's house," the 8th Mountain. An absolute "must read" for mighty men and women of God. Come, take your place, walk in the fullness of your identity and assignment, and take your place on the mountain!

Dr. Erik Kudlis
Author, Speaker, International Marketplace Minister
President and CEO, Erik's Design-Build Associates, Inc.
www.edbhomes.com

As one of the co-founders of the Vineyard Church Christian movement of healing and worship with John and Carol Wimber, in recent years I have been ministering to equip the Saints, and speaking on the Father's heart, and the return of the prodigals. It is a privilege to introduce what I believe will be one of the best books by Dr. Bruce Cook. In my 52 year ministry, there is no one in recent years that I respect and honor more than Dr. Cook, an apostle and seer prophet to the United States and the nations.

I recommend this book highly for all Christians who want to see more of the 8th Mountain in their lives and experience the fullness of their destiny in the kingdom of heaven, while walking out this life on earth with our friend, Jesus Christ. "He who wins souls is wise and will shine like the stars in the firmament forever and ever."

I believe the hand of Dr. Cook was guided from the Third Heaven by the Holy Spirit to write *The 8th Mountain*. The content is particularly relevant for the times and the seasons Christians are facing today.

Jim Campbell

Co-Founder, Vineyard Church
https://vineyardusa.org/

Bruce Cook is one of those few men in life who has a huge and positive impact on the people he encounters. Whether he is running a business, praying for the sick, or writing a book, he has the heart of Christ. Not only do I consider him one of my closest and dearest friends but I also see him as a powerful communicator of God's love and grace. *The 8th Mountain* is full of revelatory, practical, godly wisdom and truth that will bless and benefit you when applied.

Douglas F. Wall

Managing Director, Life Ventures
www.lifeventures.net
Co-founder and Director, PureForge
www.pureforge.com

Excellent! Here it is! The much needed missing piece of the 7 Mountain culture beautifully and thoroughly scribed by Dr. Bruce Cook in *The 8th Mountain*. May it function as a primer going forward for deeper spiritual contextualization. Utilize this well crafted tool and see culture influenced resulting in personal and societal transformation. Glory!

Apostle Jill Mitchell O'Brien
President/Founder, Kingdom Connections International Inc.
www.kingdom-connections.com

Dr. Bruce Cook has skillfully crafted an innovative book, *The 8th Mountain*. The number eight represents the Teacher who brings revelation knowledge that makes a person fat with abundance and prosperity. Bruce outlines the foundational elements of humility, honor, favor and faith that give leaders the ability to transcend limits of physical existence through the circumcision of the flesh. Dr. Cook explains how we are transformed by the power of God's love, wisdom, and revelation to bring forth the fruit of the spirit that empowers us to live in resurrection power, birthed into a new spiritual beginning. Bruce clarifies the process of suffering needed to develop one's character, and identity of godly sonship. The reader will journey through the disciplines of forgiveness, prayer, worship and warfare to abound in God's glory and strength. *The 8th Mountain* will empower leaders to fulfill their destiny and leave a powerful legacy and inheritance for generations to come.

Dr. Barbie L. Breathitt
President, Breath of the Spirit Ministries, Inc.
ASK BARBIE Prophetic Dream Life Coach
www.MyOnar.com Dream Interpretation
www.BarbieBreathitt.com

Dr. Bruce Cook has compiled the most imperative understanding. There is only ONE mountain that rises above all others. *The 8th Mountain* is a must-read! It causes us to ask, "Is it the highest mountain for me?" "Do I climb higher upon it every day?" In the distance, the upward path is turning... fast! It is the redefining direction of what is to come! My friend, let us continue upward and soar with unwavering perseverance.

Dr. Kluane Spake

Apostle, Speaker, Author, Ministry Mentor, and Friend
http://kluane.com

The 8th Mountain is a timely writing on the subject of the seven spheres as the Church begins to look outward to expressing His Kingdom outside of the four walls. Dr. Bruce and his team have dug deep into the Word to ground those of us who are moving into the marketplace or are already positioned there. I recommend this foundation-laying work that they have done to prepare us for the challenges ahead.

Dr. Bob Doe

President, Transformation Health Network
www.transformationhealth.net

Bruce Cook is a Kingdom thinker. He sets forth a practical paradigm detailing how one may see their sphere of influence impacted for God. This comes from an intimate relationship with Jesus. The West has been hijacked by programs, etc. Dr. Cook offers a fresh Biblical approach in how we may engage the Lord, deepen in relationship with Him and work with Him as He directs and empowers. This book warrants serious study ... and application!

The Rev'd. Dr. John Roddam

Founder and President, Pleroma International
www.pleromainternational.ca

We have experienced book after book that have come to the Body of Christ like keys unlocking greater and greater levels of revelation. *The 8th Mountain,* written by one of today's true apostles, Dr. Bruce Cook, provides us a catapult into greater realms of the Kingdom of God. We know that before the return of the Lord there will be, "The Restoration of all things." The 8th Mountain revelation brought to us by Dr. Cook comes like a supernatural trebuchet to vault us into greater understanding of the Kingdom culture, protocols and standard operating procedures. Acts 3:20-21 (NASB) says, "... that He may send Jesus, the Christ appointed for you, whom heaven must receive until the period of restoration of all things about which God spoke by the mouth of His holy prophets from ancient time."

Dan Dean
Apostolic Director, Son Rise Cultural Center
Court Rooms of Heaven Navigation Ministry
Author, "Poetry of the Dance" and "Deeper Still"
www.sonriseculturalcenter.org

The 8th Mountain is a must-read and, in my estimation, a brilliant work. With expertise in the marketplace arena of "identity," I fully understand the deep desire of leaders and organizations to connect with their unique strengths, compelling purpose and powerful contributions. With contemporary relevance, Dr. Bruce Cook reveals your DNA in Christ and His unconditional love for you. The Kingdom authority that arises from your continuous pursuit of greater intimacy with God, unleashes the clarity and depth of your identity — catapulting you into God-breathed assignments within your spheres of influence.

JoAn Risdon
CEO, Smart Image Media
TRUnorth – Destiny by Design
www.smartimagemedia.com

Dr. Bruce Cook has done a remarkable job in writing this timely and powerful book which reflects the heart of The Father in revealing how we as His "kings" on earth can forcibly advance His Kingdom from the Mountain of The Lord in heaven to the Mountains in our realms of influence in the cultures of this earth.

I highly recommend *The 8th Mountain* by Dr. Bruce Cook. This book will help us to get focused on the most important purpose for our lives and ministries. It's about fulfilling our eternal purpose in life. It's all about bringing the Kingdom of God from Heaven to Earth, as we forcibly advance the Kingdom of God in our realms of influence here on earth.

Jesus said that from the days of John the Baptist until now the kingdom of heaven suffers violence, and the violent take it by force (Matt. 11:12).

This challenging, life-changing, powerful book may be the most important book you will ever read. You will be challenged to a life of intimacy with Abba Father and discovering how to fulfill His will and purpose for your life. You will read and know the Father's will from the Mountain of the Lord in Heaven and bring His will to be done in your realm of influence on earth.

The 8th Mountain, the Mountain of the Lord in Heaven, will become a reality in our mountains of influence on earth. It is then we will be able to say: *"For the earth will be filled with the knowledge of the glory of the LORD, as the waters cover the sea"* (Hab. 2:14).

Dr. A.L. (Papa) Gill

Speaker, teacher, minister to 90 nations, and author of 28 books and manuals

President, Gill Ministries

www.gillministries.com

Every dimension of present truth requires a trumpet; a clear prophetic voice among the people of God that articulates His heart. One such voice is Dr. Bruce Cook with his latest book, *The 8th Mountain*. This book presents to us a powerful apostolic plea to come up higher. He offers revelatory insights, concepts and strategies of The Kingdom which impact our society. Dr. Bruce has penned the heart of God for our generation.

The principles and patterns in this book will equip and prepare the reader to influence and occupy the planet, rather than leave it. Dr. Bruce has written a masterpiece that will reconfigure mindsets and bring proper apostolic alignment for God's purpose in your life.

This book that you are about to read is a prophetic map which will empower you to establish the mountain of the Lord in the spheres that you are assigned to. I highly recommend this book as an invaluable resource to leaders, churches and all those who have a relentless passion to see God's Kingdom at work in the world today. Enjoy!

Dr. Mark Kauffman
CEO, Christian Chamber of Commerce of Western Pennsylvania
CEO, Butz Florists & Home Decor
Apostle, Jubilee Ministries International
www.cccwp.us
www.butzflowers.net
www.jubileeministriesint.com

The 8th Mountain is a refreshing new insight as to how to fulfill the Great Commission by impacting the 7 Mountains of Culture! Jesus said in John 5:19, *"... I tell you, the Son can do nothing by himself; he can do only what he sees his Father doing..."* Dr. Bruce Cook has been a forerunner for many years, and once again he shares valuable insights and keys as to how to receive from the Lord as we learn to ascend the most important mountain of all, the 8th Mountain!

Mark Henderson
Senior Leader, Glory House Christian Center
www.gloryhouse.net

With great care and thoughtfully crafted language, Bruce Cook has offered patterns and principles which, if applied, will cause the reader to ascend the 8th Mountain, unleashing the potential contained within the 7 Mountain Mandate. It is there we will find the strategies and keys to answer the significant challenges facing society, at last making cultural transformation a reality.

Wendy K. Walters
Motivational Speaker, Master Coach, Publishing & Branding Expert
President, The Favor Foundation
www.wendykwalters.com
www.favorfoundation.org

In his newest book, *The 8th Mountain,* Dr. Bruce Cook takes us on a scriptural journey that encourages, challenges and equips us to live out our daily lives from a place of relationship and revelation that can only come from spending intimate, quality time with the Lord. Full of biblical truths and practical application, we are taken deeper into the heart of God, and the character and nature He desires to be cultivated and developed in us so we can fulfill our destiny in the earth realm! Through these anointed pages, we are invited to "be transformed by virtue of our time on the 8th Mountain," thereby becoming empowered as agents of transformation in the 7 Mountains of Culture, so that the kingdoms of this world will truly become the kingdoms of our Lord and of His Christ (Rev 11:5)!

Jackie Seeno
President, Cyrus Land Investments, LLC
President, Jacqueline M. Seeno Construction Co., Inc.
www.seenohomes.com

The 8th Mountain is a skillfully constructed treatise that presents foundational doctrine with an emphasis on fresh *rhema* and revelation. Dr. Cook and his contributors take the reader on a new creation journey which begins with a thorough examination of the spiritual character and substance of the new spirit man, admonishing believers to grow into perfection, and ultimately pointing the spiritual sojourner to discover one's destiny in the clouds of the Mountain of the Lord.

My Spirit resonates with Apostle Cook's assertion that we are shifting into the Glory movement, even as we are emerging from the Church Age. We are the generation called to prepare the way for the coming of our Lord. To that end, I regard *The 8th Mountain* as a treasure kept in a time capsule to be released to the Kingdom of God for such a time as this. The five fold ministry has a new foundational manual to use as a spiritual tool for the development of leaders.

Frank Amedia

Apostle, Touch Heaven Ministries
www.touchheaven.com
Chairman, POTUS Shield
www.potusshield.org

The material in this book is most likely one of the first and more extensive examples of where the Body of Christ should look to understand the unfolding grace, wisdom, power and glory of the kingdom of God. *"To the intent that now unto the principalities and powers in heavenly places might be known by the church the manifold wisdom of God"* (Eph. 3:10 KJVA). While the word "manifold" is taken from the Greek term *"polupoikilos,"* meaning – multifarious and much variegated, it gives our spiritual imaginations the insight to see such ideas as "many-folds" and "various gates" in the enunciations of the words "manifold" and "variegated."

Truly, the 8th Mountain is where the unfolding of the identity of the Body of Christ is founded. If we are to be all that Jesus was and do the works that He did, and even greater works, we must expand our viewpoint of Christianity to include in our lines of sight not only a "shifting" but a "lifting" to avoid "drifting." We are indeed headed to higher thoughts, demonstrations and glory.

Dr. Bruce Cook has done an excellent job in categorizing so many of the most important elements of this upward point of view and has provided a very broad base by which believers can look at the 8th Mountain with both spiritual and practical insights. This book is definitely a "keeper" in the 7 Mountain arsenal and gives believers a greater weapon to help forcefully advance the kingdom of God. It is excellently done.

Dr. Gordon E. Bradshaw
President, Global Effect Movers & Shakers Network
Public Policy Executive and Public Safety Consultant
President, The Misrah Academy Governmental Empowerment Center
Senior Scholar of Spiritual Formation & Leadership
Hope Bible College & Seminary and Hope Schools of Ministry Consortium
www.gemsnetwork.org

Bruce Cook says, "The 8th Mountain is calling your name." But his book, *The 8th Mountain,* is more than just a call. Cook takes us to school and trains us to reach the summits of cultural influence for God's purposes. He uses a firm foundation in Scripture to demonstrate the necessary skills we can use to thrive and be successful in the unforgiving environment of the 7 Mountains of Culture. God wants to use us to bring transformation to the world but first we must be transformed. *The 8th Mountain* shows us ways to be transformed so that we can then be transformers. Thank you Bruce Cook, for showing us the way to join a community of fellow culture warriors who are establishing the kingdom of God on earth.

Dr. Tim Hamon, Ph.D.
CEO Christian International
www.christianinternational.com

Over the past two decades the church has grown in their realization of the potential of nation transformation through the increased understanding and development of the 7 cultural mountains. Men and women in every sector of society started believing in their personal calling to disciple the nations. No longer was the institutionalized church the only vehicle for God to use in the establishment of His Kingdom on earth. This was an exciting time for the church, but that season has now matured and it is time to move into the next season.

I believe that Bruce Cook has opened the door for us to walk into a new place of intimacy and divine wisdom. *The 8th Mountain* is the backdrop that will allow God's people to be the recipients of supernatural downloads. Together we could be the people who provide the answers to the questions that our world is grappling with, including poverty, corruption and injustice.

As you read this book I pray that you will boldly take that first step onto the 8th Mountain, and that you will be open and ready to receive what God is preparing for you.

My advice, take this step with caution because your life may never be the same again.

Dr. Graham Power
Founder of Global Day of Prayer & Unashamedly Ethical
www.unashamedlyethical.com
www.powergrp.co.za

Dr. Bruce Cook is a seasoned scholar, communicator, and wordsmith. His book, *The 8th Mountain,* will capture your attention and your heart. God is searching the earth to find those whose hearts are completely His so that He may show Himself strong on their behalf. Transformation is coming through those who will stand with God on the "mountain above all mountains." This book is life-transformational. Read it. Digest it. Live it.

Dr. Patricia King
Founder and President of Patricia King Ministries
www.patriciaking.com

PREFACE

Those who spend time with God and His Word and His Spirit, and who dwell in His presence and commune with Him and develop a personal relationship with Him, become transformed in the process and thus are better informed, equipped and empowered to attract, steward and exercise influence in the 7 Mountains of Culture (Arts & Entertainment, Business & Economy, Education, Family, Government & Law, Media, and Religion). That is the basic premise and thesis of this book.

Moreover, I assert that such transformation is not only possible for disciples of Christ, but, rather, it is imperative and essential to successfully fulfill our divine assignments, callings and destinies.

Several places in Scripture such as Micah 4:1 and Isaiah 2:2 mention "the mountain of the Lord" or "the mountain of the house of the Lord," that is above all the other mountains, and is the chief mountain, depending on the particular translation used. This phrase refers to the place of God's abode, or heaven, and for our purposes here, I refer to it as the 8th Mountain. Mountains in Scripture refer to kingdoms, authority, rule and dominion.

Many believe and some teach that these verses also refer to the temple mount in Jerusalem and/or a future kingdom – the millennial reign of Jesus – from Mt. Zion in

Jerusalem. This is entirely possible, since some prophecies and prophetic Scriptures have multiple applications and fulfillments, as evidenced by Jesus' and Paul's teaching about events to occur in "The Last Days" – some of which were fulfilled in 70 AD, some that have been fulfilled since 1947-1948, and yet others await fulfillment in the days and years ahead.

Jesus also taught that a season would come where there would be widespread and deep distress among the nations, with perplexity (Luke 21:25). Perplexity is from the Greek *aporia* (ap-or-ee'-a) and means anxiety, doubt, confusion – i.e., problems with no certain solution – problems that threaten the survival of a nation or a leader's rule (Strong's G640). And, as children of God, we are God's agents to bring, offer and/or provide divine solutions to these perplexing problems.

Isaiah 60 speaks of a season of intense darkness, where the Glory of God comes on His people in such a way that *"Kings will come to the brightness of your arising..."* What type of events display the glory of God in a manner that a king will personally come to experience it? Spiritual visitations with salvation, revival, healing, and miracles? Perhaps – but unlikely. Such events have occurred for centuries in different locations without attracting the attention or presence of kings. What if God's glory displayed to and manifested through His people also brought innovative, disruptive, breakthrough solutions to the perplexity of nations?

Historically, we have seen one example of what this looks like in the form and reign of King Solomon, son and royal successor of David, the *"man after God's own heart."* He asked for and received wisdom and understanding from God to be able to govern and rule his people, the nation of Israel. God was pleased with his request, priorities and motives, and so Solomon received this and much more. The result was that God so blessed Solomon and Israel that they were at peace from their enemies, prospered exceeding abundantly, and experienced a remarkable national renaissance, and the kings and rulers of nations streamed to Jerusalem to meet with King Solomon and to see and experience firsthand what the glory of God on a nation and its ruler looked like.

The Queen of Sheba was one such visitor, and her story is recorded in Scripture (1 Kings 10:1-13, 2 Chron. 9:1-12). She concluded, *"The report I heard in my own country about your achievements and your wisdom is true. But I did not believe these things until I came and saw with my own eyes. Indeed, not even half was told me; in wisdom and wealth you have far exceeded the report I heard."*

So, what will happen when God's glory is poured out upon a people group (the *ekklesia*) and not just one man or one nation? The results will be noteworthy and extraordinary, and will cause Isaiah 60 to be fulfilled. That day is now here, and it is time for the Church, the global body of Christ, to rise up, suit up, show up, and grow up into the fullness of Christ so that His incomparable, surpassing glory and wisdom can be demonstrated through us to the world.

Micah 4 and Isaiah 2 both speak of the Mountain of the Lord being exalted above the kingdoms and dominions of the earth – and that both individuals and also the leaders of the nations will come to the Mountain ("all nations will stream to it"), seeking that "He may teach us his ways, so that we may walk in his paths." As a result, there is a rule of law, justice with equity at the national level, and personal guidance. This result produces freedom from war, freedom from oppression, private property with prosperity – and even freedom of faith and religion. Micah 4:5 declares *"each man will walk in the name of his own god, but we will walk in the name of the Lord our God."*

I believe that the Mountain of the Lord, the 8th Mountain, is now being exalted above the 7 Mountains of Culture – and all of the hills as well. Around the globe, several kings and leaders of nations have now submitted their nation and their leadership or rulership to heaven and are finding solutions to perplexity. Sheep nations are now arising (Matt. 25:32-33). I believe that the 8th Mountain, and the divine wisdom that it represents, will now begin releasing or downloading breakthrough solutions to disease epidemics, food shortages, water shortages, weather changes, civil conflict (religious, racial, ethnic, gender, class), oppression and corruption, injustice, pollution, greed, family distress, educational lethargy, economic systems, corporate cultures, governments – and more! We just need to be in position and ready.

Amos 4:13 (NIV) says, *"He who **forms the mountains,** creates the wind, and reveals his thoughts to man, he who turns dawn to darkness, and treads the high places of the earth—the Lord God Almighty is his name"* (author's emphasis). So, God not only rules the mountains; He formed and created them. As the Master Designer and Creator of the Universe, God is intimately acquainted with all the mountains. I believe this applies not only to the natural, geophysical mountains, but to the cultural mountains of society as well.

This book will help teach and explain, in practical terms, how to integrate the 7 Mountains of Culture paradigm with both the realities of heaven and of daily, modern life on earth. I will attempt to provide such a tool here that can help us to bridge the perceived gaps or chasms between these dimensions or realms of existence, and to experience the "abundant life" and "greater works" Jesus spoke of in John 10:10 and 14:12, respectively. But, more importantly, and pragmatically, our goal here is to provide a tool which the Church can use to influence culture and to help effect personal and societal transformation.

For me, "abundant life" means a life well lived; it means a life of service to others, and a life of influence and purpose. The "greater works", in my opinion, are simply the works you and I do today, since Jesus ascended to heaven after being resurrected from the dead and is seated at the right hand of God. You and I are his hands and feet on earth, and He has delegated that to us as His sons and daughters, and bride—the Church. For decades, however, the Church and many theologians have been asking and teaching a one-dimensional question: Are you rapture ready?

The result has been a Church that, to a large extent in recent years, has viewed and focused on heaven as something exclusively reserved for the future and not available to us in the present as well. Fortunately, that attitude and mindset has begun to change in recent years, in part through the writings and videos of Rick Joyner, Bill Johnson, Lance Wallnau, Johnny Enlow, Kathy Walters, Kat Kerr, Shawn Bolz and others, and media ministries such as those of Patricia King, Steve Schultz and Sid Roth. Moreover, the modern Church, for the most part, has viewed and treated culture, the marketplace and government as dangerous, secular and tainted, and something to tolerate and endure as a necessary evil, and to avoid or minimize contact with as much as possible.

Not surprisingly, modern culture has experienced a significant spiritual deterioration and moral decline, and the Church has lost influence and relevance in the eyes of society and cultural elites. God is not a one-dimensional being, and neither are His Kingdom and the world we live in one-dimensional. Where are the Martin Luthers, the William Wilberforces, the Abraham Kuypers, the Martin Luther King Jrs of this age? Fortunately, God is raising up cultural champions from the Church, and beginning to reverse this trend and bring Western culture back to its roots of Judeo-Christian heritage and values.

Several more practical questions for Christians include: Are you revelation ready, are you reformation ready, are you ready to rumble in spiritual warfare, are you ready for influence, do you have a godly identity, and have you allowed God to discipline you and put to death your soulish, carnal nature so that you can humble yourself and be obedient and become spiritually mature and be promoted by God?

God is not a distant, impersonal being and heaven is not a distant, abstract promise and just a place to experience after death. No, God is very much alive and well and seated on the throne of the universe in heaven, and *"He has also set eternity in the hearts of men"* (Eccl. 3:11, NIV). God is a triune being, or Trinity—God the Father, God the Son, and God the Holy Spirit. *"For there are three that bear record in heaven, the Father, the Word, and the Holy Ghost: and these three are one. And there are three that bear witness in earth, the spirit, and the water, and the blood: and these three agree in one"* (1 John 5:7-

8). Indeed, a threefold cord or cord of three strands is not easily or quickly broken or separated (Eccl. 4:12).

Each member of the Trinity has its own unique personality and particular functions. God the Father is known by many names (see a more complete list of these below), including Abba Father, Jehovah, Elohim, Yahweh (YHWH), or simply I AM. Jesus the Son is Emmanuel, Messiah, Son of Man, Son of God, Prince of Peace, the Great Shepherd, Eternal High Priest, Advocate, Intercessor, King of Kings, and Lord of Lords. The Holy Spirit is Comforter, Counselor, Guide, and Teacher, among other roles. There is much more that could be said about each of these, but we are being intentionally brief here in order to focus on other points related to our thesis statement and basic premise, and to develop a context and framework for the reader.

There are many ways we can know God, the Master Designer and Creator of the universe and of all life. I will list just 10 of those here. First, and most importantly, we can know God through His written word or *logos* (user's or owner's manual). Second, we can know God through His spoken word or *rhema*, that we receive in our own hearts, or that comes to us through prophets or prophetic ministry. Third, we can know God through our conscience (1 John 3:19-22; see also 1 Cor. 4:4, 1 Tim. 4:1-2, 1 Pet. 3:15-17). Fourth, we can know God through nature (Rom. 1:18-20). Fifth, we can know God through the arts and sciences, which testify to the Master Designer and Architect of the universe, and give overwhelming evidence of God's existence, preeminence and sovereignty.

Sixth, we can know the Father through Jesus the Son who is the same yesterday, today and forever (John 10:30, 14:9; Heb. 13:8). Seventh, we can know God through the

Holy Spirit, who indwells us by faith as children of God. The Holy Spirit, while serving as Comforter, Counselor and Teacher, also serves as an operating system, a GUI interface, and the most powerful algorithm ever created, to enable spirit communication between God and man. 1 Cor. 2 speaks about spirit to spirit communication, and how we as humans are "wifi" enabled by the Holy Spirit to have direct communication with God's Spirit—both in sending and receiving.

Eighth, we can know God through dreams. Job 33:14-18 says, *"For God does speak—now one way, now another—though man may not perceive it. In a dream, in a vision of the night, when deep sleep falls on men as they slumber in their beds, he may speak in their ears and terrify them with warnings, to turn man from wrongdoing and keep him from pride, to preserve his soul from the pit, his life from perishing by the sword."* Several purposes of God for dreams are mentioned here in this passage: terrifying us with warnings, turning us from wrongdoing, keeping us from pride, preserving our souls from the pit, and our lives from perishing by the sword.

And, ninth and tenth, we can know God through personal experiences and spiritual encounters. Some people in the Bible entertained angels unaware, but many others were able to see and recognize and even speak with and hear angels, and today that is still the case, as dramatized and popularized by the television series *Touched By An Angel*. For example, Abraham, Sarah, Lot, Hagar, Isaac and Jacob had angelic encounters, as did Moses, Joshua, Balaam, Gideon, Elijah, Elisha, Manoah and his wife, Ezekiel, Isaiah, Zechariah the Prophet, Zechariah the Priest and father of John the Baptist, Mary the mother of Jesus, the Shepherds in the fields outside Jerusalem, Mary Magdalene, Mary the

mother of James, Salome, Jesus, Philip the Evangelist, Judas
son of James, Paul, and 11 of the original 12 apostles — all but
Judas. Gabriel was the angel who spoke to both Zechariah
and Mary (Luke 1:19, 26-28), and Abraham, Hagar, Jesus,
Peter and John all had multiple encounters with angels.

Another person who had multiple angelic encounters
was Daniel. An angel of the Lord shut the mouths of lions
for him (Dan. 6:22). Daniel had at least two encounters
with Gabriel (Daniel 8-9), and encounters with two other
unnamed angels in Daniel 7 and Daniel 10-12. Michael the
archangel helped one of these unnamed angels fight with
the prince of Persia for 21 days to be able to reach Daniel
and give him the interpretation of what he had seen in the
Spirit. The angels of the Lord surrounded an enemy army
on several occasions for the nation of Israel and either
frightened them, temporarily blinded them, routed and
defeated them, and/or caused a great slaughter among them
(2 Kings 6:16-18, 2 Kings 20:1-30, 2 Kings 19:32-37, Isa. 37:33-
38, 2 Chron. 32:20-23).

Still others, like apostles Paul and John, had Third Heaven
experiences described in 2 Cor. 12 and Rev. 4-22, respectively.
Timothy received his spiritual gifting through a prophecy
given at the laying on of hands by a council of elders (1
Tim. 4:14), which apparently included the apostle Paul (2
Tim. 1:6). Paul and Barnabas were sent out from Antioch by
the Holy Spirit, and the other leaders there fasted and laid
hands on them (Acts 13:1-3). The 12 apostles were called
and commissioned by Jesus (Matt. 10:1-4, Mark 3:13-19).
And, Jesus sent out the 70 disciples (Luke 10:1-24), just as
Moses appointed 70 elders to help him judge and rule the
people (Num. 11:16-30). Moses also had an encounter with a

burning bush where God spoke to him and called him to go to Egypt and speak to Pharaoh to let the Israelites go.

Many other people have had near death experiences, comas, or even a few reported resurrections, and have recorded and shared their testimonies and what they experienced in the afterlife before coming back to human consciousness in great detail, with many similarities in seeing bright lights and angelic beings and having sensations of feeling peaceful and loved. Some people have met with Jesus in these experiences, and have been sent back to earth to complete and fulfill their assignment and destiny, to learn or correct something in their life, or to share something with others. Unfortunately, some of these people have reported being in a dark place with fire, smoke, and hearing screams and seeing grotesque, hideous beings and having sensations of fear, repulsion, hopelessness and despair. Yes, heaven and hell are real.

So, with all of these avenues to God available to us, it is not enough just to read the user's guide or owner's manual. We also need a personal relationship with God, and that is possible for all people. James 4:8 says, *"Draw near to God, and he will draw near to you."* Jer. 33:3 says, *"Call to me and I will answer you and tell you great and unsearchable things you do not know."* Psa. 91:15 says, *"He will call upon me, and I will answer him; I will be with him in trouble, I will deliver him and honor him."* Acts 17:27 says, *"His purpose was for the nations to seek after God and perhaps feel their way toward him and find him--though he is not far from any one of us."* Micah 6:8 says, *"He has shown you, O mortal, what is good. And what does the LORD require of you? To act justly and to love mercy and to walk humbly with your God."*

Jer. 29:12-14 also says, *"'Then you will call upon Me and come and pray to Me, and I will listen to you. You will seek Me and find Me when you search for Me with all your heart. I will be found by you,' declares the LORD, 'and I will restore your fortunes and will gather you from all the nations and from all the places where I have driven you,' declares the LORD, 'and I will bring you back to the place from where I sent you into exile.'"*

We can have a real and personal relationship with God now, while on earth, just as Jesus did during his earthly life, and just as Noah, Job, Abraham, Joseph, Moses, Daniel, Nehemiah, Esther, Ruth, Deborah, David, Mary, Stephen, Lydia, Cornelius, the early apostles and countless other saints throughout history have done. The basic premise of this book is that having such a relationship with the living God while we are on earth is a basic right and responsibility of every kingdom citizen and spiritual son and daughter of the King of Kings and Lord of Lords, and that knowing God in an intimate way rather than just knowing about God on an intellectual or emotional level, will make a crucial difference and give a competitive advantage to every saint who so avails himself or herself of this reality.

For Elisha, it was a double portion and he did twice as many recorded miracles as Elijah, whose mantle he received as Elijah was taken up. For Daniel, Hananiah, Mishael and Azariah, it was a 10x factor, and it was said of them, *"In every matter of wisdom and understanding about which the king questioned them, he found them ten times better than all the magicians and enchanters in his whole kingdom"* (Dan. 1:20). For Isaac, he sowed in obedience to the word of the Lord in a time of famine and reaped a 100-fold harvest or return in the same year (Gen. 26:12). It is different for each of us depending on the measure of grace and faith that we have and operate in, and the willingness to be obedient unto death.

Knowing God and communing with God is part of our basic stewardship, birthright and inheritance as children of God and joint heirs of grace, salvation, eternal life and the kingdom of heaven with our elder brother Jesus. Just as Abraham and Enoch were known as friends of God, and David was called a man after God's own heart, and the Lord God walked with Adam and Eve in the Garden of Eden in the cool of the day, so you and I need to develop and cultivate our own intimate relationship with God. In doing so, the motives of our heart must be pure, our hands must be clean (Psa. 24:3-4), and we must be willing to lay aside our own agendas and worship Him in spirit and truth (John 4:23-24).

We are also told to enter into His gates with thanksgiving, and into His courts with praise (Psa. 100:4). Likewise, we are told that our God is a consuming fire (Heb. 12:29), and that without faith it is impossible to please God, and that those who approach Him must believe that He exists and that He rewards those who earnestly seek Him (Heb. 11:6). A picture of heaven and the throne of God as well as the four living creatures, angelic host, 24 elders and great cloud of witnesses is painted for us in Rev. 4-22 and in lesser detail in Heb. 12:22-24.

We must realize that God is not limited or confined to the 365 names of God recorded in Scripture. Those are intended and meant to teach us about the nature of God, but are not an exhaustive list of who God is. He is Yahweh (YHWH), El Chaiyim, El De'Ot, El Echad, El Emet, El Gibbor, El HaGadol, El HaKadosh, El HaKavod, El HaNe'eman, El

HaShamayim, El Kanno, El Hedem, El Mauzi, El Mishpat, El Olam, El Rachum, El Ro'I, El Sali, El Selichot, El Tehilati, El Tsadik, El Tzur, El Yerush'lem, El Yeshuati, El Yesra'el, Jehovah Nissi, Jehovah Shaphat, Jehovah Jireh, Jehovah Rapha, Jehovah Zidkenu, Jehovah Adonai, Jehovah Elohim, Jehovah Shalom, Jehovah El Elyon, Jehovah Shammah, Jehovah Gibbor, Jehovah Raah and Jehovah Sabaoth.

Indeed, He also owns the cattle on a thousand hills (Psa. 50:10), and all the gold and silver belong to Him (Hag. 2:8). God provides breath and food for every living creature (Job 12:10, 34:14; Psa. 104:27-30). God is the ultimate and pre-eminent Commander-in-Chief, Sovereign, Investor, and Entrepreneur. He has never lost a battle, and His seed investment of His Only Begotten Son, Jesus, is paying the highest return and greatest dividend in the history of the world in the form of the Church. His family franchise named Abba Father & Sons Global Enterprises Unlimited, LLC is also the largest and most valuable business franchise in the history of the world, with countless millions of franchisees. So, God is eminently — or rather, pre-eminently — qualified to speak to us about issues and questions of culture, family, marketplace and government.

Finally, this book provides an overview and strategic sampling — rather than a comprehensive or exhaustive list — of some key benefits we as sons of God can derive from a personal relationship with our Heavenly Father, the Righteous Judge of All, and the utility or usefulness of certain qualities, attributes, characteristics, and/or gifts as applied in the global marketplace of commerce, business, economics, science, technology, education, arts, entertainment, law and government to which most of us are called or assigned, and in which we earn our primary or sole income through an occupation, trade or profession. We are primarily a spirit being embodied in a physical form, rather than merely a physical being housing a spirit, as humanists and secularists would have us to believe.

As many sages throughout history have correctly noted, "Heaven is just a breath away." We have the potential to "blink in and blink out" between dimensions, as both physicists and theologians have observed. That's why we can be seated with Christ in heavenly places or realms (Eph. 2:6) in our spirit man, and at the same time, be alive and functioning on earth in our physical bodies. We are bi-vocational as kings and priests (Rev. 1:6, 5:10) and bi-locational as saints, spiritual beings and sojourners on earth (1 Pet. 2:11) whose citizenship is both in our native country of birth or origin and in the kingdom of God and heaven (Eph. 2:19, Phil. 3:20).

I invite you now to breathe in the atmosphere of heaven and take a journey with me to the Mountain of the Lord, the Mountain above all mountains, that I call the 8th Mountain® (heaven), and find the Father's heart and enjoy His presence, tenderness, warmth, love and wisdom. He has much to share with you, to teach you, and to impart. As you do this, and spend time with Him and His Word, I believe and decree that your time, effort and assignments in the 7 Mountains of Culture will become more productive, anointed and favored as a result, and that your measure of wisdom and favor, as well as your sphere of influence, will increase, and that you will be transformed in the process.

May the glory of God arise on His people – and may the kings of the earth and the leaders of the 7 Mountains of

Culture – eagerly come seeking and finding solutions to their perplexing problems.

—BRUCE COOK
Jan. 17, 2017
Co-Founder, 8thMountain®
Board Chair, KCIA
www.8thMountain.com
www.kcialliance.org

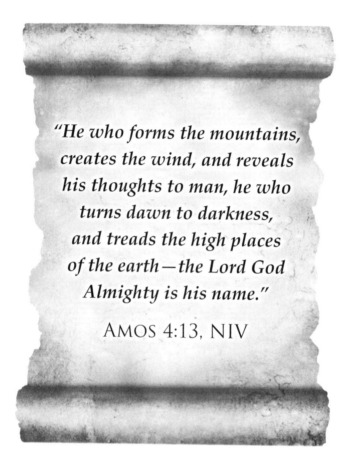

"He who forms the mountains, creates the wind, and reveals his thoughts to man, he who turns dawn to darkness, and treads the high places of the earth—the Lord God Almighty is his name."

AMOS 4:13, NIV

FOREWORD

BY DR. LANCE WALLNAU

You want to hear a wild story? I had just arrived in Aruba to meet with a friend, Lisette Malmberg, and teach in her Kingdom Leadership Institute. It was a surreal night. I went up to a flip chart and sketched two mountains and said: "The day is coming when two incompatible spiritual kingdoms are going to collide." I quoted Jeremiah who prophesied about the kingdom of Babylon saying: *"I am against you, you destroying mountain, you who destroy the whole earth," declares the LORD. "I will stretch out my hand against you, roll you off the cliffs, and make you a burned-out mountain"* (Jer. 51:25).

Drawing on the flip chart the outline of a mountain I then drew another mountain overlapping the first and read: *"In the last days the mountain of the LORD's temple will be established as the highest of the mountains; it will be exalted above the hills, and all nations will stream to it"* (Isa. 2:2).

As I said, "When these two mountains collide in the earth there will be a great shaking!" at that exact moment the power blew out in our building. In fact, the power grid over Aruba just got fried.

Now this is when it gets interesting — while the electricity was out and we were standing in the dark, a sound came booming out of the loudspeaker. It sounded like some agitated person cursing in a language I didn't understand. I asked Lisette what the voice said, assuming it was their native Papiamento dialect. She replied, "Oh, Dr. Lance, that is no language I've ever heard before!"

A moment later her housekeeper called to say the power had gone out in her house and when the power went out the housekeeper heard a loud voice saying something. She got a flashlight and looked, but didn't find anybody in the house! She wondered if she should call the police. Lisette, far from flustered, was strangely energized by what was going on. She immediately saw that this was all a sign that spiritual kingdoms were indeed colliding in her own nation and her mission to transform Aruba was being oddly confirmed by all this chaos. As we made our way out of the building, a man came forward talking frantically on his cell phone. He was the manager of the local electric utility and explained to us that the people at his facility said a surge of energy had come from deep under the island and there was a flash of light as power surged and temporarily fried the circuitry.

The power grid was out for seven hours. What was that voice? Could it have been the Strong Man assigned over the nation of Aruba? Is it possible that we can proclaim things that set spiritual forces like this in motion?

I am only in Aruba once a year, but happened to be there when Bruce contacted me to tell me about his new manuscript, *The 8th Mountain*. My mind immediately went to the experience I had when talking about the collision of the destroying mountain of Babylon and the Mountain of the Lord! I am convinced that he is writing something here that opens up a new chapter for all of us who have been talking about the 7 Mountains.

When I first began sharing the 7 Mountains, the concept was already present in the teaching of Loren Cunningham's, *Seven Mind Molders of Culture* and Bill Bright's, *Seven World Kingdoms*. In fact, Loren himself told me the story how he and Bill Bright met and discovered they both had scraps of paper in their pocket outlining the same seven sphere divine download on how to disciple nations! What happened after talking to Loren was as strange as my experience in Aruba and connects to Bruce's 8th Mountain. After talking to Loren, I had my first divine exposure to the 7 Mountain concept and the Mountain that rose above them. It happened while I was talking to Kim Clement's secretary about the resurrection of Georgia Senator Mike Crotts from the dead.

Kim was a great prophet and friend who prophesied a word over a businessman named Mike Crotts, that he would be in Georgia politics and have a son named Caleb who would walk in his steps. While on the campaign trail, Mike dropped dead of a heart attack. Not the best way to fulfill a prophecy, right? But that word Kim gave was part of what his wife, Phyllis, used to command his spirit to come back into his body. Kim's secretary, Debbie Aurin, was telling me that while in heaven, Mike was given a vision of seven islands that became mountains rising out of the ocean and suddenly an eighth mountain came up towering over the other seven as the Lord said, "Those seven mountains are seven world kingdoms, but My mountain is greater than all world kingdoms!"

Then the Lord pointed to one of the seven mountains and told Mike it was the Government Mountain and he was called to go into it ... "BUT, there must be agreement." At that moment Mike began to leave heaven and go back into his body in a hospital in Georgia where his wife was doing warfare to raise him from the dead. Anyway, after talking to Debbie I could almost see those islands that became mountains and the great mountain that rose above them. I immediately made an appointment to meet Senator Crotts and interview him. When I asked Senator Crotts (yes, he got elected) about the seven islands that became mountains he stared at me quizzically, not knowing what I was talking about. He told me about a body of water and something the Lord showed him, but it didn't match what I had heard ... and worse yet, what I was already preaching!

Seeing my confusion, he comforted me by saying that the Lord told him he would only remember part of what took place in heaven. After the interview, I immediately called Debbie to ask her where she got that story from and what she said back to me shocked me. She not only never heard that story before, she had no recollection of ever having the conversation with me in the first place! Who then was I talking to? To this day this riddle hasn't been solved. I had already been teaching the version I thought I heard about 7 Mountains and telling this story to crowds. You can hear this on recordings delivered at the first Voice of Apostles Conference in Harrisburg, Penn. It was the first time I ended my message by having everyone stand and shout, "AS ONE!" and when we did there was an angelic echo that rang back, "AS ONE!" from the ceiling. It was wild! (That's on the recording also!) I stopped telling the story about Mike Crotts, stopped selling tapes and CDs about that mountain rising above the other seven because first, Mike could not confirm it happened, second, my source denied ever speaking to me, and third and most important, because Bruce Cook was supposed to write about it!

It is interesting that Bruce wrote extensively about the apostolic before covering the 8th Mountain. I say that because there was a fresh emphasis on the word "apostolic" breaking out around 2001 when the 7 Mountains concept started to take off. I think the message has been waiting for that apostolic generation to come to the place where they can actually implement the idea. This is where Bruce's book comes in. By placing the silhouette of the "8th Mountain, the Mountain of the Lord" over the 7 Mountains that shape culture, Bruce provides a visual and conceptual bridge into a whole new chapter. The 8th Mountain is like a dome that reflects the kingdom over the 7 kingdoms that disciple each nation. It provides a capstone to the message so that apostolic leaders can begin a new phase of implementation.

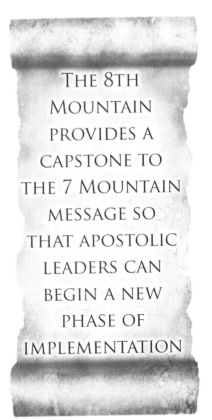

THE 8TH MOUNTAIN PROVIDES A CAPSTONE TO THE 7 MOUNTAIN MESSAGE SO THAT APOSTOLIC LEADERS CAN BEGIN A NEW PHASE OF IMPLEMENTATION

This is important because we have proclaimed, but not yet produced, a tangible manifestation of how the Church actually can disciple nations. Not that there are not testimonies in various places, there are great stories, but the truth is that in spite of our victories we've not been nearly as effective as secular political progressives who have targeted and captured the hearts of the next generation of Americans by seizing the high places of Hollywood, Media, Academia and Government.

The fault for this has to be largely placed on the Church as this is the one entity to which Christ has promised "all power in heaven and on earth" for the task of "making disciples of nations." I think there has been a maturing of an apostolic company in the earth and Bruce's 8th Mountain arrives at a time we can finally address a re-formation of how the church advances in the 7 Mountains. This re-forming of our ranks could trigger a reformation that fills the gap in our mission of discipling nations. We need to see the local church in its own sphere and the body of Christ as the extended church operates in the mountains of culture. The local church does the training, yet stands apart from culture while the people of God go forth in their various divine callings and do the actual work of bringing spheres into alignment under the 8th Mountain. In this way we go into all the world by going into all the systems.

Bruce's teaching brings a much needed next step to how this works. Have you ever noticed how many Church leaders balk at identifying themselves in the "Religion Mountain"? This reticence is for two reasons: first, many do not like the word "religion" because it lacks appeal, and second, many do not like to see themselves as having limitations applied to their scope of God-given authority. They somehow see local church leaders at the top of all the mountains. But, is this God's blueprint? Bruce does not think so, and I agree. In Daniel's words, it's "the saints who take the kingdom," not the preachers (Dan. 7:18).

The truth is, the Church is called to be a separate institution and that institution is recognized by mankind as a "religious" sphere whether you like the name or not. This separation is designed so that we never become assimilated under the dominion of earthly governments. Catholic history leading up to the Reformation and the history of England beginning with Henry the VIII shows us how messy things get when the Religion Mountain becomes enmeshed with the function of the Government Mountain. Each sphere has limits, and each sphere has its own sovereignty, accountable to God alone. There is a reason for this. Whenever a person or an institution oversteps its God-given authority, it violates the boundaries God has set up for man's benefit and protection. When you invade the sphere that belongs to someone else, you enter the realm of witchcraft – or illegitimate authority. The nature of witchcraft is intimidation, domination and control. This is the spirit of lawlessness we see running rampant. It is the very essence of the spirit of Antichrist. Where the Spirit of the Lord is there is freedom. Where the spirit of witchcraft rules (religious or otherwise) there is intimidation, domination and control. Where we fail to go, the kingdom does not come – and worse yet, in the vacuum of the Church, a counterfeit power will take control.

WHEREVER WE FAIL TO GO, THE KINGDOM DOES NOT COME

The Church in the Religion Mountain is called to be a prophetic voice that speaks truth to power, and that is why it must stand in its own sovereign space answerable to

God and not man. In the absence of this prophetic function in America, the Media Mountain has anointed itself to be the voice of truth to political power. How much truth do you think they are producing? Not much. They have been assimilated by the Government Mountain, compromised their objectivity, and lost their voice. This is what happens when the Church loses its proper function and role speaking with power to power. The Church alone has authority to speak and probe and penetrate the conscience of the nation-producing conviction and repentance toward God.

Bruce's 8th Mountain is a concept that honors the role of the Church in the Religion Mountain, yet liberates and unleashes the pent up, latent potential of the body of Christ to advance in every sphere of influence. Now we can finally begin a constructive conversation about how the *ecclesia* Jesus commissioned can operate. As Bruce describes, the Church Jesus came to build would operate as a called out company of believers with authority at the gates. The local church does the equipping, but the saints take up their outposts as the *ecclesia* in their work where they pray and wield the power of agreement to legislate the will of God in their territory over and against the will of the powers of darkness.

Now we can begin to see how apostolic and prophetic ministry can come around the saints to help them as they ascend their mountains. We see how God is now advancing the saints to become voices of counsel and advisors to the Cyrus-type leaders who are being placed in seats of authority. Now we can begin to see end time Josephs come into position. *The 8th Mountain* shows us how believers can form *ecclesias* or "micro-church" within their domain as Daniel did in Babylon when he met in his house with three

Hebrew friends serving in government (Dan. 2:17). *The 8ᵗʰ Mountain* shows us how apostolic hubs can be formed to assist the labors of leaders in the 7 Mountains.

Most importantly, *The 8ᵗʰ Mountain* is the bridge strategy that links the nuclear church to the extended Church, the body of Christ, giving Jesus that which the Father has promised – nations for His inheritance (Psa. 2:8). In the end there will be sheep nations and goat nations (Matt. 25:31). We live in the exciting time when those nations are being formed. The local church *ecclesia* and the extended Church *Ecclesia* in the 7 Mountains, make the 8ᵗʰ Mountain a reality – at the top of the Mountains (Isa. 2:2)! The coming together of these parts will fulfill what Paul wrote: *"His intent was that now, through the church, the manifold wisdom of God should be made known to the rulers and authorities in the heavenly realms"* (Eph. 3:10, NIV).

Read this book, mark it up, and let's join Dr. Bruce Cook in this powerful timely conversation.

—DR. LANCE WALLNAU
Catalytic Thought Leader
President, The Lance Learning Group
www.lancewallnau.com

ABOUT DR. LANCE WALLNAU

Dr. Lance Wallnau is an internationally recognized speaker, business and political strategist. *USA Today* reports that he is one of only three evangelical leaders to have accurately predicted Donald Trump's Presidency. Dr. Wallnau's best-selling book, *God's Chaos Candidate*, is credited as being the catalyst that mobilized thousands of Christians to vote for Donald Trump and contributed to his unprecedented election victory.

Dr. Wallnau has shared platforms with best-selling authors Ken Blanchard and John Maxwell, and lectured at universities from Harvard and M.I.T. to the London School of Theology. Merging a thirty-year background consulting in business and the non-profit sector, Lance inspires visions of tomorrow with the clarity of today—connecting ideas to action. His students represent a tapestry spanning nations and spheres: from politicians, to CEOs, entertainers and entrepreneurs. He currently directs the Lance Learning Group, a strategic teaching and consulting company based in Dallas, Texas.

Dr. Wallnau is a frequent television guest and conference keynote speaker. Thousands of leaders around the world attest to the lasting impact of their first encounter with Lance. If you've never heard him before you should join with thousands of others – just check out his regular broadcasts on Periscope and Facebook Live, under Lance Wallnau.

FOREWORD

BY DR. ALVEDA C. KING

When Dr. Bruce Cook contacted me with the invitation to write a foreword to *The 8th Mountain*, a flurry of emotions ensued. Intrigue was chased by the winds of grace as amazement, surprise and a bit of "Why me?" joined in the melee. I'd encountered Dr. Cook in some prophetic corridors with Pastor Frank Amedia and company. That is all a divine journey in and of itself. Then, just when I felt I'd mastered the urgency of conquering the 7 Mountains, in came a clarion call email from Dr. Bruce. Would I be so kind as to consider writing a foreword to *The 8th Mountain*? Talk about a kairos moment!

It wasn't like I was being asked to do a favor; I was being offered the honor of taking part in a major awakening with this new chapter in God's unfolding journey of grace. I wasn't doing a favor; I was invited to step into the favor of God surrounding the release of this book. That's just it. As you read this book, you will receive divine favor from God to be transformed in your heart and mind. You will become even more than a conqueror.

This seems unbelievable, yet it is all true. Your acceptance of the 8th Mountain, the Mountain of God, will absolutely transform you and empower you as a servant leader to influence the 7 Mountains of Culture. Isn't that just like God? Once you feel as though you are just about over the top with mastering your position of influence in the 7 Mountain journey, God takes you a step higher, from completion to new beginnings. Yes, reader, you are going from 7 to 8 and beyond. Glory to God.

While Dr. Cook holds the copyright to this book, God holds the Keys to the Kingdom, all of which is revealed throughout the pages of this journey. Each chapter is a journey until itself, each page a stepping stone to greater, higher and deeper revelation. God is releasing and revealing a higher and deeper awareness of genuine worship, obedience, submission and promotion during this season. There is a godly wave of creativity that is hovering over the body, awaiting release even as a cloudburst brings much latter rain. It's all here in these pages.

True to His nature, God leaves no stone unturned, so the housekeeping chapters of stewardship, rest, health, wealth, destiny and legacy are not to be considered afterthoughts by any means. We will understand it better as we read along, and pray continually as we do.

Somehow it seems that when life appears to be besieged by terror, God is closest to us. If we were to rely solely on human reasonings, earthbound news reports and our natural senses, we would accept the doom and gloom of the world. Yet, in this hour, God's glorious Church is arising.

At the end of his lifetime, my uncle, Rev. Martin Luther King, Jr., dreamed of Moses' Mountaintop. Even as Moses did, Uncle M.L. met God there. My daddy, Rev. A. D. King, taught me that the God of Love is ever on the mountain and in the valley. My grandfather, Dr. Martin Luther King, Sr., would often end his sermons with this phrase: "I feel my help [Holy Spirit] coming on. Keep looking up." The Psalmist penned it this way:

"I will lift up my eyes to the mountains; from where shall my help come?" (Psalm 121:1).

This book, *The 8th Mountain,* leads us to higher ground; as we follow Jesus Christ the Good Shepherd and keep looking up, God's grace is sufficiently shining upon us.

Lord lift us up, and plant our feet on higher ground, even as having hinds' feet on the highest places, we can reach Heaven by your grace. Amen.

—EVANGELIST ALVEDA C. KING
www.alvedakingministries.com
www.adkingfoundation.com
www.civilrightsfortheunborn.org

ABOUT DR. ALVEDA KING

Alveda C. King is a Christian evangelist and civil rights activist and is also known for her creative contributions in film, music, politics, education and journalism. She is also an actress, singer, songwriter, blogger, author (including KING TRUTHS, AMERICA RETURN TO GOD, KING RULES, WHO WE ARE IN CHRIST JESUS), FOX NEWS Contributor and a television and radio personality.

As a former GA State Legislator, Director of Civil Rights for the Unborn for Priests for Life, and devoted mother and grandmother, she is also a guardian of the King Family Legacy. Alveda is the daughter of Rev. A. D. King and Mrs. Naomi King, the granddaughter of Rev. Martin Luther King, Sr. and Mrs. Alberta Williams King, and the niece of Dr. Martin Luther King, Jr.

ONE

THE CHIEF MOUNTAIN

*"And it will come about in the last days That the mountain of the house of the LORD Will be established as **the chief of the mountains.** It will be raised above the hills, And the peoples will stream to it."*
(Mic. 4:1, NASB, author's emphasis)

Scripture depicts the Mountain of the Lord as "the chief of the mountains," and for good reason: it is the governing mountain above all others. The Hebrew word translated chief is *rosh* (Strong's H7218), elsewhere translated "head, top, summit, upper part, chief, total, sum, height, front, beginning." Headship conveys covering or rulership, as also denoted in 1 Cor. 11:3, Eph. 4:15, and Eph. 5:23. Scripture clearly depicts mountains as symbols of kingdoms and dominions. Micah 4 and Isaiah 2 both speak of the Mountain of the Lord being exalted above the mountains and hills – that is, the kingdoms and dominions of the earth.

Has the Mountain of the Lord always been superior to the other mountains? Is becoming the "chief of the mountains" a new event, or a new realization in "the Last Days" of an enduring situation? In either case, becoming established as the chief of the Mountains is an event with world-changing effects. With the exception of Solomon's visits from the Queen of Sheba and other rulers, there has never been a time in history when "peoples" and "Nations" have voluntarily come to the Mountain of the Lord for any extended period of time. Rather, since the Great Commission, emissaries have been going to the peoples and nations as sent ones from the Mountain of the Lord!

Micah 4 and Isaiah 2 state that the establishment of the Chief Mountain will cause both individuals and nations to voluntarily come to the Mountain ("all nations will stream to it"). What will they seek? What do they need that is unavailable anywhere else? Their expectation is summarized by two requests:

- That "He may teach us his ways."
- And that "We may walk in his paths."

What is happening now with individuals, people groups, and geopolitical entities (nations) that they are eagerly seeking guidance, instruction and even training evidenced by a commitment to ongoing learning?

Consider carefully Jesus' prophetic forecast for the "last days":

> *"And there will be ... distress of*

nations, with perplexity ..."
Luke 21:25, NKJV

"Distress" here in the Greek is *synoche*, a "narrowing" or restriction of options. "Perplexity" here is *aporia*, a state of quandary, to be without resources, to be in straits, to be left wanting, to be embarrassed, to be in doubt, not to know which way to turn. So, in Jesus' words, in the last days, nations will confront problems with limited options and without the wisdom to choose or the resources to implement the best available option. This is consistent with Isaiah's prediction of "darkness covers the earth, and gross darkness the nations" (Isa. 60:2).

So, people in darkness, and nations in perplexity and distress, will have unsolveable, intractable, perplexing problems. Sounds like a great script for a movie or reality TV show, or a great setup for someone with supernatural solutions to offer or bring to the table. Here are just a few of the intractable problems which face people and nations today:

- **Healthcare** – diabetes, obesity, hemorrhagic fever epidemics (ebola, zika, dengue), AIDS, cancer, Alzheimers, Parkinson's, contaminated air / water / land, etc.

- **Hunger** from unsafe and nutritionally deficient food supplies and famine.

- **Thirst** from unsafe and contaminated drinking water, drought, and water transportation.

- **Ideology conflicts** with racial tension, terrorism, genocide, radical Islam, communism, socialism, sexuality, immigration and refugees.

- **Human slavery** via financial oppression, corporate sweatshop operation, religious enslavement, sex trafficking, etc.

- **Wars** driven by ego, ideology, greed, and religion, with no prospects of peace in sight.

- **Environmental concerns**.

- **Political infighting**, unrest, turmoil and conflict.

- **Economic systemic stress** globally.

- **A lack of basic civility i**n public dialogue.

- **Increasing crime and violence** in urban regions and population centers.

- **An erosion of ethical and moral values** and foundations in society, and in institutions.

In these days, the Mountain of the Lord is being exalted above the kingdoms (mountains) and ideologies (hills) of mankind. Nations and people have created the problems, and have been paralyzed by an inability to solve them. Both people (individuals and ethnic / people groups) and nations need solutions. These problems, left unsolved, will potentially spell the end of civilization as we know it and terminate the rule of national leaders.

What will they find at the Mountain of the Lord? What will be the prescription for their woes? What will be the result of their quest? Will they be glad that they came? Will they be able to say that the half has not been told? Micah 4 and Isaiah 2 present a three-part solution:

- First: a common, universal framework applicable to everyone and every nation:

the rule of law, based on the "Law of the Lord" (Torah). This is an inflexible standard that displaces the vagaries, opinions, and interpretations of humans.

- Second: judgments, court rulings, decisions that settle personal and national disputes, resulting in justice with equity. This wisdom, greater than that of Solomon, settles disputes in enduring ways, and results in the perfect remediation for the injured.

- Finally: individually tailored, personal guidance, described as "the word of the Lord." In context, this is not referring solely or even primarily to the Bible – a fixed compendium of teaching and instruction – but, rather, the adaptation and application of the Lord's guidance to each unique situation. Included are prophetic words, relevant counsel, and practical insight.

What is the result? Peace and enduring freedom from war; freedom from oppression and fear; private property and prosperity – and even freedom of faith and religion. Micah 4:5 declares, *"All the nations may walk in the name of their gods; we will walk in the name of the Lord our God for ever and ever."*

Not only is the Mountain of the Lord the chief mountain, but it is **established**, according to Micah 4:1 and Isaiah 2:2. The Hebrew word for established here is *nakown*, from the root *kun* (Strong's H3559). In the case of Job 22:28, where it says to decree a thing and He will establish it, the root word used there is *quwm*, meaning to abide, accomplish, be

5

clear, make clear, continue, confirm, decree, endure, make good, help, hold, raise, remain, ordain, perform, establish, succeed, lift up, strengthen (Strong's H6965).

And, in 2 Chron. 20:20 and 1 Sam. 3:20, the root word used for establish is *'aman*, meaning to build up or support, to foster as a parent or nurse, to trust or believe, to be permanent or quiet, true or certain, to go to the right hand (Strong's H539). 2 Chron. 20:20 says that if you believe the Lord your God, you shall be established, and if you believe His prophets, you shall prosper. 1 Sam 3:20 says that Samuel was established as a prophet of the Lord. God establishes His Words, His messengers, His covenant, His ways, His nature and His mountain to give them a greater weight of authority and promise for our benefit.

Everything that God does is established at the mouth of two or three witnesses (Deut. 19:15, Matt. 18:16). Scripture is very clear on that and He will establish when it is time for your prophecies to come to pass. A few verses that touch on or address prophetic confirmation include 2 Pet. 1:19, Job 28:27, Dan. 9:12, and Isa. 44:26. 2 Pet. 1:19 states, *"We have also a more sure word of prophecy..."* The NIV version says, *"And we have the word of the prophets made more certain..."* The Greek word for more is *meizon*, an adverb meaning of greater degree, even more. It is related to the adjective *megas*, meaning larger or greater (Strong's G3185). The Greek word for sure is *bebaios* from the root word *baino*, and derivative *basis*, meaning: stable, secure, firm, steadfast, full support, certain, firmly grounded, guaranteed, more sure, unalterable, valid (Strong's G949).

In other words, as New Testament disciples and follow-ers of Christ, we have access to confirmed words that have stronger and greater influence and stability because they are foundationally built by God Himself and have the integrity, substance, and strength necessary to complete the plan and purposes of God, and to not return void or fall to the ground.

In Dan. 9:12 and Isa. 44:26, the Hebrew word for confirmed or confirmeth is *quwm* (Strong's H6965). The words of the Lord are, in themselves, a decree that affects the DNA and atomic structure of everything that is created. He causes the motives and intents of His will and purpose to be made clear after what He says demonstrates itself before the eyes of men. What He says will produce His desires. (See Isa. 46:10: *"Declaring the end from the beginning, and from ancient times the things that are not done, saying, My counsel shall stand, and I will do all my pleasures."*) Isa. 44:26 says, *"...That confirmeth the word of his servant, and performeth the counsel of his messengers..."*

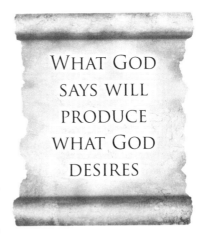

WHAT GOD SAYS WILL PRODUCE WHAT GOD DESIRES

The Hebrew word for performeth is *shalam*, meaning: to be safe in mind, body or estate; to cause to be complete; to reciprocate; to prosper, make recompense and restitution (Strong's H7999).

I believe that the Mountain of the Lord, the 8th Mountain, is now being exalted above the 7 Mountains of Culture – and all of the hills as well. Around the globe, several kings and leaders of nations have submitted their nation and its rulership to heaven and are finding solutions to perplexity. Sheep nations are now arising (Matt. 25:32-33). I believe that the 8th Mountain, and the divine wisdom that it represents, will now begin feeding or downloading breakthrough solutions to disease epidemics, food shortages, water shortages and water quality issues, weather changes, civil conflict (religious, racial, ethnic, gender, class), oppression and corruption, injustice, human slavery, sexual trafficking, pollution, greed, family distress, educational lethargy and dysfunction, economic systems malaise, corporate cultures, governments – and more!

May the glory of God arise on his people, and may the kings of the earth and the leaders of the 7 Mountains eagerly come seeking and finding solutions to their perplexing problems. Those who spend time with God and His Word and His Spirit and dwell in His presence and commune with Him and develop a personal relationship with Him, become transformed in the process, and thus are better informed, empowered and equipped to attract, steward and exercise influence in the 7 Mountains of Culture (Arts & Entertainment, Business & Economy, Education, Family, Government & Law, Media, and Religion). That is the basic premise and thesis of this book.

The remaining 20 chapters (2-21) present a strategic overview and sampling of the key resources, truths, attributes, gifts, principles, technologies and values that God has made available to us, and that you can expect to receive from Him in the Mountain of the Lord – the 8th Mountain — to aid and benefit you and others you influence in the 7 Mountains of Culture. This is essentially the "how to" and "secret sauce" and "operating system" you need to increase your influence, increase your favor, increase your effectiveness, accept your godly identity, understand your purpose, exercise your sonship, complete your assignment, get promoted to the next level, get closer to God, get closer to family and friends, find the missing piece of your own life puzzle, and/or to help bring your life into focus and order and convergence and acceleration.

Historically, all those who have come into God's presence have been changed in some way, and have been marked or imprinted in their spirit as a result. You will be, too, as you continue reading, because you cannot read, absorb, process and practice what is written in this book without being transformed (2 Cor. 3:18, Rom. 12:2) on some level. So, reader beware and continue reading at your own risk. You have been warned! Freedom, wisdom and truth are straight ahead! Contents under pressure! Extremely flammable! Potentially explosive! Handle with care! Use caution when approaching! Contents may be helpful to your life, relationships, family, education, career, vocation, occupation, profession, assignments, destiny, legacy and/or spiritual, emotional, physical and financial well-being. We now turn our attention to foundation and transformation in Chapter 2.

ALL THOSE
WHO COME
INTO GOD'S
PRESENCE ARE
CHANGED,
TRANSFORMED
BY HIS SPIRIT.

TWO

FOUNDATION AND TRANSFORMATION

"Righteousness and justice are the
foundation of your throne..."
(Psa. 89:14, 97:2, NIV)

Without a strong foundation, whatever is built will collapse and crumble eventually. Scripture tells us that the wise man built his house upon the rock, while the fool built his house upon the sand, and that when the storms, wind and waves came and crashed upon the house built upon sand, it fell and was destroyed, while the wise man's house stood firm, immovable and unshaken (Matt. 7:24-27). We are also told to "count the cost" before we begin to build, to make sure we are able to finish it and not become a public laughingstock or subject of mockery because we underestimated the cost, time, permits, labor, materials, equipment and risks involved and were unable to complete it once we started (Luke 14:25-34).

These principles apply to everything and everyone in life, including God. Therefore, God models for us what a strong foundation looks like, and makes it clear that everything He does and says has righteousness and justice as its foundation, including His throne in heaven (Psa. 89:14, 97:2). This same foundation is reiterated and reinforced throughout Scripture, including Psa. 33:5, *"He loves righteousness and justice; the earth is full of the steadfast love of the LORD."* Psa. 103:6 notes, *"The LORD works righteousness and justice for all who are oppressed."* Isa. 5:16 adds, *"The LORD of hosts is exalted in justice, and the Holy God shows himself holy in righteousness."*

Also, a prophecy about Jesus is given in Isa. 9:6-7. Verse 7 says, *"Of the increase of his government and peace there will be no end. He will reign on David's throne and over his kingdom, establishing it and upholding it with justice and righteousness from that time on and forever. The zeal of the Lord Almighty will accomplish this."* Isa. 16:5 adds, *"A throne will be established in steadfast love, and on it will sit in faithfulness in the tent of David one who judges and seeks justice and is swift to do righteousness."* God makes it very clear: like Father, like Son.

This theme has been a constant throughout God's history with Israel. Amos 5:21-23 says, *"I hate all your show and pretense—the hypocrisy of your religious festivals and solemn assemblies. I will not accept your burnt offerings and grain offerings. I won't even notice all your choice peace offerings. Away with your noisy hymns of praise! I will not listen to the music of your harps. Instead,* **I want to see a mighty flood of justice, an endless river of righteous living**" (author's emphasis).

Similar words are shared by other Old Testament prophets. Isa. 48:18 says, *"If only you had paid attention to My commandments! Then your well-being would have been like a* *river, And your righteousness like the waves of the sea."* Jer. 9:23-24 adds, *This is what the Lord says: "Let not the wise boast of their wisdom or the strong boast of their strength or the rich boast of their riches, but let the one who boasts boast about this: that they have the understanding to know me, that **I am the Lord, who exercises kindness, justice and righteousness on earth, for in these I delight"** (author's emphasis).

Jer. 22:3 records, *Thus says the LORD, "Do justice and righteousness, and deliver the one who has been robbed from the power of his oppressor. Also do not mistreat or do violence to the stranger, the orphan, or the widow; and do not shed innocent blood in this place."* And Ezek. 45:9 notes, *Thus says the Lord GOD, "Enough, you princes of Israel; put away violence and destruction, and practice justice and righteousness. Stop your expropriations from My people,"* declares the Lord GOD.

Jesus continued this theme in His earthly ministry and said to his disciples in Matt. 5:20, *"For I tell you that unless your righteousness surpasses that of the Pharisees and the teachers of the law, you will certainly not enter the kingdom of heaven."* Jesus rebuked these religious leaders with seven woes. Matt. 23:23-33 says, *"Woe to you, teachers of the law and Pharisees, you hypocrites! You give a tenth of your spices—mint, dill and cumin. But you have neglected the more important matters of the law—justice, mercy and faithfulness. You should have practiced the latter, without neglecting the former. You blind guides! You strain out a gnat but swallow a camel...You snakes! You brood of vipers! How will you escape being condemned to hell?"*

The key word Jesus spoke in the above passage besides "woe" was "hypocrites." Five times in Matt. 23:13-36, Jesus called the scribes and Pharisees hypocrites, among other things! Why? *"You shut the kingdom of heaven in men's faces.*

You yourselves do not enter, nor will you let those enter who are trying to ... You travel over land and sea to win a single convert, and when he becomes one, you make him twice as much a son of hell as you are ... You clean the outside of the cup and dish, but inside they are full of greed and self-indulgence ... You are like whitewashed tombs, which look beautiful on the outside but on the inside are full of dead men's bones and everything unclean ... [On the outside you appear to people as righteous but on the inside you are full of hypocrisy and wickedness." Jesus called these religious leaders to account and rebuked them severely because they were sinful hypocrites and were hindering others.

PERSONAL FOUNDATIONS AND TRANSFORMATION TEMPLATE

What about you and me today? Psa. 37:5-6 says, *"Commit your way to the Lord; trust in him and he will do this: He will make your righteousness shine like the dawn, the justice of your cause like the noonday sun."* Note the personalized nature of this Scripture: **"your way, your righteousness, your cause."** God is giving us a strategic key here and telling us that our foundation on earth needs to be the same as God's foundation in heaven. When that is the case, then the result is that our righteousness shines like the dawn, and the justice of our cause shines like the noonday sun. This is reminiscent of the Aaronic blessing: *"The LORD bless you and keep you; The LORD make His face shine on you and be gracious to you; The LORD lift up His face on you and give you peace"* (Num. 6:24-26).

The clear implication here is that the inverse of this proposition is also true: If you don't commit your way to the Lord and you don't trust in Him, then He will NOT make your righteousness shine like the dawn, nor the justice of your cause like the noonday sun. I.e., you will not experience the same level of favor, anointing and glory as you could have had otherwise, and your life may have a very different direction and outcome. So, these verses are a clear model or template for personal transformation.

Real, lasting transformation starts with having our foundations align with and mirror God's. This is true regardless of whether the foundations are in our friendships, marriage, family, business or job, ministry, or any other area of life. As a result, the ongoing sanctification process in each of our lives has a strong foundation to build upon, and Scriptures like Rom. 3:22-24, Rom. 12:1-2, 2 Cor. 10:3-5, 2 Cor. 3:18, Gal. 5:16-26, Eph. 4:22-5:17, Phil. 2:1-16, Phil. 4:8, Col. 2:6-18, James 1:13-15, 1 Pet. 2:1-5, 2 Pet. 1:3-9, 1 John 3:4-10 and many others have room to take effect and do their good work in our lives.

The Lord will guide us in how to build these strong foundations in each of our spheres of influence as we spend time with Him on the 8th Mountain. As a result, whatever we build on these strong foundations in each of our spheres of influence will not be shaken, for whatever is of the kingdom of God will not be shaken (Heb. 12:28)!

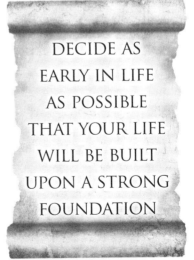

DECIDE AS EARLY IN LIFE AS POSSIBLE THAT YOUR LIFE WILL BE BUILT UPON A STRONG FOUNDATION

So, it is important to decide as early in life as possible that our life will be built upon a foundation of righteousness and justice, and that these two points will form the poles of our ethical and moral compass or GPS as we navigate life and its many decisions and relationships. This one decision will have massive ramifications, implications and consequences, and will effectively close the door to many opportunities and situations that come our way and present themselves to us, that don't meet or pass this basic test, and are less than honorable or godly. Run, don't walk, from anything that would seek to ensnare, entangle, or enslave you, and that would cause you to compromise your convictions and veer from this solid foundation. And, if you do slip, or have a momentary relapse, then quickly repent and get back on the right track.

Strong foundations cannot be shaken, and they will help you to stand the test of time, and the tests, trials and storms of life. If they are necessary and useful for God, then they are certainly essential for you and me. They are a necessary prerequisite to become a spiritual overcomer, and to walk in victory in Christ Jesus. 1 Pet. 2:3-5 says, *"As you come to him, the living Stone — rejected by humans but chosen by God and precious to him — you also, like living stones, are being built into a spiritual house to be a holy priesthood, offering spiritual sacrifices acceptable to God through Jesus Christ. For in Scripture it says: 'See, I lay a stone in Zion, a chosen and precious cornerstone, and the one who trusts in him will never be put to shame.'"*

Finally, in closing, 1 Cor. 3:11-15 says, *"For no one can lay any foundation other than the one already laid, which is Jesus Christ. If anyone builds on this foundation using gold, silver, costly stones, wood, hay or straw, their work will be shown for what it is, because the Day will bring it to light. It will be revealed with fire, and the fire will test the quality of each person's work. If what has been built survives, the builder will receive a reward. If it is burned up, the builder will suffer loss but yet will be saved— even though only as one escaping through the flames."* The only foundation worth laying and living is the one that is from God, based on righteousness and justice, and it is fireproof. If it is good enough for Abba Father and Jesus the Son and Holy Spirit, then it is good enough for you and me.

LOVE YOUR NEIGHBOR AS YOURSELF

The persistent cry of the human heart is to be known, accepted, loved and esteemed as we presently are. The greater cry is to find a hero, and to be a hero for others who are on the same journey to our destiny. We change when we are loved unconditionally, provided with a role model, and encouraged to take the risk to make the change.

Mark 12:28-31 (GW) says, *"One of the experts in Moses' Teachings went to Jesus during the argument with the Sadducees. He saw how well Jesus answered them, so he asked him, "Which commandment is the most important of them all?" Jesus answered, "The most important is, 'Listen, Israel, the Lord our God is the only Lord. So love the Lord your God with all your heart, with all your soul, with all your mind, and with all your strength.' The second most important commandment is this: 'Love your neighbor as you love yourself.' No other commandment is greater than these."*

The chapters that follow depict and illustrate facets of the life that kingdom leaders are called to live. The Golden Rule

17

is stated compactly: *"Do unto others as you would have them do unto you"* (Matt. 7:12; Luke 6:31). That's our mandate. Like a diamond that is very compact in structure, but shines brilliantly when its facets are polished and turned into the light, so the life of kingdom leaders should reflect the light emanating from the 8th Mountain as we are examined from various vantage points. Next, we will look at humility and honor in Chapter 3.

THREE

HUMILITY AND HONOR

*"The fear of the LORD is the instruction for
wisdom, And before honor comes humility."*
(Prov. 15:33, NASB)

*"Before his downfall a man's heart is proud,
but humility comes before honor."*
(Prov. 18:12, NASB)

Humility and honor are inextricably and inexorably
linked in Scripture, and in that God-appointed order,
so it is only natural and proper to write about them together.
We will first examine humility briefly, and then explore
honor in more depth. The Hebrew word for humility is
anawah (Strong's H6038). Humility is presented as a virtue
in Scripture: *"He has shown you, O man, what is good; And
what does the LORD require of you But to do justly, To love
mercy, And to walk humbly with your God?"* (Mic. 6:8, NKJV).

Humility is a foundational character trait, because it is a heart attitude, and Scripture makes it clear that *"God judges persons differently than humans do. Men and women look at the face; God looks into the heart"* (1 Sam. 16:7, MSG). Moreover, we are told, *"Guard your heart above all else, for it determines the course of your life"* (Prov. 4:23, NLT). An attitude of humility actually attracts God's favor, and one purpose and benefit of fasting is to humble or prostrate ourselves before the Lord and demonstrate repentance and mourning.

HUMILITY IS A FOUNDATIONAL CHARACTER TRAIT, BECAUSE IT IS A HEART ATTITUDE

Prov. 22:4 (NLT) says, *"True humility and fear of the LORD lead to riches, honor, and long life."* That is quite a compelling and remarkable list of benefits— riches, honor and life. The NASB version says, *"The reward of humility and the fear of the LORD Are riches, honor and life."* So, the result or reward of a lifestyle of humility and reverent fear of the Lord, are desirable, impressive and extremely valuable. Gal. 6:7 says, *"Be not deceived; God is not mocked: for whatever a man sows, that shall he also reap."*

The opposite of humility is pride, and it's the first thing on God's list of things He hates: *"These six things the Lord hates, yes, seven are an abomination to Him: **A proud look**, a lying tongue, hands that shed innocent blood, a heart that deviseth wicked plans, feet that are swift in running to evil, a false witness who speaks lies, and one who sows discord among brethren"* (Prov. 6:16-19, NIV, author's emphasis). But, God doesn't just hate pride, He actively opposes it: *"God opposes the proud but gives grace to the humble"* (Prov. 3:34, James 4:6, 1 Pet. 5:5).

The Greek word for "opposes" here is *antitassetai,* from the root *antitasso,* which means to resist, to set oneself against, eager to prevent or put an end to, disapproving of or disagreeing with, to set an army in array against, to arrange in battle order, or to be hostile toward (Strong's G498). It's no wonder then that Prov. 16:18 says, *"Pride goes before destruction, and a haughty spirit before a fall."* Psa. 31:23 adds, *"The Lord preserves the faithful, but the proud he pays back in full."* It is clear that God hates, opposes, and punishes pride.

Pride was the downfall of Lucifer, one of the chief angels, who was expelled from heaven by God and became Satan, the devil. Jesus modeled humility for us by leaving heaven and coming to earth and taking on human form. In fact, one of His names is Emmanuel, meaning "God with us" or "God incarnate". Heb. 2:9-12 says, *"But we see Jesus, who was made a little lower than the angels for the suffering of death, crowned with glory and honor; that he by the grace of God should taste death for every man. For it became him, for whom are all things, and by whom are all things, in bringing many sons unto glory, to make the captain of their salvation perfect through sufferings. For both he that sanctifieth and they who are sanctified are all of one: for which cause he is not ashamed to call them brethren, Saying, I will declare thy name unto my brethren, in the midst of the church will I sing praise unto thee."*

As a result, we are commanded and exhorted by Paul the Apostle, *"Do nothing out of selfish ambition or vain conceit, but **in humility consider others better than yourselves**. Each of you should look not only to your own interests, but also to the interests of others. Your attitude should be the same as that of Christ Jesus: Who, being in very nature God, did not consider equality with God something to be grasped, but made himself nothing, taking the very nature of a servant, being made in human likeness.*

*And being found in appearance as a man, **he humbled himself** and became obedient to death – even death on a cross! Therefore God exalted him to the highest place and gave him the name that is above every name,"* (Phil. 2:3-9, author's emphasis). The Greek word for humility here is *tapeinophrosynē* (Strong's G5012).

Jesus is our example in all things and if humility was required for His assignment, mission and destiny to be fulfilled, it will be necessary for ours also.

Once we have learned and mastered humility, and have allowed God to develop and test and refine our character, and to examine and approve our workmanship and stewardship, then we have become qualified candidates who are positioned to receive honor from God in due season. This is what will happen when we spend time with the Lord on the 8th Mountain! Humility is the key that will open the door to the honor that we need in order to make the impact that we are destined to have in the world!

In fact, you might say the kingdom of God is based upon an honor system. Some definitions and synonyms for honor include: esteem, renown, reverence, acclaim/recognition, deference/preference, glory, respect, and trust. Some ways that we can honor others are: respect, trust, obedience, prayer, service, excellence, encouragement, affirmation, acceptance, awards, promotion, recognition, kindness, mercy, grace, love, forgiveness, sharing and/or leveraging our time, talents, treasure and spiritual gifts.

Ten benefits of honor include: 1) Pleases God; 2) Blesses Others; 3) Yields Obedience to Scripture; 4) Releases Life/Unlocks Favor/Breaks Negative Cycles/ Shifts Atmospheres; 5) Long Life for Those Who Practice it (Eph. 6:3); 6) So that it May Go Well With You on the Earth (Eph. 6:3); 7) It is

Redemptive (Gen. 14:17-24; Ruth 3:1ff); 8) It is Preemptive (Gideon, Judg, 7:22-8:3); 9) It Can be Exemptive (Jesse's family was exempted from paying taxes, 1 Sam. 17:25); and 10) It is Connected to/Associated with Wisdom and Riches (1 Chron. 29:12; Prov. 8:17-18).

There are four dimensions of honor: Dishonor, Lack or Absence of Honor, True Honor, and False Honor. We will define each of those in turn (see Figure 1 for four-quadrant diagram of The Four Dimensions of Honor).

Dishonor is the state of loss of honor, fame, prestige, renown, or reputation; disgraceful or dishonest character or conduct; disgrace; ignominy; shame (Dictionary.com). Deut. 27:16 says, *"Cursed is the one who treats his father and mother with dishonor."* Psa. 4:2 says, *"O ye sons of men, **how long shall my glory be turned into dishonor**? How long will ye love vanity, and seek after falsehood?"* (author's emphasis). Psa. 44:9 says, *"Yet you have rejected us and brought us to dishonor, And do not go out with our armies."* Psa. 44:15 says, *"**My dishonor tortures me continuously**; the shame on my face overwhelms me"* (author's emphasis). Psa. 69:19 says, *"You know my reproach and my shame and my dishonor. All my adversaries are before you."* Psa. 89:34 says, *"I will not dishonor my covenant because I will not change what I have spoken."* Prov. 3:35 says, *"The wise will inherit honor, but He holds up fools to dishonor."*

Lack or Absence of Honor is the state of lack of honor, fame, prestige, renown, or reputation; or a withholding or omission of honor that is deserving or due or expected, as in a social snub or a breach of protocol. For example, Lam. 4:16 records, "The priests are shown **no honor**, the elders **no favor**" (author's emphasis). *And Jesus said to them, "A prophet is not **without honor**, except in his hometown and among his* *relatives and in his own household"* (Matt. 13:57, Mark 6:4, John 4:44, author's emphasis). It was an honor omission that kept Moses and Aaron from entering the Promised Land. Num. 20:12 says, *But the LORD said to Moses and Aaron, "Because* **you did not trust in me enough to honor me** *as holy in the sight of the Israelites, you will not bring this community into the land I give them"* (author's emphasis).

Sometimes God gives the honor to someone else because of the way you go about your assignment. Judges 4:9 records this concerning Barak, *"'Very well, Deborah said, 'I will go with you. But because of the way you are going about this,* **the honor will not be yours,** *for the Lord will hand Sisera over to a woman.' So Deborah went with Barak to Kedesh'"* (author's emphasis). On another occasion, God chastised the priests for failing to honor Him properly, or at all, with this rebuke. *"The LORD of Heaven's Armies says to the priests: "A son honors his father, and a servant respects his master.* **If I am your father and master, where are the honor and respect I deserve?** *You have shown contempt for my name!"* (Mal. 1:6, author's emphasis).

True (Godly) Honor is the real thing—genuine, authentic, pure, and uncontaminated. Honor begets honor, and has a reciprocal effect. 1 Sam. 2:30 says, *"Those who honor me I will honor, but those who despise me will be disdained (lightly esteemed)."* Prov. 3:9-10 adds, *"Honor the LORD with your possessions, And with the firstfruits of all your increase; then will your vats be full and your barns will overflow."* Giving voluntarily and cheerfully releases a powerful spiritual stimulus, and helps unlock God's blessing and generosity. Rom. 13:7 records, *"Render to all men their dues. [Pay] taxes to whom taxes are due, revenue to whom revenue is due, respect to whom respect is due, and* **honor to whom honor is due"** (author's emphasis).

Similarly, Rom. 12:10 notes, *"Be kindly affectionate to one another with brotherly love, in honor giving preference to one another."* In addition, there are other expressions of True Honor. Almsgiving or philanthropy is one such act. Prov. 14:31 says, *"He who oppresses the poor shows contempt for their Maker, but whoever is kind to the needy honors God."* How we treat our bodies is another example. 1 Cor. 6:19-20 says, *"Do you not know that your body is a temple of the Holy Spirit, who is in you, whom you have received from God? You are not your own; you were bought at a price. Therefore honor God with your body."* 1 Cor. 10:31 adds, *"So then, whether you eat or drink, or whatever you may do, do all for the honor and glory of God."*

True Honor has a cost, involves a voluntary decision and process, and is a lifestyle. 2 Tim. 2:20-21 (NASB) says, *"Now in a large house there are not only gold and silver vessels, but also vessels of wood and of earthenware, and **some to honor and some to dishonor**. Therefore, **if anyone cleanses himself** from these things, **he will be a vessel for honor**, sanctified, useful to the Master, prepared for every good work"* (author's emphasis). The

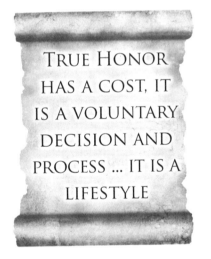

TRUE HONOR HAS A COST, IT IS A VOLUNTARY DECISION AND PROCESS ... IT IS A LIFESTYLE

word "if" is conditional, and recognizes the free will of followers and disciples of Jesus to choose the path of sanctification, obedience and holiness outlined in Scripture for all believers in Yeshua.

True Honor can also have eternal consequences. Jesus is our example in all things, and just as He honored the Father, so the Father honored the Son. *Jesus said, "I didn't make this up. What I teach comes from the One who sent me. Anyone who wants to do his will can test this teaching and know whether it's from God or whether I'm making it up. A person making things up tries to make himself look good. But* **someone trying to honor the one who sent him** *sticks to the facts and doesn't tamper with reality"* (John 7:16-19, author's emphasis).

John 8:49-50 expands on this. *Jesus said, "I'm not crazy. I simply honor my Father, while you dishonor me. I am not trying to get anything for myself. God intends something gloriously grand here and is making the decisions that will bring it about."* John 12:26 states, *"If any of you wants to serve me, then follow me. Then you'll be where I am, ready to serve at a moment's notice.* **The Father will honor and reward anyone who serves me"** (author's emphasis). Anyone includes you and me. Mark 16:19-20 records, *"Then the Master Jesus, after briefing them, was taken up to heaven, and* **he sat down beside God in the place of honor.** *And the disciples went everywhere preaching, the Master working right with them, validating the Message with indisputable evidence"* (author's emphasis).

False Honor is a very different story, and involves flattery, self-promotion, and/or wrong motives. True Honor can only be given, not taken; False Honor is focused on taking or acquiring honor for self-advancement, self-promotion, self-aggrandizement, ego gratification, financial gain, political power, ambition, or to enhance one's reputation, status, etc. The Bible speaks about this at length. Jesus and Isaiah the Prophet said, *"These people honor me with their lips, but their hearts are far from me"* (Matt. 15:8, Isa. 29:13, NIV, NLT). Prov. 25:27 records, *"It is not good to eat too much honey,* **nor is it honorable to seek one's own honor**" (author's emphasis). Heb. 5:4 notes, concerning the role or position of High Priest, *"No one takes this honor upon himself; he must be called by God…"*

Jesus also challenged the religious leaders of His day with this insightful, scathing question in John 5:44: *"How can you believe,* **who receive honor from one another, and do not seek the honor that comes from the only God?"** (author's emphasis). Jesus later taught his disciples about these same leaders in Matt. 23:5-7, *"Everything they do is done for men to see: They make their phylacteries wide and the tassels on their garments long; they love the place of honor at banquets and the most important seat in the synagogues; they love to be greeted in the marketplaces and to have men call them Rabbi."*

Jesus also had to address this topic with two of his own disciples, James and John. *"'Arrange it,' they said, 'so that we will be awarded* **the highest places of honor** *in your glory — one of us at your right, the other at your left.' Jesus said, 'Come to think of it, you will drink the cup I drink, and be baptized in my baptism. But as to awarding places of honor, that's not my business. There are other arrangements for that'"* (Mark 10:37-40, author's emphasis). Jesus further taught his disciples, *"He told them this parable: 'When someone invites you to a wedding feast, do not take the place of honor, for a person more distinguished than you may have been invited. If so, the host who invited both of you will come and say to you, 'Give this man your seat.' Then, humiliated, you will have to take the least important place. But when you are invited, take the lowest place…'"* (Luke 14:7-11). Following is a table summarizing these points.

THE FOUR DIMENSIONS OF HONOR	
DISHONOR (Insults, Slights, Curses)	**TRUE (GODLY) HONOR**
LACK / ABSENCE of HONOR	**FALSE HONOR** (Flattery or Self-Promotion)

AUTHENTICITY — More ↑ / Less ↓

AFFIRMATION — ← Less / More →

Figure 1. The Four Dimensions of Honor. ©2017 Dr. Bruce Cook.

One such application of this principle or virtue that is a direct commandment from God is to honor our fathers and mothers. This is true both in the natural or physical realm and in the spiritual realm. One of the greatest cries and needs of the human heart is to find those who are willing and able to father or mother us in the spiritual dimension in the things of God. Those who have found and entered into relationship with such an individual or individuals can testify to the profound impact and effect and critical difference that it has made in their lives.

Both the Old and New Testaments speak about this. Deut. 27:16 says, *"Cursed is the one who treats his father and mother with dishonor."* Eph. 6:1-4 adds, *"Children, obey your parents in the Lord, for this is right. Honor your father and mother, which is the first commandment with promise: that it may be well with you and you may live long on the earth. And you, fathers, do not provoke your children to wrath, but bring them up in the training and admonition of the Lord."*

A few Scriptures even speak of double honor. *"Let the elders who rule well be counted worthy of double honor, especially those who labor in the word and doctrine"* (1 Tim. 5:17). Isa. 61:7 (NLT) also records, *"Instead of shame and dishonor, you will enjoy a double share of honor. You will possess a double portion of prosperity in your land, and everlasting joy will be yours."*

The anointing breaks the yoke, and also brings honor. Acts 28:7-10 (NIV) says, *"There was an estate nearby that belonged to Publius, the chief official of the island. He welcomed us to his home and showed us generous hospitality for three days. His father was sick in bed, suffering from fever and dysentery. Paul went in to see him and, after prayer, placed his hands on him and healed him. When this had happened, the rest of the sick* *on the island came and were cured. **They honored us in many ways**; and when we were ready to sail, they furnished us with the supplies we needed"* (author's emphasis). The NLT says in verse 10, *"we were showered with honors,"* and the ESV reads, *"They also honored us greatly."*

God is the ultimate and original source of honor, favor and riches. 1 Chron. 29:12 says, *"**Both riches and honor come from You**, And You reign over all. In Your hand is power and might; In Your hand it is to make great And to give strength to all"* (author's emphasis). Psa. 84:11 adds, *"For the Lord God is a sun and shield; **the Lord bestows favor and honor**; no good thing does he withhold from those whose walk is blameless"* (author's emphasis). And, Prov. 8:17-18 records, *"I [wisdom] love those who love me, and those who seek me find me. **With me are riches and honor**, enduring wealth and prosperity"* (author's emphasis).

Who better than a king understands honor? That's why the king's honor is worth waiting for. Est. 6:6 records one of the most profound and powerful questions in Scripture. *"King Xerxes I, when he had determined that Mordecai the Jew had not yet been honored for disclosing a plot to kill the King years earlier, asked his chief royal advisor, Prince Haman: "**What should be done to the man whom the king delights to honor?**"* (author's emphasis).

Prince Haman replied, *"For the man the king delights to honor, have them bring a royal robe the king has worn and a horse the king has ridden, one with a royal crest placed on its head. Then let the robe and horse be entrusted to one of the king's most noble princes. Let them robe the man the king delights to honor, and lead him on the horse through the city streets, proclaiming before him..."* (Est. 6:7-9). Haman, of course expected this honor for himself, but the king bestowed it upon Mordecai. Now personalize this question. What should be done for you by the King of kings since God wants to honor you? It is a sobering question indeed.

Finally, Mal. 1:11 says, *"I am honored all over the world. And there are people who know how to worship me all over the world, **who honor me by bringing their best to me**. They're saying it everywhere: 'God is greater, this God-of-the-Angel-Armies'"* (author's emphasis). God expects and deserves our best in all areas of our lives as our *"reasonable service"* (Rom. 12:1). Honoring others and honoring God is a vital part of that, along with living life from a posture and attitude of humility, yet from a heart of confidence, strength and boldness.

Everyone wants a leader who is approachable, and a mentor who is successful. When Kingdom leaders model humility in the 7 Mountains of Culture, and display a life of honor, their followers find them to be approachable, credible, and inspiring, too. As a learner, and as a follower, I am encouraged by leaders who listen and share their success verbally and by example, too.

In closing this chapter, here are a few honor case studies you can read on your own for further study: 1) Abraham honored Melchizedek (Gen. 14-15); 2) King Xerxes honored Mordecai (Est. 6-10); 3) Jonathan honored David (1 Sam. 18:1-5); 4) The Queen of Sheba honored King Solomon (1 Kings 10:1-13, 2 Chron. 9:1-12); and 5) The Wise Men from the East (Magi) honored Jesus (Matt. 2:1-14). Bon appetit! Next, we turn our attention to the topic of favor in Chapter 4.

EVERYONE
WANTS A
LEADER WHO IS
APPROACHABLE,
AND A MENTOR
WHO IS
SUCCESSFUL

=== FOUR ===

FAVOR

*"For you bless the righteous, O Lord; you
cover him with favor as with a shield."*
(Psa. 5:12, ESV)

*"For the Lord God is a sun and shield; the Lord
bestows favor and honor. No good thing does he
withhold from those who walk uprightly."*
(Psa. 84:11, NIV)

Favor is defined as approval, support, preference or liking for someone or something; or, an act of kindness beyond what is due or usual; i.e., preferential treatment. Divine favor is all of this and more granted, bestowed, exhibited, and/or demonstrated by God to us, His spiritual children through the blood of Christ. Favor is a game changer and a difference maker for those who possess or enjoy it, and it represents unfair competitive advantage. Among those listed in Scripture who found divine favor were Abel, Noah, Abraham, Joseph, Job, Esther, Nehemiah, Daniel, Moses, Gideon, David, Samuel, Mary, and Jesus. You, too, may be counted by the Lord among these heroes and heroines in Scripture as one who has found divine favor, as a result of spending time with the Lord on the 8th Mountain!

Enoch and Elijah also obtained favor from God and were the only people recorded in history who did not die a physical death, but instead were taken to heaven directly by God. Arguably, two pagan kings were also given great favor by God because of their assignments, including Cyrus the Great (2 Chron. 36, Ezra 1, Isa. 44-45) and Nebuchadnezzar (Book of Daniel), both of whom bore the title King of kings.

And, since God is not a respecter of persons, you and I have access to this same favor if we are willing to pay the price required. Job 10:12 says, *"You have granted me life and favor, and Your care has preserved my spirit."* Job, the greatest man among all the people of the East, experienced a season of great hardship, loss and testing before being vindicated, restored and promoted by God. So did other great leaders like Noah, Abraham, Joseph, Moses, David, Esther and Mary. Favor does not always express itself as a bed of roses, or in pleasant circumstances, but rather as strength

SCRIPTURE IS CLEAR; THE LORD BESTOWS HIS DIVINE FAVOR UPON THE HUMBLE

to prevail and overcome adversity, and to finish and complete your assignment and mission. Jesus enjoyed great favor, but also endured tremendous opposition from the religious and political leaders of His day, and severe persecution, injustice, public humiliation, notoriety, and an agonizing and shameful death through crucifixion on a cross.

Scripture is quite clear that the Lord bestows His divine favor upon the humble, the righteous, and the wise, so you and I have a right to expect it because it is presented in Scripture as a promise to all those who meet these tests and/or satisfy these prerequisite requirements. Prov. 3:34 says, *"Toward the scorners he is scornful, but* **to the humble he gives favor**" (author's emphasis). Prov. 12:2 records, *"A good man will* **obtain favor from the LORD**, *But He will condemn a man who devises evil"* (author's emphasis). Prov. 8:35 also notes, *"For he who finds me [wisdom] finds life And* **obtains favor from the Lord**" (author's emphasis).

Prov. 3:1-4 adds, *"My son, do not forget my teaching, but let your heart keep my commandments, for length of days and years of life and peace they will add to you. Let not steadfast love and faithfulness forsake you; bind them around your neck; write them on the tablet of your heart.* **So you will find favor and good success in the sight of God and man**" (author's emphasis). And, Prov. 18:22 notes, *"He who finds a wife finds a good thing And* **obtains favor from the LORD**" (author's emphasis).

Psa. 30:5 states, *"For his anger is but for a moment, and* **his favor is for a lifetime**. *Weeping may tarry for the night, but joy comes with the morning"* (author's emphasis). The KJV says, "…in his favour is life:", and the NET Bible notes, "…his good favor restores one's life." Psa. 89:17 adds, *"For You are the glory of their strength, And by Your favor our horn is exalted."* Finally, Psa. 90:17 records a prayer of Moses we can all agree with: *"***Let the favor of the Lord our God be upon us***, and establish the work of our hands upon us; yes, establish the work of our hands!"* (author's emphasis).

Three main words are translated as favor in Scripture—two from Hebrew and one from Greek. *Ratsown* means pleasure, delight, favor, goodwill, acceptance, desire, will (Strong's H7522). *Chen* means favor, grace, charm, elegance, acceptance (Strong's H2580). And, *charis* means grace, favor, kindness, gratitude, thanks, disposed to, inclined, favorable towards, leaning towards to share benefit (Strong's G5485).

Favor has an eminently practical and measurable aspect and utility or usefulness. It is not some abstract, intangible quality

FAVOR
HAS AN
EMINENTLY
PRACTICAL
AND
MEASURABLE
ASPECT

or force. John 1:16 (AMP) notes, *"For out of His fullness (the superabundance of His grace and truth) we have all received grace upon grace [spiritual blessing upon spiritual blessing,* **favor upon favor,** *and gift heaped upon gift]"* (author's emphasis). Through Jesus we can receive not only favor, but compounded or multiplied favor.

The advantage of favor is that it is an invisible, secret weapon and a competitive advantage. It is evident to all when you have it, and when you don't. For example, U.S. President Donald Trump clearly received divine favor to help win the 2016 U.S. presidential election against all odds, and over a heavily-favored and more experienced political opponent, Hillary Clinton, who had a commanding lead in the polls. Favor can at times be subtle, but at other times create a shock and awe effect.

Approval, support, liking and preferential treatment are most often, but not always, noticeable and measurable. But, drug lords and corrupt politicians, for example, work hard to hide or cover up those kind of things for obvious reasons.

In contrast, Est. 2:15 says, *"Now Esther **won favor with everyone who saw her**"* (author's emphasis). That positive result created by favor was a great benefit and tremendous asset, not only for her, but for her people, the Jews; her uncle, Mordecai; and her husband, the king named variously Xerxes or Artaxerxes.

Similarly, Joseph found favor with both Potiphar, the captain of Pharaoh's guard, and with the unnamed chief jailer of Pharaoh's prison (Gen. 39:3-4, 21). This favor was described and expressed as both the kindness of God and prosperity. Favor toward Nehemiah by the king he served was described as mercy or compassion. It looks and acts differently with different people. Scripture records that *"Jesus kept increasing in wisdom and stature, and in favor with God and men"* (Luke 2:52). Favor is given for our assignment, and not for us personally. This is a crucial distinction, and one that we need to accept, respect, understand and steward.

Just as it is possible to receive divine favor, it is also possible to not receive favor from God (lack or absence of favor), and in fact to receive divine disfavor or judgment. Among those who received divine disfavor in Scripture were Pharaoh and his army; the several million Israelites who left Egypt with Moses and died in the wilderness — with the exception of Joshua and Caleb; Goliath; King Saul and his sons; Eli and his sons; Ahab and Jezebel; Haman and his household; Achan and his household; Balaam; Korah, Dathan, and Abiram and their families and the 250 Israelite princes who followed them; Rehoboam; Jeroboam; Baasha; Ananias and Sapphira; Judas; and Herod Agrippa, just to name a few. Jesus even said, *"I saw Satan fall like lightning from heaven"*

(Luke 10:18). So, even some angels have experienced divine disfavor.

Today, we as sons and daughters of God have received unmerited favor from God in the form of the gift of grace through the blood of Jesus and His gift of eternal life to all who believe, repent and are not ashamed to confess or profess His name before men (John 1:16, Rom. 10:9-10, Eph. 2:8, Heb. 2:10-11, James 5:16, 1 John 1:9). It is up to us to steward that gift and use it wisely, and to seek and find God's favor for our assignment(s) on earth, as well as eternal life. Figure 2 below expresses the four dimensions of favor described herein: God's Disfavor, Man's Disfavor, God's Favor, and Man's Favor. This table is designed to graphically illustrate only a few of the many dimensions of favor that potentially could be expressed, and thus is not intended to be an all-encompassing or comprehensive grid for such a complex subject.

For example, men and women who are martyred for their faith in Jesus and His Church (ekklesia) or Kingdom (basilea), appear to be in extreme disfavor with man, but are in actuality in great favor with God (Rev. 5). Likewise, those who are imprisoned, tortured, beaten, scourged and chained for their faith in Christ also appear to be in severe disfavor with man, but enjoy great favor with God (Matt. 5,6,7). Joseph, Daniel and Esther each initially appeared to be in disfavor due to their circumstances, but God quickly gave or bestowed upon them divine favor and wisdom to cause them to be promoted by man and to be used to help govern kingdoms and governments—actually, global empires, to be precise. So, spiritual discernment is required to understand the true state of an individual in their present situation or circumstance.

Joseph summarized this point well and succinctly in Gen. 50:20 (NIV) when he told his brothers, *"You intended to harm me, but God intended it for good to accomplish what is now being done, the saving of many lives."* The HCS translation says, *"You planned evil against me; God planned it for good to bring about the present result — the survival of many people."* And, the NLT translation reads, *"You intended to harm me, but God intended it all for good. **He brought me to this position** so I could save the lives of many people"* (author's emphasis).

Earlier, Joseph had explained to them the functional roles, areas of responsibility, and broad scope of his royal position (Gen. 45:8, NIV), which granted him vast authority, power and discretion: *"So then, it was not you who sent me here, but God. He made me **father to Pharaoh, lord of his entire household** and **ruler of all Egypt**"* (author's emphasis). That is quite a powerful portfolio, and one that only God could plan and bring to pass through a progressive series of assignments and promotions for a former slave with a prison record. This is a picture of triple crown glory.

Similarly, Mordecai told Esther, *"For if you remain silent at this time, relief and deliverance for the Jews will arise from another place, but you and your father's family will perish. And who knows but that **you have come to your royal position for such a time as this**?"* (Est. 4:14, NIV, author's emphasis). The NLT version says, *"If you keep quiet at a time like this, deliverance and relief for the Jews will arise from some other place, but you and your relatives will die. Who knows if perhaps you were made queen for just such a time as this?"*

How we respond to adversity, pressure, testing and stress says a lot about who we are on the inside, at our core,

HOW WE RESPOND TO ADVERSITY SAYS A LOT ABOUT WHO WE ARE

and what kind of emotional and spiritual resources and reserves we have available to us. Clearly, all adversity and testing is not at the same level of pain or severity, ranging from having a bad hair day or caffeine withdrawal or a flat tire, to being traumatized or martyred. Our God is a God of grace, a God of mercy, a God of forgiveness, love, comfort, patience, compassion, kindness, goodness, faithfulness, justice, righteousness, vengeance, holiness, provision, healing, favor, and a whole lot more. He is all you need Him to be in every situation.

Life is not always black and white; rather, it is most often multi-faceted and multi-dimensional, and requires a maturity of spiritual gifting and character to discern the presence or absence of divine favor or disfavor in an individual and their circumstances or situation. *"Indeed, all who desire to live godly in Christ Jesus will be persecuted"* (2 Tim. 3:12, NASB). *"In his kindness God called you to share in his eternal glory by means of Christ Jesus. So after you have suffered a little while, he will restore, support, and strengthen you, and he will place you on a firm foundation"* (1 Pet. 5:10, NLT). *"For our light and momentary troubles are achieving for us an eternal glory that far outweighs them all"* (2 Cor. 4:17, NIV).

Kingdom leaders who find and bestow genuine favor on their followers, attract others by their presence. Study the following table to better understand The Four Dimensions of Favor.

THE FOUR DIMENSIONS OF FAVOR		
	GOD'S DISFAVOR	GOD'S FAVOR
Greater ↑ **C O N S E Q U E N C E S** **Lesser** ↓	(Unbelief, Disobedience, Sin, Idolatry, Witchcraft, Wrath, Broken Covenants, Lack of Repentance, Judgment, Justice, Wrath, Punishment, Discipline, Banishment, Exile, Captivity, Enslavement, Righteous Anger, Lack of Rain, Famine, Plagues, Holes in Pockets, Barrenness, Lack, Poverty, Sickness, Disease, Silence, Eternal Separation, Death, Destruction)	(Innovation, Reformation, Renaissance, Anointing, Victory, Strength, Power, Might, Wisdom, Honor, Understanding, Revelation, Strategy, Order, Leadership, Teamwork, Resources, Peace, Rest, Unity, Progress, Positive Results, Advancement, Promotion, Breakthrough, Testimonies, Rejoicing, Thanksgiving, Praise, Treaties, Alliances, Covenants)
	MAN'S DISFAVOR	MAN'S FAVOR
	(Being Fired, Demoted, Passed over for Promotion, Laid Off, Put on Probation, Disciplined, Punished, Falsely Judged, Accused, Divorced, Robbed, Attacked, Assaulted, Conquered, Murdered, Raped, Enslaved, Tortured, Imprisoned, Banished, Exiled, Avoided, Shunned, Excommunicated, Blackballed, Lowballed, Marginalized, Disenfranchised, Persecuted, Discriminated, Extortion, Blackmail, Kidnaping, Ransom)	(Evil Prospering Temporarily, Recruiting, Hiring, Promotion, Advancement, Pay Raise, Salary Increase, Awards, Bonuses, Inheritances, Prizes, Rebates, Discounts, Coupons, Debt Cancellation, Acceptance by Others, Peer Pressure, Social Approval, Spiritual Approval, Agreements, Contracts, Transactions, Deals, Bribes, Graft, Corruption, Strings Attached, You Scratch My Back and I'll Scratch Yours, Quid Pro Quo, Counterfeits)
← Lesser	BENEFITS	Greater →

Figure 2. The Four Dimensions of Favor. ©2017 Dr. Bruce Cook.

The Divine Favor displayed in the 8th Mountain must be modeled and disbursed freely to others in the 7 Mountains of Culture by these Kingdom leaders. Favor is better caught than taught.

In closing, finding favor with God is a common theme in Scripture and a common cry of the human heart in all generations. Gen. 18:3 records this prayer from Abraham: *"O Lord, if I have found favor in your sight, do not pass by your servant."* That simple prayer has yielded one of the highest returns and paid some of the richest dividends in history.

Moses used his favor with God as a leverage point to gain even more favor in Exo. 33:12-14: *Then Moses said to the LORD, "See, You say to me, 'Bring up this people!' But You Yourself have not let me know whom You will send with me. Moreover, You have said, 'I have known you by name, and you have also found favor in My sight.' "Now therefore, I pray You, if I have found favor in Your sight, let me know Your ways that I may know You, so that I may find favor in Your sight. Consider too, that this nation is Your people. And He said, "My presence shall go with you, and I will give you rest."*

May the Lord bless you with His favor for your assignment and destiny as you spend time with Him on the 8th Mountain. Next, we turn our attention to the topic of faith in Chapter 5.

FIVE

FAITH

*"And without faith it is impossible to please God,
because anyone who comes to him must believe that he
exists and that he rewards those who earnestly seek him."*
(Heb. 11:6, NIV)

Faith is the bedrock of our foundation with God and the currency of our relationship with Him; without it we are spiritually bankrupt and cannot believe in God, relate to God, or please God. It is the *sine qua non* or cornerstone of the Christian life. Heb. 11:1-3 (MSG) says it well: *"The fundamental fact of existence is that **this trust in God, this faith, is the firm foundation under everything that makes life worth living.** It's our handle on what we can't see. The act of faith is what distinguished our ancestors, set them above the crowd. **By faith, we see the world called into existence by God's word**, what we see created by what we don't see"* (author's emphasis). Faith covers a vast territory and has a large, expansive portfolio. Charles Spurgeon said, "Faith obliterates time, annihilates distance, and brings future things at once into its possession."

The Amplified translation of these verses puts it this way and further defines faith: *"Now faith is the assurance (title deed, confirmation) of things hoped for (divinely guaranteed), and the evidence of things not seen [the conviction of their reality — faith comprehends as fact what cannot be experienced by the physical senses]. For by this [kind of] faith the men of old gained [divine] approval. By faith [that is, with an inherent trust and enduring confidence in the power, wisdom and goodness of God] we understand that the worlds (universe, ages) were framed and created [formed, put in order, and equipped for their intended purpose] by the word of God, so that what is seen was not made out of things which are visible."*

FAITH OBLITERATES TIME, AND BRINGS FUTURE THINGS INTO ITS POSSESSION

The process of acquiring faith is simple and straightforward: *"So then faith comes by hearing, and hearing by the word of God"* (Rom. 10:17). Eph. 2:8 adds, *"For by grace are ye saved through faith; and that not of yourselves: it is the gift of God."* Everything in this verse is the gift of God — the grace, the salvation, and the faith. Gal. 3:26-27 states, *"So in Christ Jesus you are all children of God through faith, for all of you who were baptized into Christ have clothed yourselves with Christ."*

Faith in Scripture is synonymous with the words overcome or victory or crown (John 16:33, 1 Cor. 15:57, 2 Tim. 4:8, James 1:12, 1 Pet. 5:4, Rev. 12:11, Deut. 20:4, Prov. 21:31, Psa. 118:15).

1 John 5:4-5 records, *"For everyone born of God overcomes the world.* **This is the victory that has overcome the world, even our faith.** *Who is it that overcomes the world? Only he who believes that Jesus is the Son of God"* (author's emphasis). Rom. 3:36 notes, *"Whoever believes in the Son has eternal life, but whoever rejects the Son will not see life, for God's wrath remains on him."*

As we go up to the Mountain of the Lord daily, on the 8th Mountain, we will receive the words that we need to hear that will build our faith, which will result in victory after victory in our lives that will testify of the power and greatness of our God to the world! Those who see these victories that come as a result of our faith will not be able to deny the power and fruit of our faith.

Rom. 12:3 says, *"For I say, through the grace given unto me, to every man that is among you, not to think of himself more highly than he ought to think; but to think soberly, according as* **God hath dealt to every man the measure of faith"** (author's emphasis). The Greek word for measure here is *metron*, meaning a measure, whether lineal or cubic; a measuring rod; a standard, the controlling basis by which something is determined as acceptable or unacceptable (Strong's G3358). The Greek word for faith here is *pisteos*, from the noun *pistis*, meaning faith, belief, trust, confidence, fidelity, faithfulness, divine persuasion. In secular antiquity, *pistis* meant warranty or guarantee. The root of *pistis* is *peithô*, meaning to persuade, or be persuaded (Strong's G4102).

Faith is God's warranty that guarantees the fulfillment of the revelation He births within the receptive believer, certifying that the revelation will come to pass in His way and His time. Faith is always a gift from God, and never something that can be produced by people. In short, faith for the believer is God's "divine persuasion" – and therefore distinct from human belief (confidence), yet involving it (Strong's G4102). Faith is not a virtue that can be worked up by human effort, but it can be increased and strengthened by regular use and exercise of this gift (Heb. 5:14-6:2, 2 Thess. 1:3-4). In fact, faith is intended to be a lifestyle for every follower of Christ. Rom. 1:17 says, *"For in the gospel the righteousness of God is revealed — a righteousness that is by faith from first to last, just as it is written: 'The righteous will live by faith.'"*

Scripture refers to degrees of faith, ranging from weak or little faith, to strong or great faith. Rom. 14:1 says, *"Accept the one whose faith is weak, without quarreling over disputable matters."* Matt. 14:31 notes, *Immediately Jesus reached out his hand and caught him. "You of little faith," he said, "why did you doubt?"* Matt. 15:28 records, *Then Jesus said to her, "Woman, you have great faith! Your request is granted." And her daughter was healed at that moment.* 1 Pet. 1:7 adds, *"These have come so that the proven genuineness of your faith — of greater worth than gold, which perishes even though refined by fire — may result in praise, glory and honor when Jesus Christ is revealed."*

The measure of faith you received is enough to do whatever you are called upon to do, since Jesus is the author and finisher of our faith (Heb. 12:2). In fact, faith is our recommended standard operating system for life, and comes with a lifetime warranty. 2 Cor. 5:7 says, *"For we walk by faith, not by sight."* Heb. 10:38 adds, *"Now the just shall live by faith: but if any man draw back, my soul shall have no pleasure in him."* Matt. 17:20 also records, *"Truly I tell you, if you have faith as small as a mustard seed, you can say to this mountain, 'Move from here to there,' and it will move. Nothing will be impossible for you."* Faith is so powerful that even a measure as small as a mustard seed in you can move a mountain and cast it into the sea.

This is just one of many reasons why God hates unbelief, especially among His children. To be clear, and fair, *"The Lord is not slack concerning His promise, as some men count slackness, but is longsuffering toward us, not willing that any should perish, but that all should come to repentance"* (2 Pet. 3:9). But, Jas. 1:5-8 notes, *"If any of you lacks wisdom, let him ask of God, who gives to all liberally and without reproach, and it will be given to him. But let him ask in faith, with no doubting, for he who doubts is like a wave of the sea driven and tossed by the wind.* ***For let not that man suppose that he will receive anything from the Lord;*** *he is a double-minded man, unstable in all his ways"* (author's emphasis).

A classic example of unbelief, and its disastrous consequences, is the several million Israelites who left Egypt with Moses, and perished in the wilderness, all but Caleb and Joshua, the only two spies who gave a good report to the people, spoke faith, and agreed with God. Heb. 3:16-19 records, *"And who was it who rebelled against God, even though they heard his voice? Wasn't it the people Moses led out of Egypt? And who made God angry for forty years? Wasn't it the people who sinned, whose corpses lay in the wilderness? And to whom was God speaking when he took an oath that they would never enter his rest? Wasn't it the people who disobeyed him? So we see that because of their unbelief they were not able to enter his rest."*

FAITH WITHOUT WORKS IS DEAD

According to Jas. 2:14-26 (NLT), faith without works is dead, and these two fit together hand in glove and cannot be separated. *"What good is it, dear brothers and sisters, if you say you have faith but don't show it by your actions? Can that kind* of faith save anyone? Suppose you see a brother or sister who has no food or clothing, and you say, "Good-bye and have a good day; stay warm and eat well" — but then you don't give that person any food or clothing. What good does that do? So you see, **faith by itself isn't enough. Unless it produces good deeds, it is dead and useless.**

"Now someone may argue, "Some people have faith; others have good deeds." But I say, "How can you show me your faith if you don't have good deeds? I will show you my faith by my good deeds." You say you have faith, for you believe that there is one God. Good for you! Even the demons believe this, and they tremble in terror. How foolish! Can't you see that faith without good deeds is useless?

"Don't you remember that our ancestor Abraham was shown to be right with God by his actions when he offered his son Isaac on the altar? You see, **his faith and his actions worked**

ACTIONS
MAKE FAITH
COMPLETE—THEY
WORK
TOGETHER

together. His actions made his faith complete. And so it happened just as the Scriptures say: "Abraham believed God, and God counted him as righteous because of his faith." He was even called the friend of God.

"So you see, **we are shown to be right with God by what we do, not by faith alone.** Rahab the prostitute is another example. She was shown to be right with God by her actions when she hid those messengers and sent them safely away by a different road. Just as the body is dead without breath, so also faith is dead without good works" (author's emphasis).

ABRAHAM IS THE FATHER OF FAITH FOR ALL WHO BELIEVE

No chapter on faith would be complete without examining in greater detail the singular example, contributions and influence of Abraham, the Father of Faith. Rom. 3:28-4:25 (NLT) says: *"So we are made right with God through faith and not by obeying the law. After all, is God the God of the Jews only? Isn't he also the God of the Gentiles? Of course he is. There is only one God, and he makes people right with himself only by faith, whether they are Jews or Gentiles. Well then, if we emphasize faith, does this mean that we can forget about the law? Of course not! In fact, only when we have faith do we truly fulfill the law.*

"Abraham was, humanly speaking, the founder of our Jewish nation. What did he discover about being made right with God? If his good deeds had made him acceptable to God, he would have had something to boast about. But that was not God's way. For the Scriptures tell us, **"Abraham believed God, and God counted him as righteous because of his faith."** *When people work, their wages are not a gift, but something they have earned. But people are counted as righteous, not because of their work, but because of their faith in God who forgives sinners. David also spoke of this when he described the happiness of those who are declared righteous without working for it:*

"Oh, what joy for those whose disobedience is forgiven, whose sins are put out of sight. Yes, what joy for those whose record the Lord has cleared of sin."

"Now, is this blessing only for the Jews, or is it also for uncircumcised Gentiles? Well, we have been saying that Abraham was counted as righteous by God because of his faith. But how did this happen? Was he counted as righteous only after he was

49

circumcised, or was it before he was circumcised? Clearly, God accepted Abraham before he was circumcised!

"Circumcision was a sign that Abraham already had faith and that God had already accepted him and declared him to be righteous—even before he was circumcised. So Abraham is the spiritual father of those who have faith but have not been circumcised. They are counted as righteous because of their faith. And Abraham is also the spiritual father of those who have been circumcised, but only if they have the same kind of faith Abraham had before he was circumcised.

"Clearly, God's promise to give the whole earth to Abraham and his descendants was based not on his obedience to God's law, but on a right relationship with God that comes by faith. If God's promise is only for those who obey the law, then faith is not necessary and the promise is pointless. For the law always brings punishment on those who try to obey it. (The only way to avoid breaking the law is to have no law to break!)

"So the promise is received by faith. It is given as a free gift. And we are all certain to receive it, whether or not we live according to the law of Moses, if we have faith like Abraham's. **For Abraham is the father of all who believe.** That is what the Scriptures mean when God told him, "I have made you the father of many nations." **This happened because Abraham believed in the God who brings the dead back to life and who creates new things out of nothing.**

"Even when there was no reason for hope, Abraham kept hoping—believing that he would become the father of many nations. For God had said to him, "That's how many descendants you will have!" And Abraham's faith did not weaken, even though, at about 100 years of age, he figured his body was as good as dead—and so was Sarah's womb.

"Abraham never wavered in believing God's promise. In fact, his faith grew stronger, and in this he brought glory to God. He was fully convinced that God is able to do whatever he promises. And because of Abraham's faith, God counted him as righteous. And when God counted him as righteous, it wasn't just for Abraham's benefit. It was recorded for our benefit, too, assuring us that God will also count us as righteous if we believe in him, the one who raised Jesus our Lord from the dead. He was handed over to die because of our sins, and he was raised to life to make us right with God" (author's emphasis).

In a great speech, Robert F. Kennedy declared, "There are those who look at things as they are, and ask, "Why?" I dream of things that never were, and ask, "Why not?" This is the visionary's statement of faith. The vision of the 8th Mountain describes a completed journey. The path from here to there will severely test all who undertake the journey. Kingdom leaders must bring fully tested faith to the journey, and model persistent tenacity in believing that God has prepared the way and

KINGDOM LEADERS MUST BRING FULLY TESTED FAITH TO THE JOURNEY

will provide wisdom and strategy for overcoming every obstacle that we meet along the way. Modeling faith is the charge to every Kingdom leader who would bring 8th Mountain transformation to the problems and challenges that face the leaders of the 7 Mountains of Culture.

When we know that we are loved, a gift ennobles us and empowers us. If we are unsure of the giver's motive, or unsure that we are truly loved, the very same gift can feel demeaning, belittling, and disempowering. Many who are called to become 8th Mountain kingdom leaders have recently completed an extended season of destitution, failure, and suffering to prepare them to be the grateful lovers and graceful givers in the coming season. Hebrews reminds us that Jesus is compassionate and empathetic toward us because He suffered in every way. Kingdom leaders must model love with no agenda, and giving without strings. Only in this way, will the leaders of the 7 Mountains of Culture embrace the righteousness and justice that they have personally experienced on the 8th Mountain.

In closing, it is important to keep a big picture perspective when discussing this topic. Faith is not the end goal, and is not an end in itself; it is a means to an end. *"And now these three remain: faith, hope and love. But the greatest of these is love"* (1 Cor. 13:13). So, then, faith, important and essential as it is, is superseded by love. It is not replaced, but reinforced.

God wants us to have both love and faith, so that our motives and heart are pure, righteous and holy as we operate in mighty deeds and greater works. So, He reminds us that *"...if I have a faith that can move mountains, but have not love, I am nothing"* (1 Cor. 13:2b). That is sobering. As we use and flex our faith, and are stretched by God to believe for even more, we need to keep it in the proper priority and perspective, and the 8th Mountain will help us to do that. Next, we turn our attention to love and giving in Chapter 6.

SIX

LOVE AND GIVING

"For God so loved the world that He gave His one and only Son, that whoever believes in Him shall not perish but have eternal life."
(John 3:16, NIV)

God is love, and you and I are created in His image. Love is the essence and the apex of who God is, and the basis for everything that He does, along with His foundations of justice and righteousness. Psa. 33:5 says, *"The LORD loves righteousness and justice; the earth is full of his unfailing love."* Psa. 89:14 adds, *"Righteousness and justice are the foundation of your throne; steadfast love and faithfulness go before you."*

That means everything that happens on the 8th Mountain stems from His love. That also means that everything that we receive from the Lord during our encounters with Him on the 8th Mountain will radiate with His love! 1 John 4:17-18 says, *"There is no fear in love, but perfect love drives out fear, because fear involves punishment. The one who fears has not been perfected in love.* **We love because He first loved us"** (author's emphasis).

1 John 4:7-12 (NLT) states, *"Dear friends, let us continue to love one another, for love comes from God. Anyone who loves is a child of God and knows God. But anyone who does not love does not know God, for God is love. God showed how much he loved us by sending his one and only Son into the world so that we might have eternal life through him. This is real love—not that we loved God, but that he loved us and sent his Son as a sacrifice to take away our sins. Dear friends, since God loved us that much, we surely ought to love each other. No one has ever seen God. But if we love each other, God lives in us, and his love is brought to full expression in us."* The MSG version translates verse 8: **"The person who refuses to love doesn't know the first thing about God, because God is love—so you can't know him if you don't love"** (author's emphasis).

Rom. 5:8 (NLT) adds, *"But God showed his great love for us by sending Christ to die for us while we were still sinners."* The MSG version of this verse reads, *"But* **God put his love on the line for us** *by offering his Son in sacrificial death while we were of no use whatever to him"* (author's emphasis). Rom. 8:29-30 notes, *"For God knew his people in advance, and he chose them to become like his Son, so that his Son would be the firstborn among many brothers and sisters. And having chosen them, he called them to come to him. And having called them, he gave them right standing with himself. And having given them right standing, he gave them his glory."*

2 Tim. 1:9 records, *"For God saved us and called us to live a holy life. He did this, not because we deserved it, but because that was his plan from before the beginning of time—to show us his*

grace through Christ Jesus." Eph. 1:4-5 (NLT) explains, *"**Even before he made the world, God loved us and chose us** in Christ to be holy and without fault in his eyes. God decided in advance to adopt us into his own family by bringing us to himself through Jesus Christ. This is what he wanted to do, and it gave him great pleasure"* (author's emphasis).

The MSG version of this passage reads, *"How blessed is God! And what a blessing he is! He's the Father of our Master, Jesus Christ, and takes us to the high places of blessing in him. Long before he laid down earth's foundations, **he had us in mind, had settled on us as the focus of his love, to be made whole and holy by his love.** Long, long ago he decided to adopt us into his family through Jesus Christ. (What pleasure he took in planning this!) He wanted us to enter into the celebration of his lavish gift-giving by the hand of his beloved Son"* (author's emphasis).

Wow! God's love for us is intentional, deliberate, premeditated, extravagant, eternal, unmerited, unselfish, sacrificial and unconditional, and contains or possesses both healing and redemptive qualities and attributes. And, it's free for the taking. Now, that's what I call a deal!

There are seven Greek words used to express various aspects of love: *agape, phileo* or *philia, storge, ludus, pragma, philautia* and *eros. Agape* is the word used for God's love, and means selfless love—love that is unconditional and focused on others. *Phileo* or *philia* refers to an affectionate, warm and tender platonic love. It makes you desire friendship with someone. Philia means fondness, brotherly love, or comradeship. *Storge* means affectionate, especially between parents and children. *Ludus* is playful love, or so-called "puppy love," between those newly in love or infatuated.

Pragma is longstanding love, as between mature, married couples. *Philautia* is self-love, and can refer to either healthy self-esteem, or narcissism. And, *Eros* means sexual or erotic love. Obviously, in this chapter, we are focused on *agape* love.

So, what else does God's love look like? We find in the Scriptures that *agape* love is patient, and is kind. It does not envy, it does not boast, it is not proud. It does not dishonor others, it is not self-seeking, it is not easily angered, it keeps no record of wrongs. Love does not delight in evil but rejoices with the truth. It always protects, always trusts, always hopes, always perseveres. Love never fails (1 Cor. 13:4-8a, NIV). This places love in very elite company, as most things in life, and in the universe, fail at some point. *"And now these three remain: faith, hope and love. But the greatest of these is love"* (1 Cor. 13:13).

We will be able to quickly discern whether something came from the 8th Mountain by looking at whether it is characterized by and saturated with God's love. For example, if I were to receive a strategy for my family from the Lord during my time on the 8th Mountain, it would be full of these attributes of His love as found in 1 Cor. 13:4-8a. The implementation of this strategy from the 8th Mountain would result in my family experiencing the patience of the Lord through me, the kindness of the Lord through me, the humility of the Lord through me, the truth of the Lord through me, the forgiveness of the Lord through me, and so on and so forth.

As we spend time with the Lord on the 8th Mountain, we will be transformed to become more and more like Him in His love; we will possess the nature of His love! Just as the things that come from the 8th Mountain are characterized by and saturated with God's love, so will we be! Our very essence will be full of His love. Everything we think, do, say, and feel will begin to overflow from the deep wells of His love inside of our spirits to bless everyone around us. We will become champions and conveyors of the love of God! Everything that the Lord leads us to do will become unique messages of His love to the world through us.

The nature of the love of God in us is to overflow to others to bless them, which is the foundation for giving as God intended. The ultimate example of giving that flowed from the love of God is found in John 3:16, which says, *"For God so loved the world that He gave His one and only Son, that whoever believes in Him shall not perish but have eternal life."* Just as God expressed His love to the world through giving us His only begotten Son, He will also express His love inside of us to the world by leading us to give to others—at times sacrificially.

LOVE AND GIVING ARE CLOSELY LINKED

Love and giving are inextricably and inexorably linked. We may give without love, but we cannot truly love without giving, because the nature of love is to give. Jesus said, *"It is more blessed to give than to receive."* Since we are created in the image of God, giving and loving are hardwired into our nature as human beings, and it is unnatural and unusual not to love or give. There are three main types of giving mentioned in Scripture: alms, tithes and offerings. Alms are for the poor, diseased, and crippled; tithes are for the priests; and offerings are for the needy saints – widows, orphans, missionaries, children, elderly and victims of natural disasters and wars.

These disasters include floods, famines, fires, typhoons, tsunamis, hurricanes, tornados, earthquakes, landslides, terrorist attacks, disease epidemics, ethnic cleansing, genocide, religious persecution, and wars. Uses and purposes for offerings include special cases, special collections, and special projects. Historically, offerings were used in Medieval and Renaissance times for hospitals, colleges, universities and cathedrals; and, in modern times, for building projects and capital campaigns for various nonprofits, including churches, colleges, universities, hospitals, medical centers, public charities, museums, art galleries, symphonies, ballets, operas, schools, libraries, camps, youth groups, royal societies, and think tanks, among others.

Giving is listed in Scripture as a spiritual gift (special grace). Rom. 12:6-8 (NLT) says,

GIVING IS LISTED IN SCRIPTURE AS A SPIRITUAL GIFT

"In his grace, God has given us different gifts for doing certain things well. So if God has given you the ability to prophesy, speak out with as much faith as God has given you. If your gift is serving others, serve them well. If you are a teacher, teach well. If your gift is to encourage others, be encouraging. **If it is giving, give generously.** *If God has given you leadership ability, take the responsibility seriously. And if you have a gift for showing kindness to others, do it gladly"* (author's emphasis).

God chose a Roman centurion named Cornelius (along with his household) who was faithful in almsgiving and prayer to be the first Gentile to hear the gospel, receive salvation and the baptism and infilling of the Holy Spirit, as well as water baptism (Acts 10:1-48). Verses 1-4 (NIV) notes, *"At Caesarea there was a man named Cornelius, a centurion of what was known as the Italian Cohort, a devout man who feared God with all his household, **gave alms generously** to the people, and prayed continually to God. About the ninth hour of the day he saw clearly in a vision an angel of God come in and say to him, "Cornelius." And he stared at him in terror and said, "What is it, Lord?" And he said to him, "Your prayers and your alms have ascended as a memorial before God"* (author's emphasis).

Prov. 11:25 (NIV) states, *"A generous person will prosper; whoever refreshes others will be refreshed."* The GW version says, *"A generous person will be made rich, and whoever satisfies others will himself be satisfied."* Prov. 19:17 records, *"Whoever is kind to the poor lends to the LORD, and he will reward them for what they have done."* It is impossible to outgive God. Those who have learned this are blessed indeed and abundantly satisfied and refreshed. This truth is one reason why Abraham was so blessed, because He trusted God with His son, Isaac, the child of promise, and believed God's promise even if it meant God resurrecting Isaac.

God loves cheerful givers. 2 Cor. 9:6-7 says, *"The point is this: whoever sows sparingly will also reap sparingly, and whoever sows bountifully will also reap bountifully. Each one must give as he has decided in his heart, not reluctantly or under compulsion, for God loves a cheerful giver."* We are also told to give in private. Matt. 6:2-4 says, *"So when you give to the needy, do not announce it with trumpets, as the hypocrites do in the synagogues and on the streets, to be honored by others. Truly I tell you, they have received their reward in full. But when you give to the needy, do not let your left hand know what your right hand is doing, so*

*that your giving may be in secret. Then your Father, who sees
what is done in secret, will reward you."*

With God, it is never about the size or amount of our gift,
but the attitude and motive of the heart of the giver. Mark
12:41-44 (NIV) says, *"Jesus sat down opposite the place where
the offerings were put and watched the crowd putting their money
into the temple treasury. Many rich people threw in large amounts.
But a poor widow came and put in two very small copper coins,
worth only a few cents. Calling his disciples to him, Jesus said,
"Truly I tell you, this poor widow has put more into the treasury
than all the others. They all gave out of their wealth; but she, out
of her poverty, put in everything—all she had to live on."*

Finally, God promises to provide for our needs so that we
can bless others. 2 Cor. 9:8-11a says, *"And God will generously
provide all you need. Then you will always have everything you
need and plenty left over to share with others. As the Scriptures
say, "They share freely and give generously to the poor. Their
good deeds will be remembered forever." For God is the one who
provides seed for the farmer and then bread to eat. In the same
way, he will provide and increase your resources and then produce
a great harvest of generosity in you. Yes, you will be enriched in
every way so that you can always be generous."*

THE LOVE OF GOD IS THE MOST POWERFUL FORCE IN THE UNIVERSE

As we give of our time, talent and treasure, and our wisdom,
work and wealth, to those around us, and invest in others,
as well as our local communities, we become conduits of
the love of God in whichever mountains of culture that we

are called to operate in and influence for His kingdom. In our mountains of culture, we will release (give) the love of God to the people there through whatever He leads us to do, say or pray.

The love of God is the most powerful force in the universe, and can influence, change and transform even the most stubborn areas in our mountains of culture. One of those stubborn areas may be the people who we are called, assigned or destined by God to influence. The Lord's love that is released through us and into the people who we are destined to influence will begin to transform them from the inside out! The love of God transforms people! Transformed people will carry the authority to transform the 7 Mountains of Culture to reflect the loving and giving nature of the Lord.

LIGHT YOUR TORCH!

Each of us is destined to light our torch with the fire of God's love when we spend time with Him on the 8th Mountain, and then to bring that fiery torch into the mountains of culture that we are called to in order to set the people there aflame with His love! Once people are set aflame by His love, His love will transform them into bold givers, bold healers, and bold reformers who will transform the 7 Mountains of Culture. Let us examine each one below in turn.

BOLD GIVERS

The love of God will transform people in the mountains of culture into bold givers. *"Freely you have received; freely give"*

(Matt. 10:8, NIV). When people freely receive the love and goodness of God in their lives in its various forms, they will be inspired to boldly give to others what they have received! When people in the mountains of culture become bold givers, many needs in the world will begin to be met.

These bold givers will cheerfully and generously give their finances to the Lord and to the causes in the world that are closest to their hearts, from hearts full of His love. No longer satisfied with the accumulation of wealth for themselves, they will want to channel the wealth that the Lord had blessed them with towards the betterment of the world. *"Give, and it will be given to you. A good measure, pressed down, shaken together and running over, will be poured into your lap. For with the measure you use, it will be measured to you"* (Luke 6:38, NIV).

These bold givers will also cheerfully and generously give their time to the Lord and to the people whom they are destined to impact. They will experience deep fulfillment when they make time for the Lord and for those whom they are destined to impact, as a priority in their lives, nurturing and strengthening their relationships with them. The love of God will strongly characterize each of these relationships.

Are you called to be a bold giver?

BOLD HEALERS

The love of God will transform people in the mountains of culture into bold healers. The love of God heals, so once people become healed by the love of God, He will use them to become bold healers of others. They will understand the pain that others go through, because they themselves will have gone through pain and were healed by God during or through the process! They will know how to navigate others through the pain and into the healing love of the Lord.

"Praise be to the God and Father of our Lord Jesus Christ, the Father of compassion and the God of all comfort, who comforts us in all our troubles, so that we can comfort those in any trouble with the comfort we ourselves receive from God" (2 Cor. 1:3-4, NIV).

These bold healers will have received from the Lord a crown of beauty instead of ashes, the oil of joy instead of mourning, and a garment of praise instead of a spirit of despair. They will be called oaks of righteousness, a planting of the Lord for the display of His splendor (Isa. 61:3, NIV). Then, these bold healers will possess the spiritual authority to help others receive the same from the Lord! The Lord has intended for people in the 7 Mountains of Culture to be bold healers of others, and we will see more of this become a reality as they move forward as bold healers in the mountains of culture that we are called to influence! These bold healers will do all of this from hearts full of the love of the Lord.

Are you called to be a bold healer?

BOLD REFORMERS

The love of God will transform people in the mountains of culture into bold reformers. The love of God will awaken their spirits to the reality of the world around them that needs to change for the better, as their hearts ache at the suffering and injustices in the world. The love of God will inspire them to become bold reformers in order to make the world a better place, beginning with their own spheres of influence in their mountains of culture. These bold reformers will persevere because God's perfect love will cast out all of their fears.

BOLD REFORMERS WILL BE A DISTINCTIVE BREED THAT THE WORLD HAS RARELY SEEN

These bold reformers will be bold as a lion (Prov. 28:1b). What the Lord has called them to reform will burn in their hearts day and night, and they will not back down regardless of the opposition that may come their way. They will take their stand, knowing that the Lord has raised them up "for such a time as this" (Est. 4:14) to bring reformation in their spheres of influence. In the process, they will inspire others to be bold reformers through their example! These bold reformers will be a distinctive breed that the world has only rarely seen before, and will fight for the manifestation of the purposes of God for not only their generation, but for future generations as well! As a result, future generations will be able to stand on the shoulders of these bold reformers and pick up where they have left off in the reformation of the mountains of culture.

These bold reformers will know that they will succeed in bringing reformation to their mountains of culture not by might, nor by power, but by His Spirit working in and through them (Zech. 4:6). In other words, this work of reformation will be a supernatural work of the Lord through them. In addition, every work of reformation by these bold reformers will be fueled by God's revolutionary love!

Are you called to be a bold reformer?

IT IS ALL ABOUT LOVE

In summary, not only is God's love the most powerful force in the universe, and is giving one of the primary ways to express love, but God's love is infectious, contagious, and transformative. 1 Pet. 4:8 says, *"Above all, love each other deeply, because love covers over a multitude of sins."* The MSG translation says, *"Most of all, love each other as if your life depended on it. Love makes up for practically anything."* As we experience selfless, unconditional love from God, and from some of His mature sons and daughters, and are healed, redeemed, and changed in the process, we then are able to mirror and reciprocate that, and give it away to others. In fact, one of Jesus' last prayers was for His disciples, and all believers who would enter His kingdom through them, to experience *agape* love and unity.

John 17:20-23 (NLT) records, *"I am praying not only for these disciples but also for all who will ever believe in me through their message. I pray that they will all be one, just as you and I are one—as you are in me, Father, and I am in you. And may they be in us so that the world will believe you sent me. I have given them the glory you gave me, so they may be one as we are one. I am in them and you are in me. May they experience such perfect unity that the world will know that you sent me and that you love them as much as you love me."*

Finally, Rom. 8:31-39 (MSG) states, *"So, what do you think? With God on our side like this, how can we lose? If God didn't* hesitate to put everything on the line for us, embracing our condition and exposing himself to the worst by sending his own Son, is there anything else he wouldn't gladly and freely do for us? And who would dare tangle with God by messing with one of God's chosen? Who would dare even to point a finger?

"The One who died for us—who was raised to life for us!—is in the presence of God at this very moment sticking up for us. Do you think anyone is going to be able to drive a wedge between us and Christ's love for us? There is no way! Not trouble, not hard times, not hatred, not hunger, not homelessness, not bullying threats, not backstabbing, not even the worst sins listed in Scripture:

They kill us in cold blood because they hate you.

We're sitting ducks; they pick us off one by one.

"None of this fazes us because Jesus loves us. I'm absolutely convinced that nothing—nothing living or dead, angelic or demonic, today or tomorrow, high or low, thinkable or unthinkable—absolutely nothing can get between us and God's love because of the way that Jesus our Master has embraced us." Nothing can separate us from God's love, and God desires that nothing will separate us from brotherly love among the saints as well. As we spend time with God in the 8th Mountain, we are transformed and empowered so that is possible. Next, we turn our attention to wisdom and understanding in Chapter 7.

SEVEN

WISDOM AND UNDERSTANDING

"Wisdom is the principal thing; therefore get wisdom:
and with all thy getting get understanding."
(Prov. 4:7, KJV)

It is only fitting that we cover wisdom in the seventh chapter, with seven representing the number of perfection in Scripture. *"Wisdom has built her house; she has hewn her seven pillars"* (Prov. 9:1). These are not only decorative, ornate pillars; they are also load-bearing pillars with structural integrity that can withstand pressure and weight. The Hebrew word for wisdom is *chokmah*, meaning skill, wisdom, wits (Strong's H2451). The Hebrew word for understanding is *binah,* meaning consideration, discernment, understanding, truth (Strong's H998). The Hebrew word for principal is *risheth,* meaning: beginning, chief, choicest, finest, first, foremost (Strong's H7225). Principal also means first in time, place, order, and rank.

THE ORIGINS AND SUPREMACY OF WISDOM

Wisdom occupies that supreme place as the first work of God, before the creation of the universe, and its pedigree is described in Prov. 8:22-31 (NIV): *"The Lord brought me forth as **the first of his works, before his deeds of old; I was formed long ages ago, at the very beginning,** when the world came to be. When there were no watery depths, I was given birth, when there were no springs overflowing with water; before the mountains were settled in place, before the hills, I was given birth, before he made the world or its fields or any of the dust of the earth.*

"I was there when he set the heavens in place, when he marked out the horizon on the face of the deep, when he established the clouds above and fixed securely the fountains of the deep, when he gave the sea its boundary so the waters would not overstep his command, and when he marked out the foundations of the earth. Then I was constantly at his side. I was filled with delight day after day, rejoicing always in his presence, rejoicing in his whole world and delighting in mankind" (author's emphasis).

The other main Scripture that describes the origins of wisdom is found in Job 28:20-28: *"Where then does wisdom come from? Where does understanding dwell? It is hidden from the eyes of every living thing, concealed even from the birds in the sky. Destruction and Death say, "Only a rumor of it has reached our ears."* **God understands the way to it and he alone knows where it dwells,** *for he views the ends of the earth and sees everything under the heavens.*

"When he established the force of the wind and measured out the waters, when he made a decree for the rain and a path for the thunderstorm, then **he looked at wisdom and appraised it; he confirmed it and tested it.** *And he said to the human race, "The fear of the Lord — that is wisdom, and to shun evil is understanding"* (author's emphasis). Prov. 8:13-14 adds, *"To fear the LORD is to hate evil; I hate pride and arrogance, evil behavior and perverse speech. Counsel is mine and sound wisdom; I am understanding, power is mine."*

Wisdom on earth may be in scarce supply and great demand, but in heaven or the 8th Mountain, it is abundant and bountiful, and in great measure. As we spend time with the Lord on the 8th Mountain, we will receive all of the wisdom that we need in order to fulfill our God-given assignments and destinies! Jas. 1:5 says, *"If any of you lacks wisdom, he should ask God, who gives generously to all without finding fault, and it will be given to him."* What a great promise! No limits! No favorites! And, "any" applies to us all. We have ready access to wisdom 24/7 simply by asking God for it in faith. And, God is quite willing to share it with us. But, there is more than one kind of wisdom.

WORLDLY WISDOM VS. GODLY WISDOM

Jas. 3:13-18 contrasts the wisdom of the world and godly wisdom. *"Who is wise and understanding among you? Let them show it by their good life, by deeds done in the humility that comes from wisdom. But if you harbor bitter envy and selfish ambition in your hearts, do not boast about it or deny the truth. Such "wisdom" does not come down from heaven but is earthly, unspiritual, demonic. For where you have envy and selfish ambition, there you find disorder and every evil practice.*

"But **the wisdom that comes from heaven is** *first of all* **pure; then peace-loving, considerate, submissive, full of mercy and good fruit, impartial and sincere.** *Peacemakers who sow in peace reap a harvest of righteousness"* (author's emphasis). This definition of wisdom is in stark contrast to worldly wisdom, and contains at least 10 attributes or ingredients: 1) good life, 2) deeds done in humility, 3) pure, 4) peace-loving, 5) considerate, 6) submissive, 7) full of mercy, 8) full of good fruit, 9) impartial, 10) sincere.

ONE PERSON'S WISDOM CAN SAVE A CITY

Wisdom is so powerful that even the wisdom of one person can save a city. How much more if the Church (*ekklesia*) in a city, county, state, province, region or nation wakes up

THE WISDOM OF ONE PERSON CAN SAVE A CITY

or matures and accesses the wisdom readily available to us that God freely supplies when we ask Him in faith. Prov. 21:22 (NIV) says, *"One who is wise can go up against the city of the mighty and pull down the stronghold in which they trust."* The NLT adds, *"The wise conquer the city of the strong and level the fortress in which they trust."*

Eccl. 7:19 (NIV) says, *"Wisdom makes one wise person more powerful than ten rulers in a city."* The NLT adds, *"One wise person is stronger than ten leading citizens of a town!"* Eccl. 9:15 (NIV) says, *"Now there lived in that city a man poor but wise, and he saved the city by his wisdom. But nobody remembered that poor man."* The HCS version adds, *"Now a poor wise man was found in the city, and he delivered the city by his wisdom. Yet no one remembered that poor man."* Clearly, our modern cities around the world desperately need God's wisdom sourced, delivered, displayed, modeled, transferred, and/ or imparted through God's people.

WISDOM BUILDS THE HOUSE AND IS SWEET TO YOUR SOUL, LIKE HONEY

Prov. 24:3-4 says, *"By wisdom a house is built, and through understanding it is established; through knowledge its rooms are filled with rare and beautiful treasures."* Wisdom and understanding work together like a hand in a glove; they reinforce and complement one another; and when knowledge is added, it forms a threefold cord that is not easily separated or broken. Building, establishing and filling are separate graces or gifts, but they are each necessary and add value to the whole, and work together in peace, harmony and symmetry.

The Hebrew word used for house here is *bayith*. Other meanings of *bayith* in Scripture include: temple, armory, boxes, buildings, dungeon, prison, home, homes, houses, harem, room, rooms, inside, inward, palace, place, places, tomb, treasury, and shrine (Strong's H1004). I have spoken this Scripture over couples as a blessing during their marriage ceremony on several occasions.

Prov. 24:13-14 adds, *"Eat honey, my son, for it is good; honey from the comb is sweet to your taste. Know also that wisdom is sweet to your soul; if you find it, there is a future hope for you, and your hope will not be cut off."* The writer here is using the analogy that just as honey is sweet to the taste, and brings nourishment and refreshment to the physical body, so is wisdom sweet to the soul, and attracts or produces positive, life-giving rewards and results to its possessor, including a future hope, or hope for the future. This hope is secure and certain, with wisdom acting as its warranty or guarantee, and therefore it cannot be denied, cut off, terminated or preempted. There are at least 10 known health benefits of eating honey, and similarly, wisdom conveys multiple benefits to its possessor, including honor and riches.

Kingdom leaders must access divine wisdom and display unique understanding when serving the leaders of the 7 Mountains of Culture who face distress and perplexing problems. The 8th Mountain offers not only a proven framework of law, but personal tailoring of solutions through the "word of the Lord" – a word that is steeped in revelation, prophecy, and divine wisdom. May it be that 8th Mountain kingdom leaders, like Daniel and his fellow Hebrew students, are examined and found to be "ten times better in learning and understanding" than all other candidates or choices for the King's court.

In closing this chapter, I quote the passage from Isaiah the prophet that Jesus read from the scroll in the synagogue in his hometown of Nazareth as He began His public ministry: *"The Spirit of the LORD will rest on Him,* **The spirit of wisdom** *and understanding, The spirit of counsel and strength, The spirit of knowledge and the fear of the LORD"* (Isa. 2:11, author's emphasis). Jesus, and His claim to be the fulfillment of this Scripture, were rejected by the residents of His hometown, who were so offended that they tried to throw Him off of a nearby cliff, but Jesus escaped them unharmed and left Nazareth (Luke 4:14-30).

The same Holy Spirit that Jesus was filled with is also available to you and me today. Jesus said, *"I tell you the truth, anyone who has faith in me will do what I have been doing. He will do even greater things than these, because I am going to the Father"* (John 14:12). "Anyone" includes you and me. Signs, wonders and miracles did not cease after the 1st Century. *"This salvation was first announced by the Lord, was confirmed to us by those who heard Him, and was affirmed by God through signs, wonders, various miracles, and gifts of the Holy Spirit distributed according to His will..."* (Heb. 2:3-4). The same God who affirmed His word and His messengers in the 1st Century and is still affirming them, is still God today. *"Those who know their God shall do mighty exploits"* (Dan. 11:32). Next, we turn our attention to the subject of influence in Chapter 8.

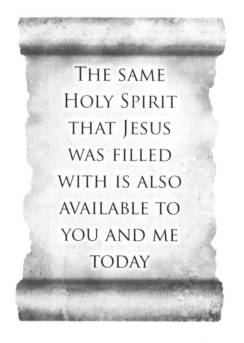

THE SAME
HOLY SPIRIT
THAT JESUS
WAS FILLED
WITH IS ALSO
AVAILABLE TO
YOU AND ME
TODAY

EIGHT

INFLUENCE

"Absalom used to get up early and stand by the road leading to the city gate...When anyone approached him and bowed down, Absalom would reach out, take hold of him, and kiss him. This is what he did for all Israelites who came to the king to have him try their case. So Absalom stole the hearts of the people of Israel."
(2 Sam. 15:2-6, GW)

"Jesus did many other things as well. If every one of them were written down, I suppose that even the whole world would not have room for the books that would be written."
(John 21:25, NIV)

Who takes your phone calls? Who follows you? Who listens to you? Who responds to your emails or texts or tweets or posts? We will explore the subject of influence from a biblical perspective in this chapter. I aim to raise as many questions as I do answers, in order to stir your thinking and action on this topic. I will begin by making two quick analogies to help prime the pump.

ONE TO MANY VS. MANY TO MANY

As a starting point, the difference between having a Rolex® and having a Rolodex® is significant, tangible and distinctive. While not mutually exclusive by any means, the former is a status symbol and one indication of financial success and personal style, and the latter is a personal network or 'book of business' of valued, trusted relationships and/or strategic contacts. A Rolex® has personal utility, meaning usefulness or benefit to the owner and/or wearer of the watch, but a Rolodex® has utility to potentially many people, depending on how it is used or stewarded by its owner or manager. So the Rolodex® potentially has more value as a tool to affect or influence others on a larger scale, depending on such factors as the audience, purpose, message and setting.

VIRAL VS. VIRUS

Similarly, the difference between influence and influenza is significant, tangible and distinctive. The first refers to the capacity to have an effect on the character, development, or behavior of someone or something, or the effect itself, while the second refers to an infectious disease caused by an influenza virus, commonly known as "the flu", of which the most common symptoms include: a high fever, runny nose, sore throat, muscle pains, headache, coughing, and feeling tired. Even a computer virus can have harmful or deadly effect on the functioning of a single computer or a network of computers. Obviously, it is far better to have influence than influenza, and to be able to exert and exercise viral capacity in communication and/or performance than to be a carrier or transmitter of a virus of any kind.

GOD IS VERY INTERESTED IN AND PROTECTIVE OF HIS INFLUENCE

God is very interested in and protective of His influence, according to Scriptures such as 1 Chron. 16:29, Ps. 29:2, Ps. 96:8, Psa. 135:13, Isa. 42:8, Isa. 48:11 and Mal. 1:11. *"I am the LORD; that is my name! I will not give my glory to anyone else, nor share my praise with carved idols"* (Psa. 42:8, NLT). *"Your name, LORD, endures forever, your renown, LORD, through all generations"* (Psa. 135:13, NLT). *"Ascribe to the LORD the glory due his name; worship the LORD in the splendor of his holiness"* (Psa. 29:2, NIV). *"Honor the LORD for the glory of his name. Worship the LORD in the splendor of his holiness"* (Psa. 29:2, NLT).

"O nations of the world, recognize the LORD, recognize that the LORD is glorious and strong. Give to the LORD the glory he deserves! Bring your offering and come into his presence. Worship the LORD in all his holy splendor" (1 Chron. 16:28-29, NLT). *"I will rescue you for my sake--yes, for my own sake!* **I will not let my reputation be tarnished,** *and I will not share my glory with idols!"* (Isa. 48:11, NLT, author's emphasis). *"For my own sake, for my own sake, I do this.* **How can I let myself be defamed?** *I will not yield my glory to another"* (Isa. 48:11, NIV, author's emphasis). *"My name will be great among the nations, from the rising to the setting of the sun. In every place incense and pure offerings will be brought to my name, because my name will be great among the nations," says the Lord Almighty* (Mal. 1:11, NIV).

Since influence is important to God, and we are created in His image, according to Gen. 1:26-28, we are also created to attract, possess and steward influence.

In fact, I suggest that influence is a candidate for the top dozen or so list of biblical virtues, desirable traits, and godly graces, coming after wisdom, love, faith, hope, honor, humility, holiness, intimacy, integrity, obedience, stewardship, discernment, favor and courage. Our God is a God of infinite and unlimited and eternal influence, reputation, renown, majesty, splendor, glory, love, wisdom, truth, mercy, compassion, righteousness, justice, patience, goodness, joy, peace, resources, knowledge, reward, promotion, vision, forgiveness, redemption, discipline, etc. God wants His children to also possess these things in abundance.

JESUS' INFLUENCE INCREASED DURING HIS LIFETIME

Jesus spent time with His Father on the 8th Mountain on a regular basis as a priority in His life, which resulted in the gradual increase of His influence on earth! May we learn from Jesus' example of spending time on the 8th Mountain as the key to increasing our influence on earth! Let us look now at several examples of the influence that Jesus had as a result of having spent time on the 8th Mountain.

Luke 2:52 says that *"Jesus grew in wisdom and stature and favor with God and man."* The words wisdom and stature and favor each imply and connote influence. For example, Eccl. 9:14-15 says, *"There was a small city with few men in it and a great king came to it, surrounded it and constructed large siegeworks against it. But there was found in it a poor wise man and he delivered the city by his wisdom."* 2 Sam. 20:13-22 similarly records the story of a wise, unnamed woman who did exactly the same thing to save her city from destruction when it was under siege by Joab and the Israelite army in pursuit of Sheba, son of Bicri.

Genesis 18 records the story of Abraham using his influence with God to negotiate the terms for the divine judgment of two nearby cities — Sodom and Gomorrah: *"So the Lord told Abraham, 'I have heard a great outcry from Sodom and Gomorrah, because their sin is so flagrant. I am going down to see if their actions are as wicked as I have heard. If not, I want to know.' The other men turned and headed toward Sodom, but the Lord remained with Abraham. Abraham approached him and said, 'Will you sweep away both the righteous and the wicked? Suppose you find fifty righteous people living there in the city— will you still sweep it away and not spare it for their sakes?' ... And the Lord replied, 'If I find fifty righteous people in Sodom, I will spare the entire city for their sake.' ... Finally, Abraham said, 'Lord, please don't be angry with me if I speak one more time. Suppose only ten are found there?' And the LORD replied, 'Then I will not destroy it for the sake of the ten'"* (Gen. 18:20-32, NLT). May we also have this kind of influence with God in our cities, spheres and mountains.

JESUS HAD SO MUCH INFLUENCE WHILE ON EARTH THAT THE WORLD COULD NOT CONTAIN IT ALL

In fact, Jesus had so much influence while on earth that John the Apostle wrote in John 21:25, *"Jesus did many other things as well. If every one of them were written down, I suppose that even the whole world would not have room for the books that would be written."* Now that's quite a testimony to the extent and scope of His influence! It takes the Library of Heaven, and heaven itself, to record and/or reveal the full measure of Jesus' influence and exploits, as even the "whole world" (*kosmon*, from the root *kosmos*, Strong's Greek 2889) cannot contain them, much less any library on earth, including the Library of Congress.

Throughout the biblical Gospels, we read accounts that various audiences marveled at Jesus. One such example is the Samaritan woman. In John 4:19 the Samaritan woman at the well said initially, after a few minutes of conversation and Q&A with Jesus, *"Sir, I perceive that You are a prophet."* But, a few verses later, after learning Jesus was also the Messiah, she took radical, immediate action. *"So the woman left her water jar and went away into town and said to the people,*

WHETHER
INFLUENCE
IS SUBTLE OR
CATALYTIC,
IT ALWAYS
PRODUCES
CHANGE

'Come, see a man who told me all that I ever did. Can this be the Christ?' They went out of the town and were coming to him" (John 4:29-30).

The result of her action and testimony? *"Many Samaritans from that town believed in him because of the woman's testimony, 'He told me all that I ever did.' So when the Samaritans came to him, they asked him to stay with them, and he stayed there two days. And many more believed because of his word. They said to the woman, 'It is no longer because of what you said that we believe, for we have heard for ourselves, and we know that this is indeed the Savior of the world'"* (John 4:39-42). This encounter is not only a living parable, but a case study of what influence looks like on a town, village or citywide scale. Influence can be subtle at times but potentially has a catalytic, explosive, viral, multiplicative, exponential effect and nature.

INFLUENCE CAUSED SALVATION AND A WEALTH TRANSFER

In Luke 19:1-10, Jesus had another encounter – this time with a tax collector named Zacchaeus. Influence caused a wealth transfer. Jesus entered Jericho and was passing through. *"A man was there by the name of Zacchaeus; he was a chief tax collector and was wealthy. He wanted to see who Jesus was, but because he was short he could not see over the crowd. So he ran ahead and climbed a sycamore-fig tree to see him, since Jesus was coming that way. When Jesus reached the spot, he looked up and said to him, 'Zacchaeus, come down immediately. I must stay at your house today.' So he came down at once and welcomed him gladly."*

All the people saw this and began to mutter, "He has gone to be the guest of a sinner." But Zacchaeus stood up and said to the Lord, "Look, Lord! Here and now I give half of my possessions to the poor, and if I have cheated anybody out of anything, I will pay back four times the amount." Jesus said to him, "Today salvation has come to this house, because this man, too, is a son of Abraham. For the Son of Man came to seek and to save the lost."

In Luke 8:1-3 it is recorded, *"Soon afterward Jesus began a tour of the nearby towns and villages, preaching and announcing the Good News about the Kingdom of God. He took his twelve disciples with him, along with some women who had been cured of evil spirits and diseases. Among them were Mary Magdalene, from whom he had cast out seven demons; Joanna, the wife of Chuza, Herod's business manager; Susanna; and many others who were contributing from their own resources to support Jesus and his disciples."* Just because Jesus said he did not have a place to lay his head (Matt. 8:20), did not mean he was financially destitute or without resources; his time share was planet Earth rather than a condo or beach house. And, Judas's job was treasurer; he was keeper of the money purse for Jesus.

INFLUENCE, COUPLED WITH FAITH, CAUSED HEALING

An example in Jesus' earthly ministry in which influence and faith caused healing, is recorded in Matt. 8:5-13.

"When he entered Capernaum, a centurion came forward to him, appealing to him, "Lord, my servant is lying paralyzed at home, suffering terribly." And he said to him, "I will come and heal him." But the centurion replied, "Lord, I am not worthy to have you come under my roof, but only say the word, and my servant will be healed. For I too am a man under authority, with soldiers under me. And I say to one, 'Go,' and he goes, and to another, 'Come,' and he comes, and to my servant, 'Do this,' and he does it."

"When Jesus heard this, he marveled and said to those who followed him, "Truly, I tell you, with no one in Israel have I found such faith. I say to you that many will come from the east and the west, and will take their places at the feast with Abraham, Isaac and Jacob in the kingdom of heaven. But the subjects of the kingdom will be thrown outside, into the darkness, where there

will be weeping and gnashing of teeth." Then Jesus said to the centurion, "Go! Let it be done just as you believed it would." And his servant was healed at that moment.''

INFLUENCE FLOWS OUT OF OUR RELATIONSHIP WITH GOD

Gen. 39:7-9 says: *"It came about after these events that his master's wife looked with desire at Joseph, and she said, "Lie with me." But he refused and said to his master's wife, "Behold, with me here, my master does not concern himself with anything in the house, and he has put all that he owns in my charge. "There is no one greater in this house than I, and he has withheld nothing from me except you, because you are his wife. How then could I do this great evil and sin against God?"*

Every great spiritual leader sees temptation and sin not as abstract or distant or impersonal, but as a sin against God. Notice that Joseph did not say, 'How can I do this great evil and sin against my master, Potiphar, or against you, his wife, or against my own self.' He properly and correctly understood that all sin is ultimately against God, and that sin separates us from God, and invites negative consequences and ultimately death.

Joseph could be trusted with influence, so he was promoted. In Gen. 45:1-11 he forgave those who had been jealous of him, and had conspired to hurt him, get rid of him, and lie about him to his father, and said this to his brothers who had betrayed him:

"Joseph could stand it no longer. There were many people in the room, and he said to his attendants, "Out, all of you!" So he was alone with his brothers when he told them who he was. Then

he broke down and wept. He wept so loudly the Egyptians could hear him, and word of it quickly carried to Pharaoh's palace. "I am Joseph!" he said to his brothers. "Is my father still alive?" But his brothers were speechless! They were stunned to realize that Joseph was standing there in front of them.

"Please, come closer," he said to them. So they came closer. And he said again, "I am Joseph, your brother, whom you sold into slavery in Egypt. But don't be upset, and don't be angry with yourselves for selling me to this place. It was God who sent me here ahead of you to preserve your lives. This famine that has ravaged the land for two years will last five more years, and there will be neither plowing nor harvesting.

"God has sent me ahead of you to keep you and your families alive and to preserve many survivors. So it was God who sent me here, not you! And he is the one who made me an adviser to Pharaoh—the manager of his entire palace and the governor of all Egypt. "Now hurry back to my father and tell him, 'This is what your son Joseph says: God has made me master over all the land of Egypt. So come down to me immediately! You can live in the region of Goshen, where you can be near me with all your children and grandchildren, your flocks and herds, and everything you own. I will take care of you there, for there are still five years of famine ahead of us. Otherwise you, your household, and all your animals will starve.'"

JESUS COULD BE TRUSTED WITH INFLUENCE, SO WAS PROMOTED. HOW ABOUT YOU?

Jesus could be trusted with influence, so was promoted. How about you? Heb. 2:9-10 says, *"But we do see Jesus, who was made lower than the angels for a little while, now crowned with glory and honor because he suffered death, so that by the grace of God he might taste death for everyone. In bringing many sons and daughters to glory, it was fitting that God, for whom and through whom everything exists, should make the pioneer of their salvation perfect through what he suffered."*

Heb. 5:8-10 adds, *"Even though Jesus was God's Son, he learned obedience from the things he suffered. In this way, God qualified him as a perfect High Priest, and he became the source of eternal salvation for all those who obey him. And God designated him to be a High Priest in the order of Melchizedek."*

Jesus' motive while on earth was to obey, honor and glorify His father, and His agenda was to build and establish the Kingdom of God on earth by sharing good news and making disciples, to bring redemption and forgiveness of sin to mankind through His atoning sacrifice on the cross, and to destroy the works of the devil. He could do this because of His humble attitude and pure motives.

Phil. 2:5-11 says, *"Let this mind be in you which was also in Christ Jesus: Who, existing in the form of God, did not consider equality with God something to cling to, but emptied Himself, taking the form of a servant, being made in human likeness. And being found in appearance as a man, He humbled Himself and became obedient to death—even death on a cross. Therefore God exalted Him to the highest place, and gave Him the name above all names, that at the name of Jesus every knee should bow, in heaven and on earth and under the earth, and every tongue confess that Jesus Christ is Lord, to the glory of God the Father."*

Consider how much more influence Jesus has now that He is the author and testator of a new covenant, is risen (resurrected) from the dead, is seated in heaven at the right hand of God, is an eternal High Priest after the Order of Melchizedek, lives forever to intercede for us, and has been given the Name above every Name and the title King of Kings and Lord of Lords, and all things in heaven and earth have been created by Him, for Him and through Him and are subject to His rule and authority and dominion.

YOU AND I ARE CREATED AND CALLED TO BE STEWARDS OF INFLUENCE

Likewise, you and I should be exercising and stewarding influence in our assigned spheres of culture. Influence comes in many shapes and forms and varieties; it can be used one-on-one or on a mass scale. It has been well said that influence is like a fulcrum; the closer you move it to what or who you want to influence, the less effort or power it requires to have an effect on or move the object of your influence.

Influence, like money, is a tool. It can be used for either positive or negative purposes, ends and/or outcomes, depending on the motives and agenda of the person or organization exercising it. Mother Teresa and Adolph Hitler both exercised influence, but from different motives and reasons, for different purposes and outcomes, and with very different results and rewards.

WE NEED TO EXERCISE AND STEWARD OUR INFLUENCE

There are many different kinds of influence, and one size or type does not fit all – domain or knowledge mastery or subject matter expertise influence, role or position influence, organizational influence, missional influence, personal influence [charisma or persuasiveness or oratorical or literary ability to move or motivate an audience], interpersonal influence [attraction, style, looks, dress, appearance] financial influence, political influence, scientific or academic [scholarly] influence, reputational influence, historical influence, leadership influence, spiritual influence, celebrity influence, media influence, peer group or reference group influence, branding influence, advertising influence, etc.

Influence can be personal or impersonal, intimate or nonintimate, direct or indirect, lasting or ephemeral, depending on the type. Influence can be an indication of intimacy. Obviously spiritual influence is linked closely with intimacy with God, but how many people can personally know a political candidate or elected official? Having more likes or followers or posts on social media does not automatically equate or correlate with influence. It obviously can, and often does, but notoriety and fame are not necessarily the same as influence; however, they provide awareness and recognition for their holders and the opportunity to exercise influence.

INFLUENCE CAN OFTEN BE COSTLY

Est. 4:15-17 says, *"Then Esther told them to reply to Mordecai, 'Go, assemble all the Jews who are found in Susa, and fast for me; do not eat or drink for three days, night or day. I and my maidens also will fast in the same way. And thus I will go in to the king, which is not according to the law; and if I perish, I perish.' So Mordecai went away and did just as Esther had commanded him."* At times it is necessary for us to risk everything – our influence and even our very lives – to obey God and to prevent great evil, such as genocide, from occurring on our watch, as Esther and Mordecai did. Dietrich Bonhoeffer, a Christian apologist, author and martyr, clearly understood and modeled this during World War II in Germany.

Daniel 2:12-23 records the story of Daniel and his friends who had come under a death sentence:

"Because of this the king [Nebuchadnezzar] became indignant and very furious and gave orders to destroy all the wise men of Babylon. So the decree went forth that the wise men should be slain; and they looked for Daniel and his friends to kill them. Then Daniel replied with discretion and discernment to Arioch, the captain of the king's bodyguard, who had gone forth to slay the wise men of Babylon; he said to Arioch, the king's commander, 'For what reason is the decree from the king so urgent?' Then Arioch informed Daniel about the matter.

"So Daniel went in and requested of the king that he would give him time, in order that he might declare the interpretation to the king. Then Daniel went to his house and informed his friends, Hananiah, Mishael and Azariah, about the matter, so that they might request compassion from the God of heaven concerning this mystery, so that Daniel and his friends would not be destroyed with the rest of the wise men of Babylon.

"Then the mystery was revealed to Daniel in a night vision. Then Daniel blessed the God of heaven; Daniel said, 'Let the name of God be blessed forever and ever, For wisdom and power belong to Him. It is He who changes the times and the epochs; He

*removes kings and establishes kings; He gives wisdom to wise men
And knowledge to men of understanding. It is He who reveals the
profound and hidden things; He knows what is in the darkness,
And the light dwells with Him. To You, O God of my fathers, I
give thanks and praise, For You have given me wisdom and power;
Even now You have made known to me what we requested of You,
For You have made known to us the king's matter.'"*

INFLUENCE IS FRAGILE AND CAN BE LOST IN AN INSTANT, SO GUARD AND STEWARD IT CAREFULLY

1 Sam. 13:8-14 records the story of King Saul and his lack of
faith, disobedience, and loss of favor and influence:

*"Now Saul waited seven days, according to the appointed time
which Samuel had set, but Samuel had not come to Gilgal; and the
people were scattering away from Saul. So Saul said, 'Bring me
the burnt offering and the peace offerings.' And he offered the burnt
offering [which he was forbidden to do]. As soon as he finished
offering the burnt offering, Samuel finally came; Saul went out
to meet and to welcome him. But Samuel said, 'What have you
done?' Saul said, 'Since I saw that the people were scattering away
from me, and that you did not come within the appointed time,
and that the Philistines were assembling at Michmash, therefore,
I said, "Now the Philistines will come down against me at Gilgal,
and I have not asked for the Lord's favor [by making supplication
to Him]."'*

"'So I forced myself to offer the burnt offering.' Samuel said to Saul, 'You have acted foolishly; you have not kept the commandment of the Lord your God, which He commanded you, for [if you had obeyed] the Lord would have established your kingdom over Israel forever. But now your kingdom shall not endure. The Lord has sought out for Himself a man (David) after His own heart, and the Lord has appointed him as leader and ruler over His people, because you have not kept (obeyed) what the Lord commanded you.'"

2 Kings 5:20-27 records the story of Gehazi, servant of Elisha, and his disobedience, sin and punishment:

"When Gehazi, the servant of Elisha the man of God, said, 'My master has spared this Naaman the Aramean (Syrian), by not accepting from him what he brought. As the Lord lives, I will run after him and get something from him.' So Gehazi pursued Naaman. When Naaman saw someone running after him, he got down from the chariot to meet him and said, 'Is all well?' And he said, 'All is well. My master has sent me to say, "Just now two young men of the sons of the prophets have come to me from the hill country of Ephraim. Please give them a talent of silver and two changes of clothes."' Naaman said, 'Please take two talents.' And he urged him [to accept], and tied up two talents of silver in two bags with two changes of clothes and gave them to two of his servants; and they carried them in front of Gehazi. When he came to the hill, he took them from their hand and put them in the house [for safekeeping]; and he sent the men away, and they left.

Then he went in and stood before his master. Elisha asked him, 'Where have you been, Gehazi?' He said, 'Your servant went nowhere.' Elisha said to him, 'Did my heart not go with you, when the man turned from his chariot to meet you? Is it a [proper] time to accept money and clothing and olive orchards and vineyards and sheep and oxen and male and female servants? Therefore, the leprosy of Naaman shall cling to you and to your descendants forever.' So Gehazi departed from his presence, a leper as white as snow."

Ananias and Sapphira were a married couple of influence and financial means in the early church. They pledged the funds from the sale of a piece of property they owned to the church in Jerusalem. However, they later conspired to keep some of the proceeds from the sale, and lied to Peter the Apostle. They not only lost influence; they lost their lives.

According to Acts 5:1-11: *"A man named Ananias and his wife Sapphira sold some property. They agreed to hold back some of the money they had pledged and turned only part of it over to the apostles. Peter asked, 'Ananias, why did you let Satan fill you with the idea that you could deceive the Holy Spirit? You've held back some of the money you received for the land. While you had the land, it was your own. After it was sold, you could have done as you pleased with the money. So how could you do a thing like this? You didn't lie to people but to God!' When Ananias heard Peter say this, he dropped dead. Everyone who heard about his death was terrified. Some young men got up, wrapped his body in a sheet, carried him outside, and buried him.*

"About three hours later Ananias' wife arrived. She didn't know what had happened. So Peter asked her, 'Tell me, did you sell the land for that price?' She answered, 'Yes, that was the price.' Then Peter said to her, 'How could you and your husband agree to test the Lord's Spirit? Those who buried your husband are standing at the door, and they will carry you outside for burial.' Immediately, she dropped dead in front of Peter. When the young men came back, they found Sapphira dead. So they carried her outside and buried her next to her husband. The whole church and everyone else who heard about what had happened were terrified."

INFLUENCE IS A FORM OF POWER: YIELD IT PRUDENTLY, GUARD IT CAREFULLY, AND USE IT FERVENTLY

In conclusion, I would suggest in all love, humility, fear of the Lord, and candor, that if you have little or no influence with God, with others, or on the world around you, then your life may have little or no spiritual substance or significance. I realize that some followers of Jesus may opt or argue for the hidden life of prayer and fasting, intercession and Bible study, and prefer to be anonymous, nameless or faceless, or may pursue the more reflective, contemplative, cloistered, communal life of religious devotees in a private community, convent, abbey, priory, or nunnery.

That can be all well and good to a point, if you are called to that, but, it is also important that our lifestyles reconcile, align and integrate with Matthew 13 and elsewhere the teachings of Jesus that the kingdom of heaven is like a sower who sowed seed in a variety of soils, like a mustard seed, like yeast hidden in a loaf, like a treasure hidden in a field, like a merchant looking for fine pearls, like a net let down into a lake which caught many fish, like a city set on a hill, like a light on a lampstand, etc. We were created to have

WE WERE CREATED TO HAVE INFLUENCE AND TO USE IT WISELY

influence, and to use it wisely and judiciously on behalf of God and His kingdom – sometimes openly and sometimes secretly or in stealth mode.

U.S. President Theodore Roosevelt famously said, *"It is not the critic who counts; not the man who points out how the strong man stumbles, or where the doer of deeds could have done them better. The credit belongs to the man who is actually in the arena, whose face is marred by dust and sweat and blood; who strives valiantly; who errs, who comes short again and again, because there is no effort without error and shortcoming; but who does actually strive to do the deeds; who knows great enthusiasms, the great devotions; who spends himself in a worthy cause; who at the best knows in the end the triumph of high achievement, and who at the worst, if he fails, at least fails while daring greatly, so that his place shall never be with those cold and timid souls who neither know victory nor defeat."*

James teaches us that faith without works is dead, being alone, and that we must mix or combine faith and deeds or works together. John 15 also says that the branches must abide in the vine to bear much fruit. And, the Scriptures are replete with analogies of the Church as a body and living organism, principles of human interaction and behavior and commerce and communication, and levels of authority and government. Clearly, God intends for His sons and daughters to be industrious and productive, to be inventive and creative and innovative, to be fruitful and multiply, to produce fruit that remains, and to have influence on others and the culture and world around us.

Influence is not optional; it is essential for leaders, and for all true [meaning authentic, genuine, legitimate] followers and disciples of Jesus. Influence is a form of power: Yield it prudently, guard it carefully, and use it fervently on behalf of others as a wise steward and master builder. The 8th Mountain's leaders must have a degree of influence where they are welcome in the palaces, courts, boardrooms, council chambers, and even homes of the leaders of the 7 Mountains of Culture.

God will not only back you up, confirm and testify of your message and of you as His messenger, but He will give you more and increase you as you are proven faithful in the little, in what is in your hand today, and so become ruler or steward over much, and thus have more influence to exercise and administer. I encourage, exhort and challenge you to become an influencer today, to grow your influence, and to use your influence to change the world and humanity – or at least your assigned portion, territory, metron or sphere thereof – for the better. This is possible as you spend time with God on the 8th Mountain and are influenced by Him. Now we turn our attention to revelation, strategy and innovation in Chapter 9.

NINE

REVELATION, STRATEGY AND INNOVATION

*"I wisdom dwell with prudence, and find
out knowledge of witty inventions."*
(Prov. 8:12, KJV)

*"Where there is no revelation, people cast off restraint;
but blessed is the one who heeds wisdom's instruction."*
(Prov. 29:18, NIV)

As I was praying recently, I was impressed by the Holy Spirit to write on the importance of revelation. Back in the day when I was a student in elementary school, we were taught the 3R's – Reading, 'Riting and 'Rithmetic. As kingdom citizens, I want to suggest a spiritual 3R's for leaders: Revelation, Relationships, and Resources, with a few others added in for good measure: Reformation, Renaissance and Resurrection. In this chapter I will focus on just the first topic, Revelation.

As kingdom leaders and disciples of Christ, we are to be living epistles "known and read of all men" (2 Cor. 3:2, KJV). That means our lives are designed and intended by God to be living revelation. Hab. 2:2 (NIV) says, *"Then the LORD replied: "Write down the revelation and make it plain on tablets so that a herald may run with it."* The NAS translation says, *"Then the LORD answered me and said, "Record the vision And inscribe it on tablets, That the one who reads it may run."* Similarly, the KJV says, *"And the LORD answered me, and said, Write the vision, and make it plain upon tablets, that he may run that readeth it."* In other words, revelation is intended to be applied and put into practice by those who read or hear it, and to be announced or shared by heralds, which can be not only official messengers, but social media, traditional media, publishers, and other outlets for mass communication and dissemination of information.

REVELATION PROVIDES AND PROJECTS A TRAINING AND A RESTRAINING FORCE OR FUNCTION IN SOCIETY

Prov. 29:18 adds, *"Where there is no revelation, people cast off restraint; but blessed is the one who heeds wisdom's instruction"* (NIV, author's emphasis). The root word for restraint in Hebrew is *para*, meaning: "let go, let loose, people, i.e. remove restraint from them; unbind head (by removing turban, sign of mourning); let alone, avoid, neglect, refrain; Niph'al Imperfect3masculine singular עֵ ם עָרְ֫מֶדִי Proverbs 29:18, the people is let loose, lacks restraint" (Strong's H6544).

I find it interesting that God's word correlates a lack of revelation with people casting off restraint, as we have seen several times in history, including the Hippie Movement of the late 1960's and 1970's in the U.S. with flower power, peace symbols, drug use, rebellion to authority and status quo, dropping out of or rejecting society and social norms, and unrestrained sexuality. Apparently, godly revelation is intended to empower or compel people to run with it, and also to preserve and protect nations and societies, and prevent or preempt the citizens or populations thereof from casting off restraint or inhibitions or conscience or the rule of law, such that *"every man did what was right in his own eyes"* (Judg. 17:6, 17:25).

Individuals, families, cities, schools, governments, churches, nations, industries, sectors, and corporations all need revelation to function and perform properly and optimally. Just ask generals, admirals, prime ministers, presidents, ambassadors, economists, attorneys, doctors, engineers, pilots, traders, hedge fund managers, or any of a myriad of other front line professionals about the critical importance and costly nature of revelation. The wrong revelation can be as bad as, or worse than, no revelation at times, and quite costly.

Just ask Britain about Neville Chamberlain's revelation of "peace in our time." It gave Germany several years' head start on arming and building an army and industrializing their nation, and almost cost England their freedom and survival in World War II. But, thank God for Winston Churchill, Rees Howells, and others God raised up that had real revelation of those times. In contrast with those who are foolish, those who heed wisdom's instruction are blessed. So, apparently there is a strong correlation between godly revelation and obedience (heeding) and receiving or being the beneficiary of the blessing of God.

THE SOURCE OF TRUE REVELATION IS GOD

Paul the Apostle says in 2 Cor. 12:6-7 (NLT), *"If I wanted to boast, I would be no fool in doing so, because I would be telling the truth. But I won't do it, because I don't want anyone to give me credit beyond what they can see in my life or hear in my message, even though I have received such wonderful revelations from God. So to keep me from becoming proud, I was given a thorn in my flesh, a messenger from Satan to torment me and keep me from becoming proud."*

Paul further states in Gal. 1:11-12 (NIV), *"I want you to know, brothers and sisters, that the gospel I preached is not of human origin. I did not receive it from any man, nor was I taught it; rather, I received it by revelation from Jesus Christ."* The NLT says, *"Dear brothers and sisters, I want you to understand that the gospel message I preach is not based on mere human reasoning. I received my message from no human source, and no one taught me. Instead, I received it by direct revelation from Jesus Christ."*

John the Apostle also received divine revelation. *"This is a revelation from Jesus Christ, which God gave him to show his servants the events that must soon take place. He sent an angel to present this revelation to his servant John, who faithfully reported everything he saw. This is his report of the word of God and the testimony of Jesus Christ"* (Rev. 1:1-2, NLT). Amos 3:7 (NASB) says, *"Surely the Lord GOD does nothing Unless He reveals His secret counsel To His servants the prophets."* Another synonym for revelation is secret counsel.

The Lord invites us to come up to the 8th Mountain to receive the revelations that we need in order to fulfill the assignments that He has given us! It pleases Him to share the revelations on His heart with those who are spiritually hungry and ready to receive these revelations, so that they may fulfill His desires for kingdom influence in their assignments.

DIVINE STRATEGY IS SUPERNATURAL

One form or expression of revelation is strategy. 2 Sam. 5:17-21 records the first victory of David over the Philistines as King of Israel, through a frontal assault. The Philistines later returned and the Lord gave David a new plan of attack. *"So David inquired of the LORD, and he answered, "Do not go straight up, but circle around behind them and attack them in front of the poplar trees. As soon as you hear the sound of marching in the tops of the poplar trees, move quickly, because that will mean the LORD has gone out in front of you to strike the Philistine army."* (2 Sam. 5:23-24, NIV). The NLT translation in 1 Chron. 14:15 says, *"When you hear a sound like marching feet in the tops of the poplar trees, go out and attack! That will be the signal that God is moving ahead of you to strike down the Philistine army."*

God told Gideon to attack a vast, superior enemy army of 135,000 with only 300 men armed with torches, lamps and shofars, and girded with swords. This divine strategy was wildly successful and the enemy forces were soundly defeated and vanquished, with losses exceeding 120,000 and the deaths of the top four Midianite leaders and kings— Oreb, Zeeb, Zebah and Zalmannua (Judg. 6-8). Naomi told her daughter-in-law Ruth the Moabitess to wash, perfume herself, and put on her best clothes and go at night and lie at the feet of Boaz on the threshing floor after he was asleep (Ruth 3:1-6). This strategy also was effective, and Ruth was redeemed by her kinsman-redeemer Boaz and then married to him and bore him a son named Obed. She was grafted into the lineage of David, and ultimately of Jesus (Ruth 4:11-22).

God told Joshua to march around the walled and fortified city of Jericho once a day for six days and seven times on the seventh day, and to have seven priests each carry and blow a trumpet (ram's horn) in front of the ark of the covenant (Josh. 6:1-5, Heb. 11:30). Joshua repeated these instructions and divine strategy to the priests, the army, and the rest of the people, and instructed them to be silent as they marched around Jericho and not to speak a word until he ordered them to on the seventh day, when they were to shout after the seventh orbit of the city (Josh. 6:6-10). Joshua and the Israelites then executed this strategy or plan, and carried it out successfully, and the walls of the city fell down, and they conquered and plundered the city as God has said, sparing only Rahab and her family (Josh. 6:11-27).

YOU AND I CAN RECEIVE DIVINE REVELATION TODAY

Similarly, you and I today should be receiving divine revelation by the Spirit on a regular basis, just as the early apostles and prophets did. Revelation is available for all of God's people and God makes it clear in His Word that He is not a respecter of persons (Rom. 2:11, Acts 10:34). Paul says in 1 Cor. 2:9-12 (NLT, author's emphasis), *"That is what the Scriptures mean when they say, 'No eye has seen, no ear has heard, and no mind has imagined what God has prepared for those who love him.' But it was to us that God revealed these things by his Spirit. For **his Spirit searches out everything and shows us God's deep secrets.** No one can know a person's thoughts except that person's own spirit, and no one can know God's thoughts except God's own Spirit. And we have received God's Spirit (not the world's spirit), **so we can know the wonderful things God has freely given us."** Please notice that in both this passage, and the verses from 2 Cor. 12 cited earlier, Paul describes godly revelation as "wonderful." Indeed it is.

For example, when I wrote my first book on the kingdom seven years ago, the Holy Spirit told me the exact date to start (Thanksgiving 2010), and within 30 minutes of sitting down to pray and listen, the Holy Spirit had given me the title and downloaded the table of contents to me for that book. I wrote that book in two months' time between 6 p.m. and 6 a.m. after working a full day beforehand. The Holy Spirit sustained me and gave me supernatural energy and rest during this time, when I averaged just a few hours sleep per night.

My job was simply to be a scribe, because the book was already written in heaven. I just needed to listen, take notes, apply Scripture references and definitions of key terms, and add a few personal anecdotes to illustrate key principles and add some color. I was writing on divine assignment and not as a personal goal or to try and become famous or rich or be considered an expert. My motives were pure. That book, *Partnering With The Prophetic*, is now in its 3rd edition. As I have been obedient to write other books on the kingdom as directed by the Holy Spirit, I have experienced similar divine downloads and favor.

As another example, while editing the five-volume *Aligning With The Apostolic*, which includes chapters from 70 modern day apostles and apostolic leaders, one evening I was working at my desk and wondering how in the world I was going to finish writing my own chapters, much less be able to organize the other 70 chapters from contributing authors, which were all Spirit-led. I wondered to myself if this challenge would affect my friendships with them, and how this great quantity of content could all possibly fit together. Early that morning, a faithful intercessor had called me to pray for a solution for this mental confusion and blockage.

That evening, I literally felt the Holy Spirit overshadow my mind and in less than one hour, about 45 minutes to be exact, God had downloaded the complete organizational structure for all five volumes, with the order and names of the 12 sections, and which chapters belonged to each section. In the natural I would never have been capable of that. But, such is the power of revelation. It's an "aha" or "eureka" experience, when the light bulb comes on, or in some cases, the entire power plant is generating energy, and the current is flowing.

GOD IS THE CHIEF INNOVATOR

God believes in and practices innovation, and He abundantly modeled it for us. He created the universe, the sun, moon and stars, the earth, the seas, the animals, insects, reptiles, mammals, birds, fish and man. God gave Noah the blueprints to build the first ark. God gave Moses the blueprints for the tabernacle, and the Ten Commandments. God gave David the blueprints for the temple, and the funds and favor for Solomon to build it. God scattered the peoples at Shinar, and confused the languages. God brought forth wisdom as the first of His works of old. Therefore, it should not surprise us when God entrusts some of His secrets, plans, technologies, blueprints, business models, strategies, etc. to His sons and daughters (you and me) to steward.

God told Isaac to sow seed in a time of famine and he reaped a 100-fold return in the same year because the Lord blessed him. It was said of him, *"The man became rich, and his wealth continued to grow until he became very wealthy. He had so many flocks and herds and servants that the Philistines envied him"* (Gen. 26:13-14). God gave Joseph a financial plan for solving the seven-year global famine crisis through a decentralized system of government-mandated and -subsidized grain storage and sharing in key cities in Egypt, along with local commissioners to enforce it. The end result was, *"And all the countries came to Egypt to buy grain from Joseph, because the famine was severe in all the world"* (Gen. 41:57).

God also chose and anointed Bezalel as a master craftsman and designer for Moses (Exo. 31:1-5) to help build the tabernacle and its furnishings. Daniel and his three Jewish friends were trained for three years by Ashpenaz, the chief court official of Babylon, and when tested and examined, were found by King Nebuchadnezzar to be *"ten times better than all the magicians and enchanters in his whole kingdom"* (Dan. 1:20). Nehemiah brought authority, integrity, confidence, determination, courage, vision and resources to the leaders of Jerusalem and the walls of the city were rebuilt in 52 days, and fear fell upon their enemies because they realized that this work had been done with the help of God (Neh. 6:15-16).

King David instituted 24/7 worship and appointed Asaph as chief musician and worship leader. Queen Esther and Mordecai drafted a royal decree for the Jews in Susa and throughout the 127 provinces of the Persian Empire to defend themselves and avenge themselves upon their enemies. The Jewish holiday of Purim celebrates this. These and other innovators helped to change and write the course of history.

THE END TIME ARMY OF BELIEVERS IS ALIVE AND WELL AND GROWING

Apostles and prophets form the foundation of the church (Eph. 2:20) and, as such, are in constant contact with the Chief Cornerstone, or Head of the Church, Jesus Christ (Eph. 2:20, 1 Pet. 2:6-7, Luke 20:17, Matt. 21:42, Mark 12:10, Acts 4:11), the apostle and high priest of our confession (Heb. 3:1). Foundations are often walked on, covered up, hidden, and out of sight, but they still serve their purpose. Without them, the rest of the building can't go up or hang together or be supported.

Apostles and prophets have spiritual gifts that are generative in nature, meaning they generate or receive revelation for the body of Christ (see *Aligning With The Apostolic, Vol. 1* as well as *The Permanent Revolution* for a more in depth treatment of this). Visions, dreams, trances, angelic encounters, intimacy with Jesus and Abba Father and the Holy Spirit, and spiritual experiences, including Third Heaven visitations, are all part of the normal lifestyle of genuine, authentic, bona fide, mature apostles and prophets. Such experiences are available to other believers as well, so long as they are willing to pay the price required to participate in and steward such things.

For every one person like Rick Joyner or Paul Cox or Kathie Walters who is a gifted writer and/or teacher on spiritual experiences, or Sid Roth or Patricia King, who host media programs to showcase such people and their experiences, there are doubtless many thousands or millions of people who have such experiences but are not called or gifted or released by God to write or speak about them. This end time body of believers is alive and well and equipped and growing, and are in position for their assignments, and are actively doing the works of God.

REVELATION ALONE IS INSUFFICIENT WITHOUT CHARACTER

However, revelation alone is not enough by itself and is not an end in itself. We must have godly character to properly handle spiritual revelation and our lives are intended and designed to be fruitful (John 15:8) and to be marked by signs, wonders and miracles following (Heb. 2:4). Even Paul was given a thorn in the flesh so that he would not be puffed up with the exceeding greatness of the revelation He received from Jesus. Scripture says, *"He that is faithful in little shall be ruler [faithful] over much"* (Luke 16:10). Therefore, steward wisely the revelation you have been given and God will give you more. The greater the revelation God shares with you or entrusts you with, the greater the humility and wisdom that will be required to steward it and implement it.

For example, Judas Iscariot did not have the character needed to implement and steward the revelation he had received from Jesus. Likewise, neither did Korah, Dathan and Abiram have the character required to steward the revelation Moses had shared from God with the Israelites (Num. 16:1-50). Nor did Achan steward the revelation he had from Joshua, nor did Ananias and Sapphira with the 1st Century apostles in Jerusalem. All of these met with disastrous consequences, and many other such examples could be cited and mentioned.

CONCLUSION: THE PURPOSES OF REVELATION

Revelation helps people to read and to run, and not to cast off restraint (that is, to voluntarily choose restraint). Revelation helps bring about reformation or lasting change, renaissance, new methods and approaches, new strategies and insights, new models and paradigms, new inventions, new technologies, new industries. Revelation is why the early church followed and obeyed the apostles' doctrine (Acts 2:42, 5:28) and grew and multiplied and prospered in so doing, because it was an ongoing, continuous flow and stream or ocean of revelation and not a static, sterile, sermon, dogma, creed, catechism, or confession.

Faced with perplexity and distress, the leaders of the 7 Mountains of Culture will seek out men and women whose reputation for explaining mysteries and solving unsolved problems, precedes them. Kingdom leaders, the emissaries of the 8th Mountain, must stay in the presence of the Lord, ready to receive and display the revelation and innovation of the Creator.

Revelation is perhaps the enemy of or at least the antidote for the status quo; the Holy Spirit is the Chief Innovation Officer of the Church, and, by extension, the culture, to use a current corporate analogy. Learn to receive, value, embrace and share godly revelation in healthy, wise ways. Stay in the secret place of intimacy and discipleship with Jesus and communion and fellowship with His Spirit on the 8th Mountain, and in mutual accountability and submission with other spiritual leaders on earth who are mature, trusted and wise. Humble yourselves under the mighty hand of God, that He may exalt you in due season. Now we turn our attention to spiritual fruits and gifts in Chapter 10.

WE MUST
HAVE GODLY
CHARACTER
TO PROPERLY
HANDLE
SPIRITUAL
REVELATION

TEN

SPIRITUAL FRUITS AND GIFTS

"Follow the way of love and eagerly desire spiritual gifts..."
(1 Cor. 14:1, NIV)

"But the fruit of the Spirit is love, joy, peace, patience, kindness, goodness, faithfulness, gentleness and self-control. Against such things there is no law."
(Gal. 5:22-23, NIV)

When we come into a saving relationship with Jesus, and repent of our sins and allow Him to put to death our carnal sin nature, we receive many benefits, not the least of which is salvation. But, there is much more available to and required of followers and disciples of Christ. Jesus wants to be Lord, and not just Savior, of every area of our lives. After all, one of His names is King of Kings, and Lord of Lords. As the Holy Spirit dwells within us, renews our spirit, and helps transform and sanctify us from the inside out into the nature and character of Christ, the fruit of the Spirit is produced in our lives in increasing measure, and in turn, we can then help others produce spiritual fruit in their lives (Rom. 12:2; 2 Cor. 3:18, 5:17-19; Gal. 5:22-23; Tit. 3:3-8).

SPIRITUAL FRUITS

Just what is this spiritual fruit, and what does it look like? According to Gal. 5:22-23 (NIV), *"But the fruit of the Spirit is love, joy, peace, patience, kindness, goodness, faithfulness, gentleness and self-control. Against such things there is no law."* 2 Pet. 1:5-9 adds, *"For this very reason, make every effort to add to your faith goodness; and to goodness, knowledge; and to knowledge, self-control; and to self-control, perseverance; and to perseverance, godliness; and to godliness, mutual affection; and to mutual affection, love. For if you possess these qualities in increasing measure, they will keep you from being ineffective and unproductive in your knowledge of our Lord Jesus Christ. But whoever does not have them is nearsighted and blind, forgetting that they have been cleansed from their past sins."*

Other spiritual fruits would include compassion, diligence, honor, respect, forgiveness, humility, steadfastness, sincerity, courage, boldness, and wisdom, just to name a few. Jas. 3:13-18 (NIV) says, *"Who is wise and understanding among you? Let them show it by their good life, by deeds done in the humility that comes from wisdom. But if you harbor bitter envy and selfish ambition in your hearts, do not boast about it or deny the truth. Such 'wisdom' does not come down from heaven but is earthly, unspiritual, demonic. For where you have envy and selfish ambition, there you find disorder and every evil practice. But the wisdom that comes from heaven is first of all pure; then peace-loving, considerate, submissive, full of mercy and good fruit, impartial and sincere. Peacemakers who sow in peace reap a harvest of righteousness."*

Spiritual fruits, then, are the qualities and attributes that are produced in a disciple's life from being made new, putting the old self to death, and taking on the nature and character of Christ, and becoming rooted, grounded and established in Christ. Eph. 2:8-10 (NLT) says, *"God saved you by his grace when you believed. And you can't take credit for this; it is a gift from God. Salvation is not a reward for the good things we have done, so none of us can boast about it. For we are God's masterpiece. He has created us anew in Christ Jesus, so we can do the good things he planned for us long ago."*

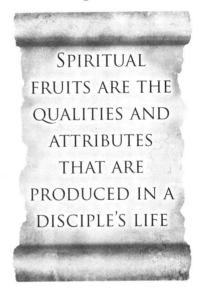

SPIRITUAL FRUITS ARE THE QUALITIES AND ATTRIBUTES THAT ARE PRODUCED IN A DISCIPLE'S LIFE

Similarly, Col. 2:9-15 (NIV) adds, *"For in Christ all the fullness of the Deity lives in bodily form, and in Christ you have been brought to fullness. He is the head over every power and authority. In him you were also circumcised with a circumcision not performed by human hands. Your whole self ruled by the flesh was put off when you were circumcised by Christ, having been buried with him in baptism, in which you were also raised with him through your faith in the working of God, who raised him from the dead. When you were dead in your sins and in the uncircumcision of your flesh, God made you alive with Christ.*

He forgave us all our sins, having canceled the charge of our legal indebtedness, which stood against us and condemned us; he has taken it away, nailing it to the cross. And having disarmed the powers and authorities, he made a public spectacle of them, triumphing over them by the cross."

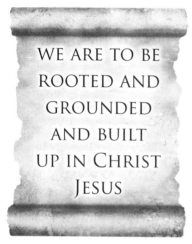

WE ARE TO BE ROOTED AND GROUNDED AND BUILT UP IN CHRIST JESUS

As long as we abide in Christ, the life-giving vine, and keep His commandments, we will receive and be richly filled and abundantly supplied with His life, Word, and Spirit, and will bear and produce much fruit, and so bring glory to Father God. John 15:1-8 (NIV) says, *"I am the true vine, and my Father is the gardener. He cuts off every branch in me that bears no fruit, while every branch that does bear fruit he prunes so that it will be even more fruitful. You are already clean because of the word I have spoken to you. Remain in me, as I also remain in you. No branch can bear fruit by itself; it must remain in the vine. Neither can you bear fruit unless you remain in me. I am the vine; you are the branches. If you remain in me and I in you, you will bear much fruit; apart from me you can do nothing. If you do not remain in me, you are like a branch that is thrown away and withers; such branches are picked up, thrown into the fire and burned. If you remain in me and my words remain in you, ask whatever you wish, and it will be done for you. This is to my Father's glory, that you bear much fruit, showing yourselves to be my disciples."*

Similarly, we are to be rooted and grounded and built up in Christ Jesus and His love (Col. 1:23, 2:7; Eph. 3:17), thus becoming stable, established and mature, as well as *"steadfast, immovable, always abounding in the work of the Lord"* (1 Cor. 15:58, NASB). The Greek word for steadfast is *hedraioi,* meaning "solidly-based, well-seated; morally fixed; firm in purpose (mind); well-stationed (securely positioned), not given to fluctuation or moving off course." The Greek word for immovable is *ametakinētoi,* meaning "without movement or change of status (location)." And the Greek word for abounding is *perisseuontes,* meaning "exceeding the ordinary (the necessary), overflowing; abundance or surplus) – properly, exceed, go beyond the expected measure, i.e. above and beyond ("more than . . . "); what goes further (more), surpasses" (Strong's G1476, G277, G4052).

The more time we spend with the Lord on the 8th Mountain on a regular basis, the more fruit of the Spirit will develop in our lives! The more fruit of the Spirit that develops in our lives, the more that the Lord will trust us and open new doors for us to exercise our spiritual gifts in a greater capacity to influence and serve more people!

SPIRITUAL GIFTS

In addition to producing spiritual fruit, we who are in Christ also receive spiritual gifts from Him. Eph. 4:7-8 (NIV) says, *"But to each one of us **grace has been given** as Christ apportioned it. This is why it says: 'When he ascended on high, he led captives in his train and **gave gifts to men.'"*** (author's emphasis). The Greek word *charis* is used here for grace and is the root word for charisma and charismatic. It means: (a) a gift or blessing brought to man by Jesus Christ, (b) favor, (c) gratitude, thanks, (d) a favor, kindness (Strong's G5485). The Greek word *domata* is used here for gifts, which is the plural version of *doma* (Strong's G1390). In fact, we are commanded by Paul the Apostle to eagerly desire spiritual gifts (1 Cor. 14:1). The Greek word *pneumatika* is used here for spiritual gifts (Strong's G4152).

Several types of spiritual gifts are listed in Scripture, with some overlap. The primary Scriptures are 1 Cor. 12:4-11, 12:27-31; Rom. 12:1-7 and Eph. 4:11. We will examine each of those now, starting with 1 Cor. 12:4-11. *"There are **different kinds of gifts**, but the same Spirit distributes them. There are **different kinds of service**, but the same Lord. There are **different kinds of working**, but in all of them and in everyone it is the same God at work. Now to each one the manifestation of the Spirit is given for the common good. To one there is given through the Spirit a message of wisdom, to another a message of knowledge by means of the same Spirit, to another faith by the same Spirit, to another gifts of healing by that one Spirit, to another miraculous powers, to another prophecy, to another distinguishing between spirits, to another speaking in different kinds of tongues, and to still another the interpretation of tongues. All these are the work of one and the same Spirit, and he distributes them to each one, just as he determines"* (NIV).

In the passage above, the Greek word used for gifts in verse 4 is *charismaton*, which signifies the charismatic nature of these nine spiritual gifts. It is important to note that they are given for the common good, to bless and serve others, and not to feed our egos, and that the recipients of these gifts do not get to pick and choose them, but God distributes them to each member of His body, just as He determines and apportions. James 1:17 says that every good and perfect gift comes from God, and this includes spiritual gifts. Matt. 7:9-11 and Luke 11:11-13 also tell us that God the Father only gives good gifts to His children.

Next, 1 Cor. 12:27-31 (NIV) continues: *"Now you are the body of Christ, and each one of you is a part of it. And God has placed in the church first of all apostles, second prophets, third teachers, then miracles, then gifts of healing, of helping, of guidance, and of different kinds of tongues. Are all apostles? Are all prophets? Are all teachers? Do all work miracles? Do all have gifts of healing? Do all speak in tongues? Do all interpret? Now eagerly desire the greater gifts."* Notice that eight gifts are listed here and that the Greek word for gifts in verses 30-31 is *charismata*. Buddy Bell has been teaching on the gift of helps for many years, for example, and there are many practitioners of divine healing, prophecy, teaching, miracles, and guidance or counseling, as well as modern day apostles.

Eph. 4:11-13 (NLT) contains a similar list of gifts: *"Now these are the gifts Christ gave to the church: the apostles, the prophets, the evangelists, and the pastors and teachers. Their responsibility is to equip God's people to do his work and build up the church, the body of Christ. This will continue until we all come to such unity in our faith and knowledge of God's Son that we will be mature in the Lord, measuring up to the full and complete standard of Christ."* These five gifts are commonly referred to and known as the "five-fold gifts" by many in ministry. And, quite obviously, these gifts are still in effect and force today, despite what some false teachers and pastors claim to the contrary, who are apparently deceived, blinded or ignorant on this matter.

Lastly, Rom. 12:4-8 states: *"For just as each of us has one body with many members, and these members do not all have the same function, so in Christ we, though many, form one body, and each member belongs to all the others. We have different gifts, according to the grace given to each of us. If your gift is prophesying, then prophesy in accordance with your faith; if it is serving, then serve; if it is teaching, then teach; if it is to encourage, then give encouragement; if it is giving, then give generously; if it is to lead, do it diligently; if it is to show mercy, do it cheerfully."* Again, the Greek word for gifts in verse 6 is *charismata,* so there is a definite pattern and consistency among these four lists.

Notice that prophecy/prophesying/prophets is the only gift listed on all four lists of spiritual gifts, and that teaching/ teachers is shared in common on three lists, while apostles are mentioned on two lists, speaking in tongues on two lists, interpretation of tongues on two lists, healing on two lists, miracles on two lists, and the other gifts – including evangelists, pastors, giving, encouraging, serving, leading, showing mercy, helping, guiding, faith, word of wisdom, word of knowledge, and discerning of spirits – are each mentioned only on one list.

This totals 19 distinct spiritual gifts of 29 gifts listed when they are cross referenced against the four lists. A few of these gifts such as serving and leading could also apply to many or most of the other ones. Scripture is quite clear that God has given us these spiritual gifts to bless and serve others, and glorify God, as well as the spiritual fruits to go along with them, so that we will be effective witnesses for Him when we speak and act, and more likely to be received and believed.

REDEEMING THE TIME

According to several of the Gospels, there will be wars and rumors of war until the time of Jesus' return (Matt. 24:6; Mark 13:7). That is certainly true today. God has also promised us that everything that can be shaken will be shaken, and so the present shakings, tremors, rumblings and aftershocks on planet Earth to the world's financial and political and cultural and legal systems, while disturbing and unsettling to some, should come as no surprise to those who are led by the Spirit and familiar with the word of God. That being the case, the question presents itself: How should we as believers live so as to redeem the time, and to please the One who has called us unto Himself and into His body to a life of service to others (Eph. 5:15-17)?

Jesus is quite clear in the Parable of the Talents and other Scriptures that He expects and calls us to live as stewards of all that He has entrusted to us, and to be profitable servants as His sons and daughters who are kings and priests in the Order of Melchizedek, and joint heirs of eternal life with Jesus. Much of Matthew 13, for example, is devoted to providing various analogies of how kingdom citizens are to use their influence to bring change and/or make a positive difference on the earth to those around them in their spheres of influence.

Many Christians, unfortunately, appear to suffer from a common malady named Arrested Development (aka Stunted Growth). They are content and comfortable to stop at knowing Jesus as their Savior, when that is just the starting point of the Christian life, and not the finish line. Knowing who I am in Jesus is the gospel of salvation. This informs me of the benefits I receive in the Great Exchange such as grace, mercy, forgiveness of sins, regenerated spirit, redemption, unconditional love, the indwelling of the Holy Spirit, the gift of tongues, and eternal life. But, there is much more involved, according to Scripture.

SANCTIFICATION

The deeper work of the Spirit in producing discipleship, spiritual maturity and lasting fruit in the lives of saints, begins after salvation. Otherwise, Paul the Apostle would not have had to write his numerous epistles to the 1st Century churches and John the Revelator would not have had to write to the seven churches of Asia, with each apostle giving these churches, respectively, correction, instruction, warning, admonition, and exhortation.

Sanctification follows salvation, and is a lifetime process. Although we have been convicted of our sinful condition, have repented and asked Jesus into our heart, have confessed Him with our mouth, and our spirit has been regenerated and we have become a new creation as a part of our salvation experience, our soul – mind, will and emotions – remains in the same state as before our conversion to Christ. Therefore, we have to be willing to change and to enter into an ongoing process of transforming and taking captive our thoughts, speech, actions, attitudes, habits, dreams, will and desires by voluntarily surrendering and submitting them to the Lordship of Jesus and the ministry of the Holy Spirit (Rom. 12:1-2; 2 Cor. 10:3-5).

Indeed, there is a vast difference in knowing Jesus as Lord and knowing him as Savior. Knowing who I am in Christ is equivalent to elementary school and junior high school studies and curricula, to use an education analogy. Knowing who Christ is in me is equivalent to high school and college or university studies and curricula. It is significantly more advanced training, and training for a specific purpose with tangible fruit and measurable results.

MEMBERSHIP VS. CITIZENSHIP

Spiritual training is for reigning, not complaining, feigning, abstaining, gainsaying or fainting. Knowing who I am in Jesus is **membership.** Knowing who Jesus is in me is **citizenship.** Both are important but obviously God, and the world, need and would prefer that we function as citizens also, and not just as members. *"So then you are no longer strangers and aliens, but you are **fellow citizens** with the saints **and members** of the household of God,"* (Eph. 2:19, ESV, author's emphasis).

Members can quit or drop out anytime they feel tired, weary, exhausted, unappreciated, unloved, misunderstood, discouraged, disillusioned, disgruntled, discontented, depressed, offended, oppressed or bored, and either transfer their membership elsewhere, choose to isolate or hibernate and not fellowship with other saints, or start or join a home fellowship or cell group or support group which may or may not have a biblical authority structure and leadership accountability.

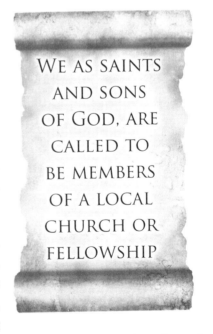

WE AS SAINTS AND SONS OF GOD, ARE CALLED TO BE MEMBERS OF A LOCAL CHURCH OR FELLOWSHIP

Citizens, on the other hand, understand their duty and responsibility, and serve others. They vote, work, pay taxes, engage in public discourse on public issues and public policy, run for elected office, lead, innovate, earn money, invest, save, create companies, create jobs, hire employees, respect authority, and volunteer their time, talent and treasure to build, protect and defend their communities and nation. We as saints and sons of God, are called to be members of a local church or fellowship, AND citizens of a global kingdom. It's not either/or; it's both/and.

The global Church, and the broader Kingdom of God, need citizens who can bring ideas, creativity, experience, energy, passion, wisdom, discernment, leadership and other gifts, talents, abilities and attributes to the table. Members of organizations usually expect to receive services, to pay dues, and to meet and connect with other like-minded individuals who share a common or similar mission, vision and set of values. Citizens, in contrast, serve others, and seek the public good and/or the public benefit, as they understand and define those terms.

Jesus is not one-dimensional, and neither are we. He is King of kings, Lord of lords, Prince of Peace, Son of God, Son of Man, Emmanuel, the Christ, our Redeemer, our Chief Advocate and eternal High Priest, Savior, the Lamb of God, and so much more. Likewise, we are kings and priests, saints and sons (this gender-neutral term includes daughters), members and citizens.

SPIRITUAL LEADERSHIP

Anyone who has ever served on a sports team, a corporate team, or in the military, knows that teamwork requires discipline, focused effort, humility, honor, respect for authority, effective communication and character development. It is no different in being a Christian and living life as a Christian. Scripture says, *"What we do see is Jesus, who was given a position 'a little lower than the angels'; and because he suffered death for us, he is now 'crowned with glory and honor. Yes, by God's grace, Jesus tasted death for everyone. God, for whom and through whom everything was made, chose to bring many children into glory. And it was only right that he should make Jesus, through his suffering, a perfect leader, fit to bring them into their salvation"* (Heb. 2:9-10, NLT).

Scripture also says, *"Though outwardly we are wearing out, inwardly we are renewed day by day. Our suffering is light and temporary and is producing for us an eternal glory that is greater than anything we can imagine"* (2 Cor. 4:16-17, God's Word, author's emphasis). *"And since we are his children, we are his heirs. In fact, together with Christ we are heirs of God's glory. But if we are to share his glory, we must also share his suffering"* (Rom. 8:17, NLT, author's emphasis). *"But rejoice insofar as you share Christ's sufferings, that you may also rejoice and be glad when his glory is revealed."* (1 Pet. 4:13, ESV).

Many Christians want God's glory without the suffering; they want God's promotion without the obedience and sacrifice and testing and discipline and faithfulness required for refinement and character development and becoming effective, accountable spiritual leaders. Joseph, Esther, Daniel, Moses, Joshua, David and so many others, patiently endured the process and were found faithful in their assignments, then were promoted into the fullness of their destiny from God.

2 Tim. 2:20-21, NLT, (author's emphasis) says, *"In a wealthy home some utensils are made of gold and silver, and some are made of wood and clay. The expensive utensils are used for special occasions, and the cheap ones are for everyday use. If you keep*

yourself pure, you will be a special utensil for honorable use. Your life will be clean, and you will be ready for the Master to use you for every good work." Obviously, God will not force you to become ready for honorable use and for every good work, or to actually do such work when invited by Him. Those are intentional, deliberate, conscious decisions you must voluntarily choose to make. Spiritual leadership costs something, and the price is always some form of death (John 12:24).

MAKING DISCIPLES VS. GROWING NUMBERS

It has been well said that whatever is worth doing is worth measuring, and that we tend to get more of whatever behavior or outcome we measure. The modern Church has measured and documented responses to evangelistic campaigns and soul-winning crusades with excellence and precision, but failed miserably at measuring or documenting discipleship and mentoring programs and processes to produce maturity, character, identity and sonship in future leaders by true spiritual fathers and mothers. This status quo is obviously out of balance and it's no wonder, then, that the Church has lost ground in its perceived influence, credence, and relevance to the broader culture over the last 50+ years.

Jesus did not focus on numbers; instead, He focused on discipling 12 men, and a small handful of other inner circle followers, including several women and the 70. He was faithful to both His assignment and His Father. As our churches and spiritual leaders begin to shift from a primary or exclusive focus on membership and numbers to a more balanced approach of both soul-winning AND producing kingdom citizens and disciples in equal measure, then we will see the Church regain lost ground and momentum, and the Kingdom regain and reclaim its distinctiveness and influence, and true leaders – not only captains, commanders and generals but statesmen, diplomats and ambassadors – emerge from our ranks.

RETURN TO THE ANCIENT PATHS

This book is a clarion call and clear trumpet sound to this generation to return to the ancient paths, and the ancient foundations of righteousness and justice. Then, we can again expect and see reformation, transformation and a spiritual renaissance on the earth in our lifetime. This is what the LORD says: *"Stand at the crossroads and look; ask for the ancient paths, ask where the good way is, and walk in it, and you will find rest for your souls"* (Jer. 6:16, NIV). *"If my people, who are called by my name, will humble themselves and pray and seek my face and turn from their wicked ways, then I will hear from heaven, and I will forgive their sin and will heal their land"* (2 Chron. 7:14, NIV).

It's not too late Church, but it is time to wake up, grow up, suit up, and show up. Let's take our place at the tables and in the gates, and use our influence to help transform, reform and redeem society and culture as citizens of His kingdom.

Both the world and the kingdom of God need and deserve your best. Jesus set the example and modeled transformation for us. He purchased our freedom and redemption and victory and inheritance with His own blood, and His own life. He gave His best; we can do no less. The Church is God's only plan for the earth; there is no Plan B. We have everything we need to get the job done, so it's time to stop making excuses and feeling sorry for ourselves. As warriors and championship-winning teams know, the best defense is a good offense. It's time for the Church to play offense again.

And, here's the game plan and heaven's winning strategy. *"So Christ himself gave the apostles, the prophets, the evangelists, the pastors and teachers, to equip his people for works of service, so that the body of Christ may be built up until we all reach unity in the faith and in the knowledge of the Son of God and become mature, attaining to the whole measure of the fullness of Christ"* (Eph. 4:11-13, NIV). That sounds like discipleship training and mentoring to me, and a functionally-diversified Church structure and government.

This passage of Scripture is every bit as strategic and important as the Great Commission for the mission and purpose and assignment of the Church, but receives far less attention, focus and resources, in comparison, for a variety of reasons, which we will not go into here. That is unfortunate, to say the least, and that disparity needs to change, now, for the Church to achieve its potential and successfully carry out and fulfill its mission. In fact, Paul told Timothy, *"You have heard me teach things that have been confirmed by many reliable witnesses. Now teach these truths to other trustworthy people who will be able to pass them on to others"* (2 Tim. 2:2).

This again sounds like discipleship and equipping from a five-fold ministry leader. The 8th Mountain's leaders are its gifts to the leaders of the 7 Mountains of Culture, and their divine gifts are made desirable when packaged in the fruit of the Spirit.

In closing this chapter, I echo the words of Paul the Apostle: *"My dear children, for whom I am again in the pains of childbirth until Christ is formed in you,"* (Gal. 4:19, NIV). It's time to become the bride of Christ, not just the body of Christ. One of the main ways we can do that is to spend time with God on the 8th Mountain. Make yourself ready, Church. You and I are God's answer, God's solution and God's wisdom to the world's woes and thorny, perplexing questions, dilemmas and policy issues. He wants to manifest His glory through you. We have been given access to all we need to get the job done. It's time and God's design to shine even brighter as the darkness increases (Isa. 59:19, 60:1-3). Now we turn our attention to character, discipline, process and suffering in Chapter 11.

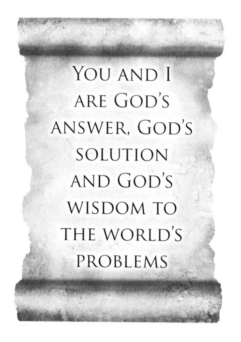

YOU AND I
ARE GOD'S
ANSWER, GOD'S
SOLUTION
AND GOD'S
WISDOM TO
THE WORLD'S
PROBLEMS

ELEVEN

CHARACTER, DISCIPLINE, PROCESS AND SUFFERING

"No discipline seems pleasant at the time, but painful. Later on, however, it produces a harvest of righteousness and peace for those who have been trained by it."
(Heb. 12:11, NIV)

A few summers ago as I was working in my office, I received a phone call from Dr. Karl Bandlien. It was the first time I had met Dr. Bandlien and he was calling to complete the application process to join KCIA, where he had been referred by a mutual friend and Board member. After a few minutes of getting acquainted and sharing information, Dr. Bandlien abruptly said, "As I was praying, I received a word for you from the Lord."

"What is it?" I asked. "Feel free to share it with me."

"The Lord says to tell you that He has chosen you to lead KCIA because you have suffered much, and been willing to suffer for Him; therefore, He can trust you with increased spiritual authority," said Dr. Bandlien.

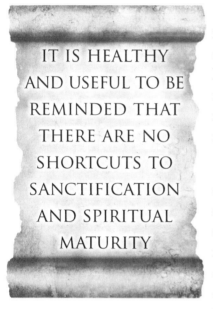

IT IS HEALTHY AND USEFUL TO BE REMINDED THAT THERE ARE NO SHORTCUTS TO SANCTIFICATION AND SPIRITUAL MATURITY

I felt this word impact my Spirit as it was being delivered and received, and have since thought about it several times, and have meditated and reflected upon it in some detail.

I had not previously equated or correlated suffering with spiritual leadership, but soon realized that the Bible is full of such connections and comparisons, especially concerning Jesus (see Isa. 53:1-12, Phil. 2:5-11). In this modern age where hyper grace and cheap grace are being preached and taught and extolled by some Christian leaders, I think it is healthy and useful to be reminded that there are no shortcuts to sanctification and spiritual maturity, and that real grace, while free, is costly, as Dietrich Bonhoeffer so eloquently wrote about prior to his martyrdom. Many of us want to experience the glory but not the suffering. It doesn't work that way in the Kingdom of God. They go together.

As we spend time with the Lord on the 8th Mountain, He will teach us the benefits and rewards of the suffering that we have undergone that He will use in our lives to mature our character, deepen our faith, and advance His kingdom in our spheres of influence.

Even with the original mandate God gave Adam in the Garden of Eden (Gen. 1:26-30), suffering is involved in walking that out in our lives and seeing it manifest and come to pass. Regarding Joseph, Psa. 105:19 (NLT) says, *"Until the time came to fulfill his dreams, the Lord tested Joseph's character."* God tests us through discipline, suffering and process. Now, don't get me wrong. I am not saying we should seek out or enjoy suffering. Far from it. But, when it comes, we must be willing to endure *"hardships and suffering as a good soldier of Jesus Christ"* (2 Tim. 2:3, AMP). In fact, suffering is intertwined and interconnected with character, according to Rom. 5:2b-5a, (NIV), *"And we boast in the hope of the glory of God. Not only so, but we also glory in our sufferings, because we know that suffering produces perseverance; perseverance, character; and character, hope. And hope does not put us to shame."*

Following are several more Scriptures which speak to this subject. I pray they will encourage, enlighten and empower you.

"The Spirit himself testifies with our spirit that we are God's children. Now if we are children, then we are heirs—heirs of God and co-heirs with Christ, if indeed we share in his sufferings in order that we may also share in his glory. I consider that our present sufferings are not worth comparing with the glory that will be revealed in us" (Rom. 8:16-18, NIV). *"For our light affliction, which is but for a moment, worketh for us a far more exceeding and eternal weight of glory"* (2 Cor. 4:17, KJV).

"In bringing many sons and daughters to glory, it was fitting that God, for whom and through whom everything exists,

should make the pioneer of their salvation perfect through what he suffered. Both the one who makes people holy and those who are made holy are of the same family. So Jesus is not ashamed to call them brothers and sisters" (Heb. 2:10-11, NIV). *"In fact, everyone who wants to live a godly life in Christ Jesus will be persecuted"* (2 Tim. 3:12, NIV). *"Therefore, since Christ suffered in his body, arm yourselves also with the same attitude, because whoever suffers in the body is done with sin"* (1 Pet. 4:1, NIV).

"But rejoice inasmuch as you participate in the sufferings of Christ, so that you may be overjoyed when his glory is revealed" (1 Pet. 4:13, NIV). *"But let none of you suffer as a murderer, or as a thief, or as an evildoer, or as a busybody in other men's matters. Yet if any man suffer as a Christian, let him not be ashamed; but let him glorify God on this behalf"* (1 Pet. 4:15-16, KJV). *"I want to know Christ—yes, to know the power of his resurrection and participation in his sufferings, becoming like him in his death, and so, somehow, attaining to the resurrection from the dead"* (Phil. 3:10-11, NIV).

"Be alert and of sober mind. Your enemy the devil prowls around like a roaring lion looking for someone to devour. Resist him, standing firm in the faith, because you know that the family of believers throughout the world is undergoing the same kind of sufferings. And the God of all grace, who called you to his eternal glory in Christ, after you have suffered a little while, will himself restore you and make you strong, firm and steadfast" (1 Pet. 5:8-9, NIV).

We are told in Scripture that all disciples of Jesus will suffer hardships, and to view hardship and adversity as divine discipline. *"They encouraged them to continue in the faith, reminding them that we must suffer many hardships to enter the Kingdom of God"* (Acts 14:22, NLT). *"Endure hardship as discipline; God is treating you as his children. For what children are not disciplined by their father? If you are not disciplined— and everyone undergoes discipline—then you are not legitimate, not true sons and daughters at all. Moreover, we have all had human fathers who disciplined us and we respected them for it. How much more should we submit to the Father of spirits and live! They disciplined us for a little while as they thought best; but God disciplines us for our good, in order that we may share in his holiness."* (Heb. 12:7-10, NIV). In the next section we will examine adversity, and possible ways we can respond to it.

ADVERSITY IS OFTEN UNEXPECTED AND UNPREDICTABLE

Adversity comes in many shapes and forms, and often takes us by surprise, unexpectedly, since life is not always fair or predictable or a bed of roses. It could be a sick child, a chronically-ill spouse, an abusive family member or relative, a cranky or ill-tempered boss, a jealous or insecure co-worker, a dishonest or lazy employee or business partner, an angry neighbor, an unrighteous judge, an unfriendly or unfaithful pastor, an unreasonable or egotistical client.

Or, it could be loss of a job, loss of income, loss of a friendship, loss of a spouse or other loved one, loss of a pet, or even loss of health, loss of food and shelter, loss of freedom, loss of memory, an auto accident, a sports or recreational injury, a wound in military service, a work-related accident, a natural disaster, act of terrorism, project deadline, budget cut, reduction in force (RIF), unjust criticism or accusation or conviction, a demotion or being passed over for a promotion or raise, or being robbed, assaulted, kidnaped, imprisoned, raped, tortured, or martyred.

How we respond to adversity, pressure and stress says a lot about who we are on the inside, at our core, and what kind of emotional and spiritual resources and reserves we have available to us. Clearly, all adversity is not at the same level of pain or severity, ranging from having a bad hair day, flat tire or caffeine withdrawal, to being traumatized or martyred. Our God is a God of grace, a God of mercy, a God of forgiveness and love and comfort and patience and a whole lot more. He is all you need Him to be in every situation.

But, for those of us who are human, sons of God, in the process of being sanctified and becoming like Jesus, we may be lacking or have a deficit in one or more of these divine attributes or qualities, and fruits of the Spirit (Gal. 5:22-23), even as a leader. Peter the Apostle was certainly not immune from such fleshly reactions, nor was Paul the Apostle, nor James and John, the "sons of thunder." It should come as no surprise, then, that you and I may have need of refinement and purification of our soulish, fleshly, carnal nature which we are commanded to "put to death" (Col. 3:5-10; Rom. 8:12-13; see also Eph. 6:16-17; 2 Thess. 2:13; 1 John 1:5-10; Rom. 3:23; Gal. 3:5). This nature was figuratively put to death in our baptism by crucifixion, according to Scripture (Rom. 6:3-7, 1 Pet. 3:21, Col. 2:12), but literally we get to walk it out each day we live and "work out your salvation with fear and trembling" (Phil. 2:12).

Sometimes we have to put the old sin nature to death more than once...at times in the same day. Paul said, *"I die [face death] daily"* (1 Cor. 15:31). He also said, *"But I discipline my body and keep it under control, lest after preaching to others I myself should be disqualified"* (I Cor. 9:27). Character doesn't just appear out of thin air or develop in isolation or by wishful thinking or by watching television or movies or frequenting Facebook. It is developed by training the spirit man, by which a foundation of justice and righteousness is laid.

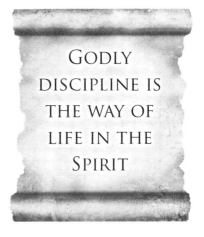

Godly discipline is the way of life in the Spirit, and it is for our own good, and produces a harvest of righteousness and peace. Heb. 12:7-11 (NIV) says, *"Endure hardship as discipline; God is treating you as his children. For what children are not disciplined by their father? If you are not disciplined (and everyone undergoes discipline), then you are not legitimate, not true sons and daughters at all. Moreover, we have all had human fathers who disciplined us and we respected them for it. How much more should we submit to the Father of spirits and live! They disciplined us for a little while as they thought best; but God disciplines us for our good, in order that we may share in his holiness. No discipline seems pleasant at the time, but painful. Later on, however, it produces a harvest of righteousness and peace for those who have been trained by it."*

Character is also further developed by adversity or pressure – what some have called "the school of hard knocks." Adversity teaches lessons that are not soon forgotten, and has the potential to bring forth greatness in a person, by causing them to examine themselves and look outside themselves for answers and solutions, and to either bring them to God, or cause them to go deeper in

God. Adversity also strengthens our prayer life. Solomon said that both prosperity and adversity come from God. *"In times of prosperity be joyful, but in times of adversity consider this: God has made one as well as the other, so that no one can discover what the future holds"* (Eccl. 7:14, NET Bible). Quite obviously, we can choose several ways to deal with the adversity we encounter in life. Below are four such choices and their consequences.

FOUR POSSIBLE RESPONSES TO ADVERSITY

Choice 1: We Can Become Bitter

The first way we can respond to adversity is to become bitter. Unfortunately, many people choose this option, even among followers of Christ. This is a recipe for disaster. Heb. 12:15 says, *"See to it that no one comes short of the grace of God; that no root of bitterness springing up causes trouble, and by it many be defiled."* Eph. 4:31-32 adds, *"Let all bitterness and wrath and anger and clamor and slander be put away from you, along with all malice. Be kind to one another, tender-hearted, forgiving each other, just as God in Christ also has forgiven you."*

Acts 8:23 records, *"For I see that you are in the gall of bitterness and in the bondage of iniquity."* Jas. 3:14 notes, *"But if you have bitter jealousy and selfish ambition in your heart, do not be arrogant and so lie against the truth."* Prov. 17:25 says, *"A foolish son is a grief to his father and bitterness to her who bore him."* Isa. 38:17 states, *"Lo, for my own welfare I had great bitterness; It is You who has kept my soul from the pit of nothingness, For You have cast all my sins behind Your back."*

1 Sam. 30:6 records the story of Ziklag being burned with fire, and all of the livestock, women and children being taken by the Amalekites. David's own men were so distraught and bitter that they spoke of stoning him. *"Moreover David was greatly distressed because the people spoke of stoning him, for all the people were embittered, each one because of his sons and his daughters. But David strengthened himself in the LORD his God."* Great leaders have to rise above circumstances and the threats or doubts of their followers, and take action.

Gen. 27:34 states, *"When Esau heard the words of his father, he cried out with an exceedingly great and bitter cry, and said to his father, "Bless me, even me also, O my father!"* Esau was so bitter over Jacob stealing his birthright, that Jacob had to flee for his life to another country and live with and serve a distant kinsman for many years.

Finally, Job 7:11 says, after he had suffered great pain and anguish of soul, *"Therefore I will not restrain my mouth; I will speak in the anguish of my spirit, I will complain in the bitterness of my soul."* He later adds in Job 10:1, *"I loathe my own life; I will give full vent to my complaint; I will speak in the bitterness of my soul."* I.e., Job had a flesh fest—he had a pity party because he could not rationalize or accept or justify his losses, pain and suffering. But, God had mercy on him after awhile and restored to him double all that he had lost. That was quite a lot because he was the wealthiest man of the East in his day and time.

Choice 2: We Can Become Butter

A second way we can respond to adversity is to become like butter. Butter melts and runs under heat and pressure, and is yellow, which is the color of cowardice.

2 Tim. 1:7 says, *"For God gave us a spirit not of fear but of power and love and self-control"* (ESV). The God's Word translation says, *"God didn't give us a cowardly spirit but a spirit of power, love, and good judgment."* So, this is not an effective, God-honoring choice. Giving in to pressure and circumstances and giving up on life and/or on God never works. Just ask Jonah. It is a futile and cowardly response which lacks faith and hope, and admits defeat. God is not glorified in such attitudes and actions. His plan is to turn your test into a testimony. But, first you have to stand your ground and wage a good warfare, as Paul the Apostle told Timothy.

Choice 3: We Can Become Battered

Third, we can respond to adversity by becoming battered, which is when we enable an abuser or voluntarily choose to stay in an abusive relationship. The Bible teaches us not to become unequally yoked with unbelievers, and to not associate with those who are divisive and quarrelsome, and stir up strife, but to warn them, and gently entreat them, and then to mark them in the spirit and tell the church (report them) if they do not repent (Rom. 16:17, Tit. 3:10). So, this is also not a viable, healthy option. Some nations have civil laws to protect the victims of domestic violence, and to try and help prevent such abuse, while others do not.

We are also told to avoid those with violent tempers and easily-angered spirits, or with those who struggle with or are subject to addictions of various types. Those suffering abuse need to seek and find shelters, refuges, and other safe places which offer counsel, encouragement, legal assistance, security, resources and support. Obviously, there is a huge difference in voluntarily choosing to remain in an abusive relationship, and in involuntarily being battered and abused, and enabling this dysfunctional and destructive behavior to continue by not reporting it to the proper authorities or agencies, and/or not seeking help for yourself. Here we are speaking of the latter and not the former.

It also goes without saying that there are those who are being tortured or martyred for the gospel's sake as a missionary or evangelist or pastor in a hostile environment geographically, culturally, ethnically, politically or religiously. Obviously, such treatment is also involuntary in nature, and at times cruel, sadistic and inhumane.

Choice 4: We Can Become Better

The fourth and best choice is to respond rather than react to adversity, and in so doing, become a better person. This assumes we have the emotional and spiritual capacity to guard our hearts and maintain some degree of control over our emotional and mental state of being, rather than just reacting to circumstances from the fleshly, carnal nature either in what we say or what we do. This response takes more thought, more self-control, more creativity, more wisdom, more sobriety and more empathy than simply reacting, but pays far higher dividends, and is the way Jesus modeled and taught, as well as the original apostles and Paul once they matured in their faith and were entrusted by the Holy Spirit to write parts of the New Testament. This may be easier or more natural for some than others, but it is possible for all believers through Christ.

In 2 Cor. 5:16-17, Paul says, *"Wherefore henceforth know we no man after the flesh: yea, though we have known Christ after the flesh, yet now henceforth know we him no more. Therefore if any man be in Christ, he is a new creature: old things are passed away; behold, all things are become new."* Job suffered more than his share of adversity and had this to say initially: *"Then Job arose and tore his robe and shaved his head, and he fell to the ground and worshiped. He said, "Naked I came from my mother's womb, And naked I shall return there. The LORD gave and the LORD has taken away. Blessed be the name of the LORD"* (Job 1:20-21).

Prov. 17:17 notes, *"A friend loves at all times, And a brother is born for adversity."* We are created to need each other as the body of Christ on earth and to live in community and covenant with one another. Heb. 12:14 says, *"Pursue peace with all men, and the sanctification without which no one will see the Lord."* Rom. 12:17-21 adds, *"Recompense to no man evil for evil. Provide things honest in the sight of all men. If it be possible, as much as lieth in you, live peaceably with all men. Dearly beloved, avenge not yourselves, but rather give place unto wrath: for it is written, Vengeance is mine; I will repay, saith the Lord. Therefore if thine enemy hunger, feed him; if he thirst, give him drink: for in so doing thou shalt heap coals of fire on his head. Be not overcome of evil, but overcome evil with good."*

Jas. 1:19-20 says, *"Wherefore, my beloved brethren, let every man be swift to hear, slow to speak, slow to wrath: For the wrath of man worketh not the righteousness of God."* Jas. 1:2-4 records, *"Consider it all joy, my brethren, when you encounter various trials, knowing that the testing of your faith produces endurance. And let endurance have its perfect result, so that you may be perfect and complete, lacking in nothing."* John 16:33 adds, *"These things I have spoken to you, so that in Me you may have peace. In the world you have tribulation, but take courage; I have overcome the world."* Psa. 55:22 says, *"Cast your burden upon the LORD and He will sustain you; He will never allow the righteous to be shaken."*

1 Cor. 10:13 adds, *"No temptation has overtaken you but such as is common to man; and God is faithful, who will not allow you to be tempted beyond what you are able, but with the temptation will provide the way of escape also, so that you will be able to endure it."* Psa. 46:1 notes, *"God is our refuge and strength, A very present help in trouble."* Psa. 34:8 says, *"O taste and see that the LORD is good; How blessed is the man who takes refuge in Him!"*

Rom. 8:35 states, *"Who will separate us from the love of Christ? Will tribulation, or distress, or persecution, or famine, or nakedness, or peril, or sword?"* Psa. 50:15 adds, *"Call upon Me in the day of trouble; I shall rescue you, and you will honor Me."* Psa. 145:14 says, *"The LORD sustains all who fall And raises up all who are bowed down."* Psa. 34:17 notes, *"The righteous cry, and the LORD hears And delivers them out of all their troubles."* Isa. 40:31 records, *"Yet those who wait for the LORD Will gain new strength; They will mount up with wings like eagles, They will run and not get tired, They will walk and not become weary."*

Matt. 11:28 promises, *"Come to Me, all who are weary and heavy-laden, and I will give you rest."* Jas. 1:12 says, *"Blessed is a man who perseveres under trial; for once he has been approved, he will receive the crown of life which the Lord has promised to those who love Him."* 1 Pet. 4:12-13 records, *"Beloved, do not be surprised at the fiery ordeal among you, which comes upon you for your testing, as though some strange thing were happening to you; but to the degree that you share the sufferings of Christ, keep on rejoicing, so that also at the revelation of His glory you may rejoice with exultation."*

CONCLUSION

If you haven't found your blind spots, hot buttons, lenses, filters, walls, triggers, boiling point, bursting point or breaking point yet, don't worry; you will. Just keep living long enough for it to happen. Then, you will discover God is still on the throne, He's a whole lot wiser and more loving than you, and you will find out rather quickly who your true friends are, and what you are made of, and how big God really is. He loves you enough to heal you, to sanctify you, to set you free, to speak the truth in love, and to cause you to walk in wholeness, freedom and maturity. His plan is to prosper you and not harm you, to give you a hope and a future (Jer. 29:11). *"The Lord delights in the prosperity of His servant."* But, He also delights to heal you. *"Healing is the children's bread."*

As God cares enough about you to heal you from the inside out – in your heart, emotions and memories – and to reveal areas of blind spots or weaknesses or sins where you need to change, respond by repenting, asking His forgiveness, and seeking to make amends to any you have hurt, caused an offense, or sinned against. *"So if the Son sets you free, you are truly free"* (John 8:36, NLT). *"Therefore if the Son makes you free, you shall be free indeed"* (John 8:36, NKJV). Gal. 5:1 (MSG) adds, *"Christ has set us free to live a free life. So take your stand! Never again let anyone put a harness of slavery on you."* The God's Word version says, *"Christ has freed us so that we may enjoy the benefits of freedom. Therefore, be firm in this freedom, and don't become slaves again."*

Those who would become the 8th Mountain's leaders must model grace in suffering, and exercise persistence, humility and courage in finding and receiving their own healing. It is a requirement of leaders, and disciples, to model and practice what one teaches or preaches. Paul the Apostle famously said, *"Follow me as I follow Christ"* (1 Cor. 11:1). With these graces, the 8th Mountain's leaders can display patience, humility and love in helping the broken, battered, and bruised people in the 7 Mountains of Culture become whole.

Resolve to become better by His grace, love, strength, wisdom, power and mercy, rather than becoming bitter or butter, or being battered, whenever you face adversity. Spending time on the 8th Mountain with God will help you to do this by being transformed into His nature and character, and allowing His love, grace, and wisdom and power to heal you. In that way we are changed from glory to glory and renewed and transformed in our thoughts and mind, according to 2 Cor. 3:18 and Rom. 12:2. *"But he said to me, "My grace is sufficient for you, for my power is made perfect in weakness. Therefore I will boast all the more gladly about my weaknesses, so that Christ's power may rest on me"* (2 Cor. 12:9). Next, we will explore the topic of forgiveness and reconciliation in Chapter 12.

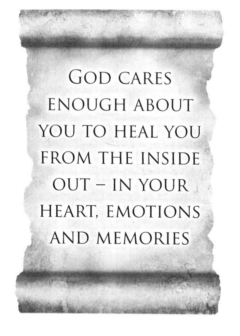

GOD CARES
ENOUGH ABOUT
YOU TO HEAL YOU
FROM THE INSIDE
OUT – IN YOUR
HEART, EMOTIONS
AND MEMORIES

TWELVE

FORGIVENESS AND RECONCILIATION

*"Forgive one another as quickly and thoroughly
as God in Christ forgave you."*
(Eph. 4:31, MSG)

*"Make allowance for each other's faults, and
forgive anyone who offends you. Remember, the
Lord forgave you, so you must forgive others"*
(Col. 3:13, NLT)

*"If you forgive those who sin against you, your
heavenly Father will forgive you. But if you refuse to
forgive others, your Father will not forgive your sins."*
(Matt. 6:14-15, NLT)

For most people, including Christians, forgiving may be one of their least favorite things to do, and is sometimes easier said than done. After all, it goes against our human (carnal) nature, and in that sense, is unnatural. But, those who have taken on the nature and character of Christ, have learned to forgive instinctively and as often as necessary, as part of their new nature. The more we forgive, the easier and more natural it becomes. One thing is certain: Disciples of Christ must walk in forgiveness to be pleasing to God, and obedient to Christ.

Perhaps the classic question in Scripture about this subject came from Simon Peter, who asked Jesus how often we must forgive others who hurt or offend us. Matt. 18:21-35 (NLT) says, *Then Peter came to him and asked, "Lord, how often should I forgive someone who sins against me? Seven times?" "No, not seven times," Jesus replied, "but seventy times seven!*

"Therefore, the Kingdom of Heaven can be compared to a king who decided to bring his accounts up to date with servants who had borrowed money from him. In the process, one of his debtors was brought in who owed him millions of dollars. He couldn't pay, so his master ordered that he be sold—along with his wife, his children, and everything he owned—to pay the debt. "But the man fell down before his master and begged him, 'Please, be patient with me, and I will pay it all.' Then his master was filled with pity for him, and he released him and forgave his debt.

"But when the man left the king, he went to a fellow servant who owed him a few thousand dollars. He grabbed him by the throat and demanded instant payment. "His fellow servant fell down before him and begged for a little more time. 'Be patient with me, and I will pay it,' he pleaded. But his creditor wouldn't wait. He had the man arrested and put in prison until the debt could be paid in full.

"When some of the other servants saw this, they were very upset. They went to the king and told him everything that had happened. Then the king called in the man he had forgiven and said, 'You evil servant! I forgave you that tremendous debt because you pleaded with me. Shouldn't you have mercy on your fellow servant, just as I had mercy on you?' Then the angry king sent the man to prison to be tortured until he had paid his entire debt. "That's what my heavenly Father will do to you if you refuse to forgive your brothers and sisters from your heart."

In this parable, Jesus made the point to his disciples that there are no limits on our forgiving others, just as God has not placed any limits on how often or how many times He is willing to forgive us, and that Christ has already paid the debt of sin on behalf of the whole world, that none of us would have ever been able to repay; therefore, we should be willing to forgive our brothers and sisters in Christ their debts, when they are unable to repay them. For an economic analysis of how these two amounts of debt (10,000 talents vs. a few hundred denarii) would compare in modern times, see Philip Massey, "The Parable of the Two Debtors in Modern Terms," Oct. 27, 2010, Biola University Chimes. http://chimes.biola.edu/story/2010/oct/27/parable-two-debtors/

FORGIVING OTHERS

"For he has . . . brought us into the kingdom of the Son he loves, in whom we have redemption, the forgiveness of sins"
(Col. 1:13–14, NIV).

On our journeys on the 8th Mountain, we're challenged when we harbor resentment against others. When we hold onto bitterness, our vista from its slopes is enshrouded by a fog of deceit. Forgiveness, though, dispels deceptions with light pouring from the beacon of hope found in the cross. Forgiveness is the sherpa of the Himalayas, leading us with the clarity of Christ's light.

"But if we walk in the light, as he is in the light, we have fellowship with one another, and the blood of Jesus his Son cleanses us from all sin" (1 John 1:7, ESV). The mountains of kingdoms, authority, rule and dominion are occupied with authority only when we walk in the light of Christ. That light is found in appropriating grace for others, just as it has been extended to us. *"Make allowance for each other's faults, and forgive anyone who offends you. Remember, the Lord forgave you, so you must forgive others"* (Col. 3:13, NLT).

Remember, we can discern whether something came from the 8th Mountain by looking at whether it is characterized by and saturated with God's love. Which offenses are covered by the blood of Christ? They're all forgivable. They're all forgiven. Every sin and offense is covered by His blood, regardless of magnitude. The redemptive act of Christ on the cross covers every transgression. While dying on the cross, Jesus said, *"Father, forgive them, for they don't know what they are doing..."* (Luke 23:34, NLT). Every act of forgiveness is saturated with His love.

True forgiveness isn't about a contrived erasure of offenses. Our memories carry emotions, both positive and negative. But, in order to think and pray clearly, we need to let go of hurts inflicted by others. Forgiveness is a crisis of the will.

Unfinished business opens the door for resentment to build in our hearts, and over time become a root of bitterness. When we pray, that bitterness hinders or blocks the flow, and affects the quality, of our dialogue. But, when we forgive, our conversations with the Lord flow without interruption. When we forgive others, we clear distractions and hindrances from our dialogues with Christ. Praying from a position of grace, our minds, wills, and emotions operate more clearly and with more wisdom as we're filled with His presence.

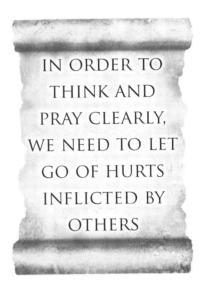

IN ORDER TO THINK AND PRAY CLEARLY, WE NEED TO LET GO OF HURTS INFLICTED BY OTHERS

"If it is possible, as far as it depends on you, live at peace with everyone" (Rom. 12:18). Jehovah-Shalom releases His calm certainty in our relationships. In the process, well-being is reshaped in our minds, and healing is set in motion.

Our Kingdom rule and dominion are diminished when we're in the myopic space of tending to our wounds. Conversely, each act of forgiveness and reconciliation matures us and empowers us to gain a high-level kingdom view. 8th Mountain leaders always take the path of peace. That peace is found in the humility of relinquishing pride for reconciliation, of being right for seeing the relationship healed and restored. Reconciliation shifts atmospheres in cities, states, nations, tribes, peoples, and tongues.

Reformation is seated in 8th Mountain mercy released in the Mountains of Business, Government, Education, Media, Entertainment, Family and Religion. Love begets forgiveness. Forgiveness begets unity. Unity begets progress. Progress begets reformation.

When we forgive, our times of rest and restoration operate from the place of Christ's peace, because our souls are in alignment with His Spirit. *"Be angry and do not sin; do not let the sun go down on your anger"* (Eph. 4:26, ESV). When we forgive, we arise from our times of quiet intimacy awakened and refreshed with the power to govern our respective Mountains with Christ-centered authority.

When times of intimacy are filled with God's Word, we're dialed in to the GPS of True North. Scripture brings us back to the supernatural work of the Holy Spirit in ourselves and others. Scripture is inerrant. Scripture declares our need to be complete and whole in Christ.

"Consider it pure joy, my brothers and sisters, whenever you face trials of many kinds, because you know that the testing of your faith produces perseverance. Let perseverance finish its work so that you may be mature and complete, not lacking anything" (Jas. 1:2-4, NIV). When we persevere in our relationships, we have the power to speak wisdom into peers, as they grow on integrous paths for His name's sake. Perseverance in relationships fosters maturity and completion as we become more Christ-like, bearing an orchard of the spiritual fruit of patience.

When we forgive from the heart, we're free to live without regret or bitterness. Joseph modeled this for us with his brothers in Egypt in Gen. 45:1-15. He forgave them, wept over them, embraced them and kissed them. Then he showed mercy and kindness to them, gave them gifts and supplies and donkeys, and provided land for them and their families in Goshen, as well as his father Jacob. This type of response to injustice, jealousy and betrayal demonstrated that his trust in the Lord was secure, and that his heart was healed.

Similarly, when we forgive from the heart others who have wronged us, we're free to live without regret or bitterness, and it shows that we are growing spiritually or have matured in Christ. If God permits or allows us to get hurt or be wounded, He's inviting us to grow and be perfected, and to forgive as His Son forgave.

Forgiveness is not only important to extend to others, but also to appropriate for ourselves.

FORGIVING OURSELVES

Sometimes the hardest person to forgive is ourselves. When we give Him permission, God reaches deep into the dark hurts of guilt and shame and leads us up and out to sunlight-bathed clearings of freedom and grace. Here, the Holy Spirit's words spill onto the pages of our Book in Heaven (Psa. 139:13-18) and renew us so that we can become agents of renewal for others.

When we make a commitment to encourage others toward a lifestyle of self-acceptance and self-directed grace, we welcome renewal arising from the infilling of the Holy Spirit. When we don't accomplish kingdom assignments with perfectly neat strokes or polished words, we can celebrate the tangible, realized presence of the Holy Spirit in that chapter of our Book in Heaven.

We can expect outrageous encounters with the brilliant Redeemer. He has seen everything we've been through. Everything. And, He never wastes pain. Never. He can take anything and everything we've been through and transform it into raw beauty. He uses even the most peculiar and the most unlikely for His glory.

When we humbly and openly extend grace and mercy to ourselves and others, an atmosphere of acceptance and grace forms the core of our culture. When that happens, we celebrate authentic, safe places to grow in our homes, businesses, ministries, schools, and communities.

8th Mountain shifts are all about a culture of forgiveness. A culture of forgiveness is found in a community that values honor, humility, grace and relationship above an egocentric win. The 8th Mountain win is a space of outward-affirming, forward-reaching God encounters. The Lord sees us in terms of who we're becoming as individuals and corporately. Jesus celebrates us and relates to us based not on our current position, but our future promotion.

Godly humility honors one another above ourselves. Forgiving always promotes us in the Kingdom.

The grace we extend to ourselves and others attracts all of heaven and opens up our hearts to futures laden with God-possibilities. God sweeps kingdom possibilitarians forward with the hope-filled sounds of His relentless, inexorable, empowered Spirit.

Our hard-won victories have the capacity to resonate with the next generation. They will become confident and strong when we encourage them to see and experience the Creator, His love, and their identity as forgivers.

In our Book in Heaven, we can set aside chapters for Jesus, the Author and Perfecter of our faith, to make the next silent stroke of His pen on our pages. Air time to broadcast forgiveness encounters, is an open invitation to exact an enormous amount of retribution against the enemy, released by the blood of the Lamb and the word of our testimony (Rev. 12:11).

Perhaps on some days God does more than lavish His grace upon us and pour His grace into us through Jesus; occasionally, He pours us into Olympic-size swimming pools of His grace. Immersed in these 8th Mountain grace-pools, together we can celebrate one another's discovery that there is no force that can separate us from the love of God that is in Christ Jesus our Lord (Rom. 8:35-39).

FORGIVING GOD

Most of us form our images of God, in part or whole, from our experiences with the fathers, or father figures, in our lives. These can include biological fathers, stepfathers, adoptive fathers, or other male relatives such as an uncle or grandfather, or even a trusted authority figure such as a teacher, coach, priest, bishop, pastor, or rabbi. There are healthy, mature, godly fathers and unhealthy, immature, or dysfunctional fathers, including missing fathers, absent fathers, unavailable fathers, abusive fathers, addictive fathers, angry fathers, controlling fathers, etc.

As we get older and become adults, we may not realize that our views and expectations of God have been tainted, influenced, compromised, distorted, and/or colored by our earlier experiences with father figures in our lives.

Such influences – whether positive or negative – will undoubtedly affect and color our expectations of God, and our assumptions about God, regardless of how much intellectual knowledge we have or do not have about God. It is really the emotional feelings, memories, and lies we have believed and agreed with about God, and about ourself, and the inner vows we have made, as well as the ancestral bloodline sins and generational curses in our family lineage, that must be repented of and renounced, and replaced with forgiveness and truth, and God's love, mercy and grace.

This means getting rid of and dismantling or destroying lies, myths, half-truths, deceptions, rumors, and innuendos about God in our own minds and hearts and souls, as well as severing and shattering shame cycles, blame cycles, guilt, fear, pride, ego, self-condemnation, self-sabotage, orphan spirits, victim and poverty mindsets and identities, and learning to trust and believe and love and respect and honor God in a much greater dimension and increased capacity. As we gain a clearer picture and perspective on who God really is, and learn His nature and character and ways, then we can relate to Him on a much deeper level, and in a much healthier and stronger manner and relationship.

As we forgive God, we are truly set free. And, in removing the limitations and distortions we have placed on God, and the lies we have believed about Him, this has a reciprocal effect on us, and our futures, by properly aligning us with God, and being transformed into His true image, from glory to glory, rather than from story to story. As we see God for who He is, then we can truly see ourselves for who He has designed and created us to be in His image. Psa. 36:9 says, *"For with you is the fountain of life; in your light we see light."*

RECONCILIATION

Reconciliation is an additional step beyond forgiveness – and is separate but related. Reconciliation seeks to restore or rebuild the relationship between two parties where a breach or sin or offense has occurred. Time does not heal all wounds; however, God can, if both parties are willing to take the necessary steps. Therefore, it is always best to offer to reconcile, and to make the effort and attempt to repair the relationship and rebuild the bridge whenever possible. Depending on the nature and severity of the offense, and the amount of time that has gone by since it occurred, most people appreciate such overtures and efforts to "bury the hatchet" and "mend the fence," and often surprising results and seemingly miraculous healings of hearts can occur with God's help, sustained and effectual prayer, and genuine repentance.

Jesus said in Matt. 5:21-26 (NASB), *"You have heard that the ancients were told, 'YOU SHALL NOT COMMIT MURDER' and 'Whoever commits murder shall be liable to the court.' "But I say to you that everyone who is angry with his brother shall be guilty before the court; and whoever says to his brother, 'You good-for-nothing,' shall be guilty before the supreme court; and whoever says, 'You fool,' shall be guilty enough to go into the fiery hell. "Therefore if you are presenting your offering at the altar, and there remember that your brother has something against you, leave your offering there before the altar and go;* **first be reconciled to your brother, and then come and present your offering.** *"Make friends quickly with your opponent at law while you are with him on the way, so that your opponent may not hand you over to the judge, and the judge to the officer, and you be thrown into prison. "Truly I say to you, you will not come out of there until you have paid up the last cent"* (author's emphasis).

Apparently reconciliation between brothers (or sisters) in Christ is more important to God than whatever offering (or sacrifice) you have to present to Him. He's more interested in the condition of your heart than your offering, and He desires for you to walk in unity and peace with other believers, and with other people in general, as much as it is possible within you (Rom. 12:18). Learn to be a peacemaker, and develop those skills. There's a promised blessing in that. Matt. 5:9 (NLT) says, *"God blesses those who work for peace, for they will be called the children of God."*

Yes, it does take some work from time to time to keep and maintain peace in our relationships. We may have to clear

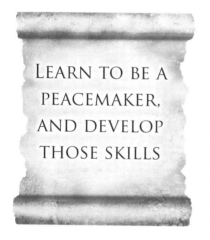

LEARN TO BE A PEACEMAKER, AND DEVELOP THOSE SKILLS

up a misunderstanding, or clarify a miscommunication, or reset or redefine an expectation, or apologize for an insensitive remark or comment, or just admit to being tired or feeling upset or having a bad day. Be quick to forgive, but also be quick to apologize and repent. Jesus died not only for our sins, but for our unity (John 17), and it's worth it. Relationships are the capital and currency of God's Kingdom.

It's far too easy to "unfriend" someone on Facebook, or "unfollow" them on Twitter, and remove them from the speed dial of your phone. Learn to have mastery of your emotions and emotional state, and be the bigger person. What works between individuals also works between nations, and my friend Amb. Clyde Rivers is a Goodwill

Peace Ambassador for Golden Rule International, as well as the Ambassador at Large for the nation of Burundi, and the Interfaith Peace Initiative of the United Nations. He travels and helps mediate and resolve conflicts and disputes between nations, and between warring factions within nations.

Jesus also laid out the process for us in Matt. 18:15-17 (NLT) to resolve conflicts between believers. *"If another believer sins against you, go privately and point out the offense. If the other person listens and confesses it, you have won that person back. But if they will not listen, take one or two others along, so that 'every matter may be established by the testimony of two or three witnesses.' If they still refuse to listen, tell it to the church; and if they refuse to listen even to the church, treat them as you would a pagan or a tax collector."* Apparently Jesus thinks working through conflict and offense as believers is an important thing to do, and part of what it means to function as a body with one head and many parts.

While this model is excellent, it is only as useful as the maturity levels of the parties involved. Healing the offense is only a part; the bigger picture is healing and preserving the relationship and taking it to a deeper level, and learning so as not to repeat the same issue in the future. If needed, the witness or witnesses should be peacemakers, and be people of proven character and wisdom who are known to be impartial. We are encouraged to be gentle and to speak the truth in love, rather than being harsh, critical or judgmental toward others. Gal. 6: 1 (NLT) says, *"Dear brothers and sisters, if another believer is overcome by some sin, you who are godly should gently and humbly help that person back onto the right path. And be careful not to fall into the same temptation yourself."*

155

Prov. 18:19 (KJV) states, *"A brother offended is harder to be won than a strong city: and their contentions are like the bars of a castle."* The NIV says, *"A brother wronged is more unyielding than a fortified city; disputes are like the barred gates of a citadel."* The NLT adds, *"An offended friend is harder to win back than a fortified city. Arguments separate friends like a gate locked with bars."*

Unfortunately, it is not always possible to reconcile with someone you have forgiven, for a variety of reasons. All you can do is your part, to take the initiative and try. That is all you are responsible for before God. The other party or parties may be dead; they may be unavailable; they may be missing or in hiding; they may be incarcerated; they may not be open or willing to reconcile; they may be immature, disobedient and/or not willing to be accountable; they may be under a court order to have no contact with you; they may be deeply wounded or traumatized and are healing, and the timing is not right; your sin may have affected more than one person and they are making decisions as a group; and, they may not have forgiven you yet. God's grace, love, mercy and forgiveness are always available, but are always a choice.

The 8th Mountain's leaders are governmental ambassadors – ambassadors of reconciliation. Our charge is to live reconciled with each other, and serve the leaders of the 7 Mountains of Culture in reconciling their differences with one another. Next, we turn our attention to prayer, intercession and spiritual warfare in Chapter 13.

THIRTEEN

PRAYER, INTERCESSION AND SPIRITUAL WARFARE

"You will also decree a thing, and it will be established for you; And light will shine on your ways."
(Job 22:28, NASB)

"And I sought for a man among them, that should build up the wall, and stand in the gap before me for the land, that I should not destroy it: but I found none."
(Ezek. 22:30, NIV)

"In the same way, the Spirit helps us in our weakness. We do not know what we ought to pray for, but the Spirit himself intercedes for us through wordless groans."
(Rom. 8:26, NIV)

TWO KINGDOMS IN CONFLICT

There are two spiritual kingdoms – the kingdom of darkness and the kingdom of light – and their respective forces are warring for our souls, identities, destinies and futures, as well as those of every other human on planet Earth. This is the basis and cause of spiritual warfare. These kingdoms are in conflict and are diametrically opposed. As followers and disciples of Jesus, we have a price on our heads – one from God and one from Satan (the devil). The question and choice is: Whose price will you pay? This is the nature and reality of the spiritual warfare we each must face and deal with, and we ignore or downplay it at our own risk and detriment. Prayer, intercession and spiritual warfare are obviously important to God, because He has a lot to say about them in His word, and we will explore that in the following pages.

WHOSE PRICE WILL YOU PAY?

First of all, the Lord Jesus has paid the ultimate price for each of us by His death on the cross for our sins, and by having His body broken and His innocent blood shed on our behalf as well as the sins of the whole world. Jesus said, *"I am the good shepherd. The good shepherd lays down his life for the sheep"* (John 10:11, NIV).

Scripture says, *"Therefore, since we are surrounded by such a great cloud of witnesses, let us throw off everything that hinders and the sin that so easily entangles. And let us run with perseverance the race marked out for us, fixing our eyes on Jesus, the pioneer and perfecter of faith. For the joy set before him he endured the cross, scorning its shame, and sat down at the right hand of the throne of God. Consider him who endured such opposition from sinners, so that you will not grow weary and lose heart"* (Heb. 12:1-3, NIV).

Rom. 5:6-8 (KJV) says, *"For when we were yet without strength, in due time Christ died for the ungodly. For scarcely for a righteous man will one die: yet peradventure for a good man some would even dare to die. But God commendeth his love toward us, in that, while we were yet sinners, Christ died for us."* John the Apostle said, *"Greater love hath no man than this, that a man lay down his life for his friends"* (John 15:13, KJV). *"Hereby perceive we the love of God, because he laid down his life for us: and we ought to lay down our lives for the brethren"* (1 John 3:16, KJV).

This is one of the secrets and mysteries of God and a seeming contradiction. It is in losing our lives in the service of God and for the benefit of others that we find life in the Kingdom. *"If you grasp and cling to life on your terms, you'll lose it, but if you let that life go, you'll get life on God's terms"* (Luke 17:33, MSG). *"Whoever tries to keep their life will lose it, and whoever loses their life will preserve it"* (Luke 17:33, NIV). *"I assure you, most solemnly I tell you, Unless a grain of wheat falls into the earth and dies, it remains [just one grain; it never becomes more but lives] by itself alone. But if it dies, it produces many others and yields a rich harvest"* (John 12:24, AMP).

Paul the Apostle said, *"You were bought with a price [purchased with a preciousness and paid for, made His own]. So then, honor God and bring glory to Him in your body"* (1 Cor. 6:20, AMP). He also said, *"You were bought with a price [purchased with a preciousness and paid for by Christ]; then do not yield yourselves up to become [in your own estimation] slaves to men [but consider yourselves slaves to Christ]"* (1 Cor. 7:23, AMP).

Paul also said, in Gal. 2:20 (NIV), *"I have been crucified with Christ and I no longer live, but Christ lives in me. The life I now live in the body, I live by faith in the Son of God, who loved me and gave himself for me."* Col. 3:3-4 (AMP) says, *"For [as far as this world is concerned] you have died, and your [new, real] life is hidden with Christ in God. When Christ, Who is our life, appears, then you also will appear with Him in [the splendor of His] glory."*

BECAUSE WE ARE SONS OF GOD WE ARE THEREFORE A THREAT TO THE EVIL ONE

Because we are sons of God, and joint heirs with Jesus, and are called to exercise dominion in the earth, to rule and reign with Christ, to make disciples of all nations, to be fruitful and multiply, to fill the earth and subdue it, to prosper and be in health, to exercise righteousness and justice, to abound and increase in every good work, to bind and loose, to decree and declare and establish, to possess and occupy, to be wise and faithful stewards, and to walk in authority on the earth, we are therefore a threat to the evil one and the enemy of our souls, and he has placed or put a bounty (price) on our heads as well.

Even though the devil has no legal authority over us, because we are citizens of the Kingdom of God and have sworn our allegiance to Christ Jesus and His Kingdom, and have been washed and cleansed by the blood of Jesus, the kingdom of darkness hopes to win us back or get us to compromise or sell out or fall short of our purpose and destiny, or even just to neutralize us and have us be ineffective and unfruitful in our faith. Moreover, the devil may still have legal access to us through unrepented sins we have committed or lies we have believed after (since) we were saved, or through the unrepented sins and iniquities in our ancestral bloodline, otherwise known as generational curses.

In recent years, Robert Henderson has done the body of Christ a great service by writing his book series on the Courts of Heaven, and I recommend those to you. If the demonic lie and false doctrine of "once saved, always saved" were actually true, there would have been no need for Jesus to teach His disciples about Satan's nature and tactics, or for the 1st Century apostles to teach the saints on spiritual warfare, or to send warnings and to write letters of correction to the early churches, or for Peter the Apostle to say, *"Be alert and of sober mind. Your enemy the devil prowls around like a roaring lion looking for someone to devour"* (1 Pet. 5:8, NIV). There would also be no need for deliverance and inner healing ministries today.

THE WEAPONS OF SATAN'S WARFARE

Satan's aim and goal is to disqualify us through any means at his disposal. He doesn't fight fair and he and his demons use deception as a primary weapon and strategy. He preys upon the weak, cowardly, fearful, untrained, uninformed, unaligned, unaccountable, unsubmitted, the proud, arrogant, angry, bitter, guilty, shamed, wounded, victimized, traumatized, and those at greatest risk to their faith, and he uses every opportunity to exploit our weaknesses. Jesus said, *"The thief comes only in order to steal and kill and destroy. I came that they may have and enjoy life, and have it in abundance (to the full, till it overflows)"* (John 10:10, AMP).

Jesus later said, when speaking to the Jewish religious leaders of His day, *"You are of your father, the devil, and it is your will to practice the lusts and gratify the desires [which are characteristic] of your father. He was a murderer from the beginning and does not stand in the truth, because there is no truth in him. When he speaks a falsehood, he speaks what is natural to him, for he is a liar [himself] and the father of lies and of all that is false"* (John 8:44, AMP). Satan is also called the accuser of the saints, which apparently is one of his chief roles. Rev. 12:10 (NLT) states, *"For the accuser of our brothers and sisters has been thrown down to earth — the one who accuses them before our God day and night."*

BELIEVERS ARE TO BE BLAMELESS

That's quite a rap sheet (criminal history) and m.o. (*modus operandi*, method of operation) on the devil. In contrast, God calls us, redeems us and qualifies us in and through Christ Jesus, the Lamb of God, who committed no sin. Spiritual warfare and sanctification are necessary in order that we may be blameless before God. 1 Cor. 1:8-9 notes, *"He will also keep you firm to the end, so that you will be blameless on the day of our Lord Jesus Christ. God, who has called you into fellowship with his Son Jesus Christ our Lord, is faithful."* 1 Cor. 5:23 (NIV) states, *"May God himself, the God of peace, sanctify you through and through. May your whole spirit, soul and body be kept blameless at the coming of our Lord Jesus Christ."*

Eph. 1:4 (NIV) says, *"For he chose us in him before the creation of the world to be **holy and blameless** in his sight"* (author's emphasis). Phil. 1:9-10 adds, *"And this is my prayer: that your love may abound more and more in knowledge and depth of insight, so that you may be able to discern what is best and may be pure and blameless for the day of Christ."* Phil. 2:14-15 adds, *"Do everything without complaining or arguing, so that you may become blameless and pure, children of God without fault in a warped and crooked generation..."* 2 Tim. 5:7 records, *"Give the people these instructions, **so that no one may be open to blame**"* (author's emphasis). Some of those listed in Scripture as blameless include Noah, Abraham, Job and Jesus. Today, we can each qualify by the blood of Jesus.

Rom. 6:23 (NLT) says, *"For the wages of sin is death, but the free gift of God is eternal life in Christ Jesus our Lord."* Similarly, Prov. 10:16 says, *"The wages of the righteous is life, but the earnings of the wicked are sin and death."* Those are very different outcomes and rewards. James the Apostle said, *"When tempted, no one should say, 'God is tempting me.' For God cannot be tempted by evil, nor does he tempt anyone; but each person is tempted when they are dragged away by their own evil desire and enticed. Then, after desire has conceived, it gives birth to sin; and sin, when it is full-grown, gives birth to death"* (Jas. 1:13-15, NIV).

U.S. President John F. Kennedy said in his inaugural address Jan. 20, 1961, "Let every nation know, whether it wishes us well or ill, that we shall pay any price, bear any burden, meet any hardship, support any friend, oppose any foe to assure the survival and the success of liberty."

How much more should we, as sons of God, citizens of heaven, and soldiers in service to Christ, be vigilant, diligent, and sober-minded to hold fast to our confession of faith, repentance and forgiveness of sin, and salvation unto eternal life which has been purchased at a high price by Jesus — the cost of His own life and broken body and shed blood — to maintain our liberty in Christ under the law of grace through faith, and to resist all claims, counterfeits, and counteroffers from the evil one, Satan, the enemy of our souls and accuser of the brethren.

THE WEAPONS OF OUR WARFARE

Among the primary weapons of our spiritual warfare as saints of God are the blood of Jesus, intercession, prayer, the Word of God, the armor of God, our testimony, the gift of tongues, and the Holy Spirit. Paul the Apostle referred to these weapons as "weapons of righteousness" in 2 Cor. 6:7. Holy angels are also available to assist those who are the heirs of salvation, but we will discuss angels separately in a later chapter. So, first of all, the weapons we fight with are not natural (carnal or worldly) weapons. Jesus made that clear in the Garden of Gethsemane when he told an unnamed disciple to sheath his sword, and said, *"Those who use the sword will die by the sword"* (Matt. 26:52, NLT).

2 Cor. 10:3-5 (NIV) adds, *"For though we live in the world, we do not wage war as the world does. The weapons we fight with are not the weapons of the world. On the contrary, they have divine power to demolish strongholds. We demolish arguments and every pretension that sets itself up against the knowledge of God, and we take captive every thought to make it obedient to Christ."* Our weapons are from God, and they have divine power as

opposed to natural power. For example, resurrection power is the strongest force in the universe; it is stronger than nuclear power, thermonuclear power, solar power, wind power, wave power, water power, hydroelectric power, electric power, chemical power, magnetic power, jet power, fire power, etc.

Eph. 6:11-13 (NIV) states, *"Put on the full armor of God, so that you can make your stand against the devil's schemes. For our struggle is not against flesh and blood, but against the rulers, against the authorities, against the powers of this world's darkness, and against the spiritual forces of evil in the heavenly realms. Therefore take up the full armor of God, so that when the day of evil comes, you will be able to stand your ground, and having done everything, to stand…"* Col. 1:16 (N IV) adds, *"For by him all things were created: things in heaven and on earth, visible and invisible, whether thrones or powers or rulers or authorities; all things were created by him and for him."*

Rom. 8:28 mentions demons and angels and powers; Col. 2:15 mentions powers and authorities. This latter verse is also translated variously principalities and powers, and spiritual rulers and authorities. These four Scriptures provide a ranking of entities in the spiritual realm, all of which are involved in spiritual warfare. This is part of the reason we need the angel armies of heaven to help us while on earth. For more detail in this area, please refer to Dr. Gordon E. Bradshaw, *I See Thrones!*, 2015, Kingdom House Publishing.

Eph. 6:14-18 (NIV) continues, *"Stand firm then, with the belt of truth buckled around your waist, with the breastplate of righteousness in place, and with your feet fitted with the readiness that comes from the gospel of peace. In addition to all this, take up the shield of faith, with which you can extinguish all the flaming arrows of the evil one. Take the helmet of salvation and the sword of the Spirit, which is the word of God. And pray in the Spirit on all occasions with all kinds of prayers and requests. With this in mind, be alert and always keep on praying for all the Lord's people.*" We war and pray from a place of strength, stability, and security, undergirded by truth, righteousness, peace, faith, salvation, and the Word of God.

CHRIST JESUS IS OUR ETERNAL HIGH PRIEST, ADVOCATE AND INTERCESSOR

Rom. 8:34 says, "*Who then is the one who condemns? No one. Christ Jesus who died — more than that, who was raised to life — is at the right hand of God and is also interceding for us.*" Heb. 7:24-26 (NIV) adds, "*...but because Jesus lives forever, he has a permanent priesthood. Therefore He is able also to save completely those who draw near to God through Him, because He always lives to intercede for them. Such a high priest meets*

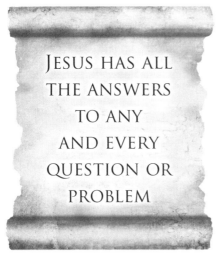

JESUS HAS ALL THE ANSWERS TO ANY AND EVERY QUESTION OR PROBLEM

our need — one who is holy, blameless, pure, set apart from sinners, exalted above the heavens." 1 John 2:1 notes, "*My dear children, I am writing this to you so that you will not sin. But if anyone does sin, we have an advocate who pleads our case before the Father. He is Jesus Christ, the one who is truly righteous.*" Jesus is our ultimate trump card. He has all the answers, and all the power, to any and every question or problem, and in any and every situation or circumstance.

WE ARE SEATED WITH CHRIST IN HEAVENLY PLACES

Eph. 2:4-6 (NIV) says, *"But because of his great love for us, God, who is rich in mercy, made us alive with Christ even when we were dead in transgressions — it is by grace you have been saved. And God raised us up with Christ **and seated us with him in the heavenly realms** in Christ Jesus,…"* (author's emphasis). Similarly, Col. 3:1-2 (NIV) adds, *"Since, then, you have been raised with Christ, set your hearts on things above, where Christ is, seated at the right hand of God."* The NLT version reads, *"Since you have been raised to new life with Christ, set your sights on the realities of heaven, where Christ sits in the place of honor at God's right hand."* I like to say in this regard that we have dual citizenship – both in the nation of our birth or our parents' citizenship, as well as the kingdom of heaven (Phil. 3:20). We are bilocational (our bodies are on earth but our spirits have access to heaven) as well as bivocational (we are kings and priests). By the way, both Christ and His Father, Abba, are each seated on a different throne, and you have access to a throne also in the spirit dimension (Bradshaw, *I See Thrones!*, 2015).

Authority is granted (delegated) to every believer by Jesus, and we have all the spiritual authority needed for our assignments and destinies on earth. Mark 16:17 says that two signs of believers in the kingdom age are casting out demons and speaking in tongues. I.e., this should be commonplace and normal practice for the Church and kingdom citizens. John 14:12-13 says, *"Truly, truly, I say to you, he who believes in Me, the works that I do, he will do also; and greater works than these he will do; because I go to the Father. Whatever you ask in My name, that will I do, so that the Father may be glorified in the Son..."* Increased spiritual authority is also granted to godly, mature leaders, including Eph. 4:11 five-fold ministers (an extra measure of grace, honor, respect, influence, wisdom and/or power due to spiritual rank and maturity). For more detail on spiritual rank and spiritual authority, see books by Naomi Dowdy, John Eckhardt, Dr. Bruce Cook, Dr. Kluane Spake, and Dr. Gordon E. Bradshaw.

DEVELOP AN ACTIVE LIFESTYLE OF PRAYER

One of the keys to living a victorious life is praying daily, and not just for ourselves, but for other people. Prayer is mentioned more than 650 times in Scripture, and is a key part and central component of the victorious, overcoming, faith-filled lives of the saints. Edwin Orr noted, "History is silent about revivals that did not begin with prayer." Martin Luther added, "Work, work, from morning until late at night. In fact, I have so much to do that I shall have to spend the first three hours in prayer." My friend Dave Hodgson, CEO of Paladin Corp., a group of 32 companies, spends one day a week in prayer – the whole day. He interacts with God, listens, receives divine counsel and answers to his questions and business issues, and deepens his intimacy with the Almighty. He is an 8th Mountain leader who is making a major difference in his nation and globally.

Elisabeth Elliot said, "Prayer lays hold of God's plan and becomes the link between His will and its accomplishment on earth. Amazing things happen, and we are given the privilege of being the channels of the Holy Spirit's prayer."

Rom. 8:26 (NIV) states, *"In the same way, the Spirit helps us in our weakness. We do not know what we ought to pray for, but the Spirit himself intercedes for us through wordless groans."* Eph. 6:18 (NIV) says, *"And pray in the Spirit on all occasions with all kinds of prayers and requests. With this in mind, be alert and always keep on praying for all the Lord's people."* The NLT version adds, *"Pray in the Spirit at all times and on every occasion. Stay alert and be persistent in your prayers for all believers everywhere."*

1 Tim. 2:1-4 (NIV) records, *"I urge, then, first of all, that requests, prayers, intercession and thanksgiving be made for everyone — for kings and all those in authority, that we may live peaceful and quiet lives in all godliness and holiness. This is good, and pleases God our Savior, who wants all men to be saved and to come to a knowledge of the truth."* 1 Thess. 5:16-18 (NIV) also says, *"Be joyful always; pray continually; give thanks in all circumstances, for this is God's will for you in Christ Jesus."* It is clear from these Scriptures that God wants and expects us to be praying frequently; praying fervently; praying for a large number and a wide variety of people – including both believers and nonbelievers; praying for different kinds of situations, efforts and initiatives; and praying not only in our native language(s), but also praying in the Spirit. There is quite obviously a vast amount that could be, and has been, written on this subject, and I will try to be as brief and concise as possible.

TYPES OF PRAYER

There are numerous types or styles of prayer, including the following basic, common types. An acronym that I use to help me memorize these is BACTIPS – Blessing, Adoration, Confession or Contrition, Thanksgiving, Intercession, Petition and Supplication. Blessing is typically praying blessings for others, including our enemies. Adoration is glorifying, praising, extolling, honoring and/or magnifying God for who He is, and expressing our reverence and affection for Him. Confession or Contrition is confession of sin, penitence or repentance, and humbling or prostrating oneself before God in spirit.

Thanksgiving is offering God thanks and appreciation, and expressing gratitude. I use this prayer often and thank God in advance for things that I have not yet seen in the natural, but that have been promised to me or others in His word, or mentioned specifically in prophecies, dreams, or visions, and so I have seen, believed and received them already by faith. Intercession is praying on behalf of another person, or for a larger group, such as a neighborhood, city, county or province, region, state, nation, or people group (ethnos). Intercession literally means standing in the gap for, or taking on the burdens of, someone else. Petition is requesting or asking God for something. Supplication is similar to petition but usually

THANKSGIVING IS OFFERING GOD THANKS AND APPRECIATION, AND EXPRESSING GRATITUDE

involves kneeling down and bending down in which someone makes a humble, earnest, heartfelt petition or an entreaty to God of a weighty or serious nature. Jesus was in supplication prayer in the Garden of Gethsemane, and sweated drops of blood.

THE PRAYERS OF PAUL

Romans 1, Ephesians 1, Philippians 1, Colossians 1 and 1 Thessalonians 1 provide us great examples of a leader, Paul the Apostle, praying for other believers. *"First, I thank my God through Jesus Christ for you all, because your faith is being proclaimed throughout the whole world. For God, whom I serve in my spirit in the preaching of the gospel of His Son, is my witness as to how unceasingly I make mention of you, always in my prayers making request, if perhaps now at last by the will of God I may succeed in coming to you"* (Rom. 1:8-10, NIV). This is thanksgiving prayer, intercession prayer, and petition prayer.

"For this reason, ever since I heard about your faith in the Lord Jesus and your love for all God's people, I have not stopped giving thanks for you, remembering you in my prayers. I keep asking that the God of our Lord Jesus Christ, the glorious Father, may give you the Spirit of wisdom and revelation, so that you may know him better. I pray that the eyes of your heart may be enlightened in order that you may know the hope to which he has called you, the riches of his glorious inheritance in his holy people, and his incomparably great power for us who believe..." (Eph. 1:15-19, NIV). This is thanksgiving prayer, intercession prayer, and petition prayer.

"I thank my God every time I remember you. In all my prayers for all of you, I always pray with joy because of your partnership in the gospel from the first day until now, being confident of this, that he who began a good work in you will carry it on to completion until the day of Christ Jesus...And this is my prayer: that your love may abound more and more in knowledge and depth of insight, so that you may be able to discern what is best and may be pure and blameless for the day of Christ, filled with the fruit of righteousness that comes through Jesus Christ — to the glory and praise of God" (Phil. 1:3-6, 9-11, NIV). This is thanksgiving prayer, intercession prayer, and petition prayer.

"We always thank God, the Father of our Lord Jesus Christ, when we pray for you, because we have heard of your faith in Christ Jesus and of the love you have for all the saints..." (Col. 1:3-4, NIV). This is thanksgiving prayer.

"For this reason, since the day we heard about you, we have not stopped praying for you and asking God to fill you with the knowledge of his will through all spiritual wisdom and understanding. And we pray this in order that you may live a life worthy of the Lord and may please him in every way: bearing fruit in every good work, growing in the knowledge of God, being strengthened with all power according to his glorious might so that you may have great endurance and patience,..." (Col. 1:9-11, NIV). This is intercession prayer and petition prayer.

"We always thank God for all of you, mentioning you in our prayers. We continually remember before our God and Father your work produced by faith, your labor prompted by love, and your endurance inspired by hope in our Lord Jesus Christ" (1 Thess. 1:2-3, NIV). This is thanksgiving prayer, and intercession prayer, and perhaps some blessing prayer mixed in.

TYPES OF INTERCESSORS AND STYLES OF PRAYER

Tommi Femrite listed in her 2011 book, *Invading The Seven Mountains With Intercession*, the following 12 Types of Intercessors and prayer styles, including:

1. List Intercessors (praying from a list of items)
2. Crisis (praying for crisis situations)
3. Issues (praying for social justice causes/issues)
4. Salvation (praying for salvation for people)
5. Personal (praying for one or more individuals
6. Financial (praying for financial/economic issues
7. Mercy (asking God to show compassion)
8. Warfare (spiritual warfare, 3rd heaven)
9. Worship (praying from worship)
10. Government/Apostolic (decrees, courts)
11. People Group (Ethnic) (tribes, races)
12. Prophetic-Seers (visions, prophecies)

Try these on and see which ones fit, and are most natural or comfortable for you. Ask Holy Spirit and trusted mentors to confirm what they sense or discern for you about which type or types from this list of 12 that you flow best in in prayer. Most people fit several of these categories, and over a lifetime, you may change your core prayer styles or add new ones. Be led by the Spirit, and avoid rote prayers as much as possible.

CREATE YOUR OWN PRAYER PORTFOLIO

One way that I have found helpful to think about, approach and steward prayer is to create a prayer portfolio. We can each have a prayer portfolio in the same way that we can have an investment portfolio in one or more asset classes and investment strategies. For example, such a prayer portfolio could include, among other things:

- Health/Healing
- Family & Friends
- Local Church or Churches in Your City or Region
- Finances
- Purpose & Significance
- Crisis
- Ethnos (People Groups)
- Nations
- Rulers, Government & Laws
- Culture
- Injustice
- Religious Freedom
- Revival, Reformation and/or Transformation

DIFFERENT LEVELS OF PRAYER

In closing this chapter, I will mention that there are different levels of prayer, and that not all prayers are created equal. We all pray by the same Spirit, and the same God hears them all, and He is not a respecter of persons (Acts 10:34). However, some prayers are effectual, some are ineffectual, and some are prayers amiss, while others are laser-guided smart bombs and drone strikes in the spirit realm that hit the bullseye and cause maximum effect. Some prayers are trial balloons and some are heat seeking missiles. Some prayers have little or no faith in them, and Rom. 14:23b says, *"Everything that does not come from faith is sin."* That's why Jesus had to send unbelieving bystanders out of the room when he prayed for a dead girl in Matt. 9:24-26. Peter the Apostle did the same thing before raising Dorcas from the dead in Acts 9:39-41.

One of my favorite prayers is the one Nehemiah prayed when the king asked him the question, *"'What is it you want?' Then I prayed to the God of heaven, and I answered the king ..."* (Neh. 2:4-5, NIV). This was a nonverbal, split-second prayer, and then Nehemiah answered the king's question, with a favorable result. Of course, this prayer and favor followed a time of mourning, prayer and fasting by Nehemiah (Neh. 1:4).

Another short, effective prayer was when Jesus prayed, *"Peace be still,"* in the midst of a storm in a boat on the Sea of Galilee. Instantly the winds and the waves calmed. Jesus also prayed another three-word prayer with great effect, *"Lazarus, come forth!"* In the Garden of Gethsemane, Jesus prayed, *"If it be possible, let this cup pass from me; nevertheless, not my will, but yours be done."*

175

The model prayer Jesus taught His disciples is found in Matt. 6:6-13 (NKJV). *"But you, when you pray, go into your room, and when you have shut your door, pray to your Father who is in the secret place; and your Father who sees in secret will reward you openly. And when you pray, do not use vain repetitions as the heathen do. For they think that they will be heard for their many words. Therefore do not be like them. For your Father knows the things you have need of before you ask Him. In this manner, therefore, pray:*

'Our Father in heaven, Hallowed be Your name. Your kingdom come. Your will be done On earth as it is in heaven. Give us this day our daily bread. And forgive us our debts, As we forgive our debtors. And do not lead us into temptation, But deliver us from the evil one. For Yours is the kingdom and the power and the glory forever. Amen.'"

Jesus told a parable to his disciples about a persistent widow to teach them to always pray and not give up. Luke 18:1-8 (NKJV) says, *"Then He spoke a parable to them, that men always ought to pray and not lose heart, saying: "There was in a certain city a judge who did not fear God nor regard man. Now there was a widow in that city; and she came to him, saying, 'Get justice for me from my adversary.' And he would not for a while; but afterward he said within himself, 'Though I do not fear God nor regard man, yet because this widow troubles me I will avenge her, lest by her continual coming she weary me.'" Then the Lord said, "Hear what the unjust judge said. And shall God not avenge His own elect who cry out day and night to Him, though He bears long with them? I tell you that He will avenge them speedily. Nevertheless, when the Son of Man comes, will He really find faith on the earth?"*

Jesus also told his disciples the following parable about prayer, and the contrasting heart attitudes and mindsets of two Jewish men, and God's perspective, in Luke 18:10-14: *"Two men went up into the temple to pray, one a Pharisee and the other a tax collector. "The Pharisee stood and was praying this to himself: 'God, I thank You that I am not like other people: swindlers, unjust, adulterers, or even like this tax collector. 'I fast twice a week; I pay tithes of all that I get.' "But the tax collector, standing some distance away, was even unwilling to lift up his eyes to heaven, but was beating his breast, saying, 'God, be merciful to me, the sinner!' "I tell you, this man went to his house justified rather than the other; for everyone who exalts himself will be humbled, but he who humbles himself will be exalted."* Now here are five different levels of prayer.

Level One

First, there is personal prayer or prayer between a husband and wife, or a family unit. Next, there is corporate prayer led by a chaplain, the owner, a member of management, or in many cases, by an employee or group of employees. There can also be voluntary intercession teams for businesses which are usually led by the owner, a member of senior management, or a volunteer. And, there is liturgical prayer, which is reading Scripture aloud by a priest, minister, rabbi, bishop, pastor or other clergy member, followed by a congregational response, also spoken aloud in unison.

Level Two

Most churches of any size have intercessors, and an organized intercession team or group to pray for the church services, the pastor, priest, minister, rabbi, bishop or other senior leader and their family, and the needs of the members. Such teams or groups may or may not have a designated or appointed leader. Sometimes the senior clergyman leads these groups, or occasionally a prayer pastor at larger churches which can afford such a position, will lead them. Most often, however, if there is an intercession team leader, it is either a volunteer, unpaid church member gifted in and called to prayer, or the senior clergyman or their spouse.

Level Three

The next level is city, regional, and state intercession teams, some of which are territorial or geographic, and voluntary, and some of which are more missional, and may have a paid director. Co-Labor Ministries and Serving Our Neighbors (SON) in Portland, Ore. are good examples. Kingdom League International in Renton, Wash. and their 1Church1Day initiative is another example. They have just developed and released a prayer app called United We Pray which can be downloaded and used by individuals, churches and other ministries. www.kingdomleague.org/1church1day

The Fellowship in Seattle, Wash. has been having weekly prayer meetings since 1935, and hosts the National Prayer Breakfast annually in Washington, DC. Bethel Church in Redding, Calif. has had Sozo ministry teams for a number of years, and Dan Dean leads a Courts of Heaven ministry team through SonRise Cultural Center in Yakima, Wash. There are far too many such groups globally to research and list them all here.

Level Four

The next level is national and global intercession teams. Examples of such groups include National Day of Prayer, Global Day of Prayer, the International Prayer Connect (IPC), Reformation Prayer Network (RPN), various prayer congresses held annually around the world by different denominations and religious groups and organizations, POTUS Shield, Intercessors for America (IFA), Watchmen for the Nations, Congressional Prayer Caucus, Kansas City IHOP, YWAM. Many of these groups either have on staff, develop and train internally, or recruit externally, strategic level intercessors, who are gifted, called and seasoned prayer warriors, usually led by one or more prayer generals, depending on their size and/or budget.

South Korea in particular, and Asia in general, have long been hot beds and leaders in prayer, as has Africa. The frequency and duration of prayers and prayer meetings there is legendary. There are even Prayer Mountains dedicated to prayer. In Jakarta and Indonesia, there are even groups and teams of praying children.

Level Five

Finally, the last level is professional intercessors who are paid by their clients to pray in the Spirit on either a full-time or part-time basis, whether that is hourly, monthly or annually, or project-based. Such groups are primarily composed of apostles and prophets, and started originating and appearing around 15-20 years ago in North America. Included are Michelle Seidler and Ancient Paths; Charles and Liz Robinson and WISE Ministries International; Apostolic Intercessors Network (AIN), founded by Tommi Femrite, and currently led by Al Hauck, President, and Norma Johnson, Vice President, assisted by Diane Emmons, COO and an extended team of contract intercessors.

Divine Exchange is led by Ralph and Sharon Gerlach, and assisted by Dennis and Katie Wiedrick and an extended team of contract intercessors; and Kingdom Congressional International Alliance (KCIA), led by Dr. Bruce Cook, Chair, and John Anderson, President, with Team Leader and Director Dr. James Brewton, and an extended team of contract intercessors. There may be other groups offering such contract intercession services, but these are the ones of which I am currently aware.

Professional level intercessors focus primarily on the marketplace. Some people and organizations have not yet accepted this model, or do not believe in the concept of paid prayer, while others are eagerly and enthusiastically on board and running with it. This model is not for everyone, but then, it doesn't try to be. Who are professional level, strategic intercessors? Dr Gayle Rogers said the following are some criteria that identify them:

- MUST know their true and authentic identity as son/daughter & the power and authority that comes with this revelation (Luke 10:19) "I give you power..."

- Spend quality time in the Presence of God. The 8th Mountain is the place of partnership with God. He speaks to us on the 8th Mountain.

- Understand their call to intercession, and more importantly "marketplace intercession"; also some may be called specifically to the Business & Economy Mountain.

- Understand the type of intercession to which they are called (i.e., warfare, crisis, financial, list, worship, prophetic, people group, etc.)

- Understand their divine privilege to present a matter in the courtroom of heaven appearing before the righteous judge agreeing, decreeing, declaring, & proclaiming God's word.

- Train their mind/thoughts how to see/visualize the resolution through understanding God's word of a matter and then declaring the answer (using God's word) into existence, without doubting or unbelief.

- Are in agreement with apostle/pastor/ ministry leader/business owner you're assigned to; community, city, region, nation

- Help marketplace leaders disciple, train, and shift their communities, cities, and nations, in a variety of ways.

Intercessors from all five levels of prayer have an equal chance to make a difference in their spheres of influence and the 7 Mountains of Culture through effectual, fervent, faith-filled prayer. God is not limited and we need to remind ourselves as we pray that unless we become as little children, we cannot enter the kingdom, much less pray and decree its fulfillment, establishment, and expansion (Matt. 18:3).

God, please give your children wisdom, revelation and understanding to pray Your heart and Your word, and to engage in spiritual warfare in a prepared and safe way. This concludes Chapter 13. Next, we turn our attention to intimacy, worship and sacraments in Chapter 14.

PRAYER IS A KEY
COMPONENT
OF THE
VICTORIOUS,
OVERCOMING,
FAITH-FILLED
LIVES OF THE
SAINTS

FOURTEEN

INTIMACY, WORSHIP AND SACRAMENTS

"But an hour is coming, and now is, when the true worshipers will worship the Father in spirit and truth; for such people the Father seeks to be His worshipers. God is spirit, and those who worship Him must worship in spirit and truth."
(John 4:23-24, NIV)

"So in Christ Jesus you are all children of God through faith, for all of you who were baptized into Christ have clothed yourselves with Christ."
(Gal. 3:26-27, NIV)

God wants relationship with us. It's one of the many reasons He created mankind. Intimacy with God is available 24/7, 365 days a year, and most of the time, He is waiting on us to disengage and disentangle from our busy lives, schedules, priorities, and agendas, and come away or "steal away" with Him for some uninterrupted time and fellowship and communion together – Father-son talks, coaching calls, friendship discussions, and even "pillow talk," if you will, as the intimacy grows and deepens. We use different names for these times, such as our "quiet time," "sacred time," "devotional time," "listening time," "journaling time," "prayer time," "worship time," or "Word time." In this chapter we will explore intimacy with God as expressed in life, worship, baptism, and communion. We will begin with worship.

Once while my wife and I were recording a worship CD of prophetic songs the Lord had given us to share, Holy Spirit asked me to write a song about lingering in His presence, so I wrote a song called "Linger" to express that and help others experience it, which was included on our 2004 CD, *Daddy's in the House* (Glory Realm Music). I got to co-create with God! What a joy, delight, honor and privilege! My wife and I also wrote a song on that CD from Song of Songs, called "Steal Away," which describes lovers stealing away in secret to be intimate with one another, as well as "Beautiful," "Heartbeat," "Procession of Glory," "Come As You Are," "Song of Heaven," "Daddy's in the House," and others.

Steve Swanson, who has recorded over two dozen original worship CDs and leads worship for many different Christian ministries and conferences, as well as the Asaph School of Worship, and Friend of the Bridegroom Worship

Ministries, taught on worship recently at a conference I spoke at in California, and described leading worship like "entering the on ramp" on an interstate highway and then accelerating to merge with existing traffic flow. In other words, worship is happening all the time in heaven, and our job is to find or create the right frequency and flow in the atmosphere that matches what is happening in heaven, and to join in and release that on earth. That requires spiritual sensitivity, gifting, timing, and teamwork, and being willing to yield to and honor the Holy Spirit at all times.

There's nothing like joining the flow of heaven in bringing our hearts and lives to Him, giving Him all that we are, and pouring ourselves out as an offering before the Lord, in song and praise and worship. This type of ministry and service to the Lord enriches us – body, soul, and spirit. We are refreshed in the flow as we find ourselves embraced in His arms of love, and at times wrapped or bathed in His glory. Sometimes in worship as we are singing and playing our musical instruments, we sense, see or hear the presence of angels, and them joining us in worship. At such times, there is a richness and fullness and resonance in the chords, notes and harmonies that surpass the ability of human voices and instruments. I have experienced this many times over the years in private, in live worship, in the recording studio, and during the mixing and mastering of audio tracks. And, I am sure it must be similar in recording live video or film as well, and in editing anointed video or film files.

Worship leader Sylvia Blair said this, "Worship is what flows out of our hearts and into God's heart when we connect with the flow of Heaven. It is pure love poured out like hot, molten gold and silver flowing from the holy fires inside us out to God, who in turn lavishes more love and fire on us." Indeed, high praise and worship are exhilarating! But, there's much more to worship than just those moments in church services, conferences, concerts, studio sessions, and audio or video recordings. God desires relationship with us so much that He sent His only son, Jesus, to die for us to redeem us to Himself. God is seeking daily intimacy with us, drawing us, wooing us, to come to Him and spend time together. He seeks true worshippers, and He wants this personal, covenant relationship with us more than we want it.

TRUE WORSHIP COMES FROM THE PLACE OF LOVE AND INTIMACY

"But an hour is coming, and now is, when the true worshipers will worship the Father in spirit and truth; for such people the Father seeks to be His worshipers. God is spirit, and those who worship Him must worship in spirit and truth" (John 4:23-24, NIV).

True worship comes from the place of love and intimacy, spirit to spirit, where truth and honesty are valued above all and honored. There is a strength that flows out of relationship with God and that strength comes from the deep place where you spend time with Him, pouring out your honest heart, all that is in you, allowing Him to wash and refresh you in His love and His life, pouring Himself into you.

In fact, it's a two-way street. We pour our hearts and lives into Him and He pours back into us. It's a process that takes time and builds. The more we worship God, the more we build our relationship with God. Much like building muscles in the body, over time we develop greater capacity to move in the flow and power of relationship with Him. And, although we can never outgive God in any area, including worship, it is fun to try.

Music producer, worship leader and recording artist Nick Coetzee, President of Rain Music, said, "Our corporate worship needs to be directed toward God and not man. The ministry of the Psalmist flows from God to man but the Worship Leader puts one hand in the hand of the congregation, the other in the hand of God, then brings them together and gets out of the way."

Thomas Carlyle said, "Wonder is the basis for worship." That moment when you first began to realize how big God is and how little you are and just how amazing His love is – that's worship. That place in your life when you were overwhelmed and gasping for air, desperately crying out for help, and the comfort of God swept you up in His peace and left you astonished and grateful for His goodness – that's worship. Those times in your life when He was calling you to lay down your own agenda and pour out your life in obedience to him – that's worship. Out of these life moments and into our daily thoughts and prayers, the presence of our loving God inhabits our hearts moving us into the intimacy of worship. Each new revelation of who God is brings us to a new depth of devotion and desire for more of Him.

Have you ever danced with the Lord? It's amazing and He loves to lead. This is heaven on earth, when you learn to spend time with Him and learn to run and laugh and dance and let Him show you new steps, new places in your heart you didn't know existed, already prepared for time with the King. There is a flow of worship in heaven that never stops and He invites us daily, moment by moment, to join Him in that flow. It's just a matter of opening up your heart to Him.

"Enter his gates with thanksgiving and his courts with praise; give thanks to him and praise his name" (Psa. 100:4, NIV). Worship is a state of mind, an attitude, a condition or posture of the heart toward God. We make the choice to draw close to God and seek Him because He is worthy of all our worship. We set our desire on Him, to know Him and pursue Him. As we draw near to Him, He draws near to us (James 4:8). As we call to Him, He will answer us, and tell us great and unsearchable things that we do not know (Jer. 33:3).

DAVID WAS A WORSHIPPER

King David knew the power of worship and the strength of intimate relationship. While the rest of Israel cowered in fear before the Philistines, and their champion Goliath, David's heart was on fire for the honor of God, the One who he knew would deliver him from the hand of his enemies. This strength, this sureness and trust in God, comes from a heart of worship.

When David and his troops returned home to Ziklag from a raiding party and found their families and possessions stolen, and their homes burned, the troops were understandably upset and spoke against David and even threatened to kill him. David had one course of action – to trust and inquire of God.

"Moreover David was greatly distressed because the people spoke of stoning him, for all the people were embittered, each one because of his sons and his daughters. But David strengthened himself in the Lord his God" (1 Sam. 30:6, NASB).

Exhausted from battle and grieving for his lost wives and children, David took refuge in God's presence and received the knowledge, direction, and strength to go and take back everything that was stolen. *"Pursue and recover all!"* was the rhema word He received.

Today, we have the same needs and the same answer, to worship God. He is calling you, drawing you, wooing you, and patiently waiting for you. He wants you more than you can possibly imagine and He has prepared a table just for you, to sit and spend time with Him. Rise up in your spirit man and go to God and commune with Him. Spend time with God. Cultivate a deep, intimate relationship with Him. Spend time in His Word, meditate on His truth, worship Him as you read of His love and provision for you. Receive His counsel, correction, and comfort.

If we're going to influence mountains (domains, spheres) for the Kingdom of God, we must have the strength that comes from such a relationship. Joshua was still in the Tabernacle when Moses left to go back to the camp. He was building the relationship with God that he would need later to take the promised land.

"So the Lord spoke to Moses fact to face, as a man speaks to his friend. And he would return to the camp, but his servant Joshua the son of Nun, a young man, did not depart from the tabernacle" (Exo. 33:11, NASB).

Abraham, our father of faith, set the standard for worship and intimacy when he took his son up the Mountain of the Lord (Gen. 22:14; Rom. 4:16; Gal. 3:7). Once they climbed that mountain, and came back down, God guaranteed Abraham's legacy and succession in the earth, and the multiplication of their seed, and he and Isaac both prospered exceedingly abundantly.

Abraham said to his young servant men, *"Stay here with the donkey, and I and the lad will go over there; and we will worship and return to you"* (Gen. 22:5, NASB).

Abraham offered his son, Isaac, in worship through sacrifice, his son of many great promises, with the full confidence that he and his son would return. Where did this confidence come from? Abraham had a deep abiding relationship with God, built on time spent with Him and obedience to what God said, building trust upon trust. *"Abraham reasoned that if Isaac died, God was able to bring him back to life again. And in a sense, Abraham did receive his son back from the dead"* (Heb. 11:19, NLT).

God's response to Abraham's worship is clear – God blessed Abraham and prospered him, and made him the father of many nations by multiplying his seed to be like the sand on the seashore, and the stars in the heavens — vast and innumerable.

"… By Myself I have sworn, declares the Lord, because you have done this thing and have not withheld your son, your only son, indeed I will greatly bless you, and I will greatly multiply your seed as the stars of the heavens and as the sand which is on the seashore; and your seed shall possess the gate of their enemies. In your seed all the nations of the earth shall be blessed, because you have obeyed My voice" (Gen. 22:16-18, NASB).

Your worship and intimacy with God is your foundation for achieving your purpose in life, your ability to take the mountain of your destiny. You are building Kingdom strength and endurance as you turn your focus to God and make Him the number one priority in your life. The Psalmist David said, *"Let everything that has breath praise the Lord!"* (Psa. 150:6). Both heaven and earth – all of creation – worships the Lord. Even the last chapter of the Bible says, *"...Worship God!"* (Rev. 22:9, NIV).

YOU ARE BUILDING KINGDOM STRENGTH AND ENDURANCE AS YOU TURN YOUR FOCUS TO GOD

Lana Vawser, a prophet from Australia, recently wrote, "Invite Him in through your intimacy with Him, your total surrender, praying in the Spirit, and renewing your mind with the Word to prepare you for the new that is upon you." (Lana Vawser email and Internet post, "The Pathway Into the 'New Thing' God is Doing," July 15, 2017).

Abraham, Joshua, and David are examples of worshippers and warriors. They exemplified leadership and dependence on God. They lived lives of dedication to His purposes and they knew God from the deep place of intimacy and worship. Do you want to beard the lion and kill the Goliath in your life? Can you face the loss of everything in your life and turn to God like David? Will you take your promised land like Joshua and will you receive the fulfillment of

God's promises like Abraham when he and Sarah were well past their prime?

SACRAMENTS

Jesus lived his life on earth in intimacy with Father God. He spent time on the mountain gaining strength and direction through long nights of prayer and direction and strength for the long days ahead. The sacraments we have come from this – Jesus' life of intimacy with the Father. "The word 'sacrament' comes from the Latin *sacramentum*, which in the classical period of the language was used in two chief senses: (1) as a legal term to denote the sum of money deposited by two parties to a suit which was forfeited by the loser and appropriated to sacred uses; (2) as a military term to designate the oath of obedience taken by newly enlisted soldiers. Whether referring to an oath of obedience or to something set apart for a sacred purpose, it is evident that *sacramentum* would readily lend itself to describe such ordinances as Baptism and the Lord's Supper." www.biblestudytools.com/dictionary/sacraments/

The word sacrament means "a visible sign of an inward grace, especially one of the solemn Christian rites considered to have been instituted by Jesus Christ to symbolize or confer grace: the sacraments of the Protestant churches are baptism and the Lord's Supper" (Dictionary.com). Roman Catholic and Greek Orthodox churches have a longer list of seven sacraments that they observe, including marriage. But, generally speaking, such things as baptism, communion (also known as the Lord's Supper or Eucharist), ordination and commissioning are the most commonly-accepted sacraments or rites of the Christian faith.

In submitting Himself to baptism as an example to us in all things, Jesus modeled our submission to death and resurrection (Matt. 3:13-17; Mark 1:9-11; Luke 3:21-22; John 1:32-34). We receive the washing and cleansing through the shedding of His blood, His atoning, redeeming sacrifice on the cross, and His resurrection. As the waters cover us in baptism, we enter into his death and as we rise from the water as He rose from the dead, we are lifted up to heaven as He was in our spirit man and we take our place beside him, "seated with Him in heavenly places" (Eph. 2:6). Death is intimate. Resurrection is intimate. And, new life in Jesus is intimate. Meditating on this truth – His life for ours and our resurrection with Him – will take you deep into communion with Him.

"For you are all children of God through faith in Christ Jesus. And all who have been united with Christ in baptism have put on Christ, like putting on new clothes. There is no longer Jew or Gentile, slave or free, male and female. For you are all one in Christ Jesus. And now that you belong to Christ, you are the true children of Abraham. You are his heirs, and God's promise to Abraham belongs to you" (Gal. 3:26-29, NLT).

Acts 2:37-38 (NIV) says, in response to Peter's inspired, extemporaneous preaching on the Day of Pentecost, *"When the people heard this, they were cut to the heart and said to Peter and the other apostles, "Brothers, what shall we do?" Peter replied, "Repent and be baptized, every one of you, in the name of Jesus Christ for the forgiveness of your sins. And you will receive the gift of the Holy Spirit."* Many other examples of baptism are found in Scripture, including Philip and the Ethiopian Eunuch (Acts 8:26-40), Cornelius and his household (Acts 10:47-48), Saul (Acts 9:18-19), Crispus and his household (Acts 16:8), Lydia (Acts 16:13-15), the Philippian jailer (Acts

16:31-34), 12 male disciples in Ephesus (Acts 19:5), and numerous others.

"For Christ also suffered once for sins, the righteous for the unrighteous, to bring you to God. He was put to death in the body but made alive in the Spirit. After being made alive, he went and made proclamation to the imprisoned spirits— to those who were disobedient long ago when God waited patiently in the days of Noah while the ark was being built. In it only a few people, eight in all, were saved through water, and this water symbolizes baptism that now saves you also--not the removal of dirt from the body but the pledge of a clear conscience toward God. It saves you by the resurrection of Jesus Christ," (1 Pet. 3:18-21, NIV).

This communion of identity in Christ through baptism continues as we partake of the bread and the cup, remembering His costly sacrifice and what He accomplished for us in His death, burial and resurrection. 1 Cor. 10:16 (KJV) says, *"The cup of blessing which we bless, is it not the communion of the blood of Christ? The bread which we break, is it not the communion of the body of Christ?"*

Paul the Apostle gives the church at Corinth (and the Church universal) explicit instructions about the necessity for partaking of communion in a worthy manner in 1 Cor. 11:17-33. He even said that some in the Corinthian church had become weak and sick, and fallen asleep (died) because of partaking of the Lord's Supper in an unworthy manner, and of turning the love feast of Christ into a feast of gluttony and drunkenness. *"For anyone who eats and drinks without recognizing the body of the Lord eats and drinks judgment on himself...But if we judged ourselves, we would not come under judgment"* (vs. 29, 31, NIV).

Jesus instructed his disciples at the Last Supper that when anyone takes communion, to "do this in remembrance of me" (Luke 22:19-20, NIV). *"For whenever you eat this bread and drink this cup, you proclaim the Lord's death until he comes"* (1 Cor. 11:26, NIV). There is no clear instruction in Scripture on the frequency of communion – although it seemed to be a regular part of the early Church – just on the manner and attitude in which it is partaken. Therefore, some saints take communion daily, some weekly, some monthly, some quarterly, and some annually. It is more a matter of the heart and personal or denominational preference.

The sacrament of communion brings us to the place of truth in our lives and realignment with the One who is Truth. We confess our sins and receive His forgiveness as we remember His blood poured out and His body broken beyond recognition for us. This is the atonement, satisfaction of debt owed, for the evil we've done. *"This is love: not that we loved God, but that he loved us and sent his Son as an atoning sacrifice for our sins"* (1 John 4:10, NIV). Redemption! Jesus

THE SACRAMENT OF COMMUNION BRINGS US TO THE PLACE OF TRUTH IN OUR LIVES

enacted and instituted a new covenant of abundant life, purchased with perfect blood, overcoming and overtaking the former covenant that ended with death (Heb. 9:15-28).

"For this reason Christ is the mediator of a new covenant, that those who are called may receive the promised eternal inheritance—

now that he has died as a ransom to set them free from the sins committed under the first covenant. In the case of a will, it is necessary to prove the death of the one who made it, because a will is in force only when somebody has died; it never takes effect while the one who made it is living" (Heb. 9:15-17, NIV).

There is power in the blood of Jesus, overcoming power, and we need to remember this. Communion is the sacrament that helps us to remember the power and strength that He gives us in the intimacy of relationship, responding to His call to go deeper in Him.

We have the honor and privilege of receiving the Savior's sacraments, and of worshipping the One True God. We have the astonishing invitation and ability to draw close to the Immortal, Invisible, Omnipotent Creator of all that is, in fellowship and worship and intimacy on the 8th Mountain. Although the leaders of the 7 Mountains of Culture can choose to "walk each in the name of their own God" (Micah 4:5a, ESV), our authenticity and reverence presents to them an invitation to join us as "we [will] walk in the name of the Lord our God for ever and ever." (Micah 4:5b, ESV).

The Lord invites us to enter into a time of intimacy, worship, and sacraments on the 8th Mountain regularly. When we accept this invitation, we will be transformed from glory to glory, and we will never be the same! Next, we turn our attention to the subject of promotion in Chapter 15.

FIFTEEN

PROMOTION

"For promotion cometh neither from the east, nor from the west, nor from the south. But God is the judge: he putteth down one, and setteth up another."
(Psa. 75:6-7, KJV)

Promotion is an important part of life and is part of the nature of God. Receiving a promotion typically requires or at least implies mastery at some level, whether of skill, knowledge, experience, wisdom, technical prowess, acumen, or character, or some combination thereof. Promotion can happen in several different ways, and it is important to differentiate here between natural promotion in the marketplace and governmental and educational systems, and spiritual promotion. These can and do overlap or coincide at times, but not always. Natural promotion is most often based on seniority, rank, tenure, merit, and ability, and criteria can include community service and character, but unfortunately, it can also be abused and based on sexual favors, political favors, bribes, corruption, graft, cronyism, racism, and other forms of discrimination, dishonesty and/or self-gain. Spiritual promotion, on the other hand, is different.

Psa. 75:6-7 (KJV) says, *"For promotion cometh neither from the east, nor from the west, nor from the south. But God is the judge: he putteth down one, and setteth up another."* The word promotion here is *harim* or *rum* in Hebrew, which means: to be high or exalted, rise (Strong's H7311). Most modern translations use the word exalt here. So, God is the ultimate source of promotion, although most often there are human intermediaries or agents involved. It is true that in some settings and cultures, Christians are discriminated against and overlooked or bypassed for promotions, or targeted and selected for early retirement or attrition, as we saw recently during the Obama administration in the U.S., where many senior officers of the U.S. military who were leaders of faith, were forced into early retirement.

Luke 16:10-12 says, *"Whoever is faithful with very little will also be faithful with much, and whoever is dishonest with very little will also be dishonest with much. If, then, you have not been faithful with worldly wealth, who will entrust you with true riches? And if you have not been faithful with the belongings of another, who will give you belongings of your own?"* Faithfulness, integrity, and incorruptibility are beyond the reach of Mammon, at any price. And, as Gal. 5:22-23 points out, such personal qualities or attributes serve as a defense and protection against natural laws: *"But the fruit of the Spirit is love, joy, peace, forbearance, kindness, goodness, **faithfulness,** gentleness and self-control. **Against such things there is no law"*** (author's emphasis).

Similarly, Matt. 25:19-30 records the Parable of the Talents. *"After a long time, the master of those servants returned to settle accounts with them. The servant who had received five talents came and presented five more. 'Master,' he said, 'you entrusted me with five talents. See, I have gained five more.' His master replied, 'Well done, good and faithful servant! You have been faithful with a few things; I will put you in charge of many things. Enter into the joy of your master!' Then the servant who had received two talents also came and said, 'Master, you entrusted me with two talents. See, I have gained two more.' His master replied, 'Well done, good and faithful servant! You have been faithful with a few things; I will put you in charge of many things. Enter into the joy of your master!'*

"Finally, the servant who had received one talent came and said, 'Master, I knew that you are a hard man, reaping where you have not sown, and gathering where you have not scattered seed. So in my fear, I went and hid your talent in the ground. See, you have what belongs to you.' 'You wicked, lazy servant!' replied his master. 'You knew that I reap where I have not sown and gather where I have not scattered seed. Then you should have deposited my money with the bankers, and on my return I would have received it back with interest. Therefore take the talent from him and give it to the one who has ten talents. For everyone who has will be given more, and he will have an abundance. But the one who does not have, even what he has will be taken away from him. And throw that worthless servant into the outer darkness, where there will be weeping and gnashing of teeth.'

Many people try to take shortcuts in life, bypass or accelerate God's process, and either promote themselves or sell out some part of themselves to get a rung up the ladder of fame and fortune for so-called success. There are many possible reasons for this — impatience, greed, envy, pride, lust for power or position, ambition, ego, need for recognition or attention, desperation, dissatisfaction, etc. Even Jesus had to deal with this with some of his own disciples, James and John. *"Teacher," they said, "we want you to do for us whatever we ask. What do you want me to do for you?" he asked. They replied, "Let one of us sit at your right and the other at your left in your glory." You don't know what you are asking," Jesus said* (Mark 10:35-38).

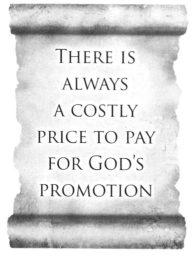

THERE IS ALWAYS A COSTLY PRICE TO PAY FOR GOD'S PROMOTION

Many times in life, we may not know what we are asking when we seek promotion prematurely or from the wrong motives. It might even cost us our life, as we see throughout history with people like Haman the Agagite, Judas Iscariot, Balaam, Absalom, Adonijah, and Joab. There is always a costly price to pay for God's promotion, and you need to decide now whether to choose and pay God's price and receive His reward, or whether to choose and pay Satan's or the world's price, and receive a much different reward.

God's methods of promotion are not always pleasant or what we might expect, and His choices of who to promote often surprise us. For example, God chose a murderer and shepherd named Moses to be a deliverer and leader of His people when it was time for the Israelites to exodus Egypt. He chose a barren womb and childless couple in Zechariah and Elizabeth to conceive, birth and parent John the Baptist. He chose a man named Gideon from the smallest tribe and the smallest clan and the smallest family to deliver, lead and judge Israel. He chose a young shepherd boy named David who became one of the greatest kings in history and a man after God's own heart. He chose a slave girl name Hadassah, or Esther, to become a queen and the redeemer of her people, the Jews. He chose a nomad shepherd and tent dweller named Abram to become the father of faith, and a father of nations and the Jewish people, who later had his named changed to Abraham. God also chose a virgin maiden named Mary to become the mother of Jesus, and He chose a fasting and praying cupbearer named Nehemiah serving a pagan king to be the apostolic rebuilder of Jerusalem, whose walls were built in 52 days.

Another example is Shadrach, Meshach and Abednego. Their refusal to bow down and worship an image of gold 90 feet high and 9 feet wide that was set up by King Nebuchadnezzar of Babylon, brought them to a crisis of belief. When faced with death after their civil disobedience, they loved not their lives more than death, and fearlessly and famously gave this reply to the pagan king after hearing his ultimatum in Dan. 3:16-18: *"King Nebuchadnezzar, we do not need to defend ourselves before you in this matter. If we are thrown into the blazing furnace, the God we serve is able to deliver us from it, and he will deliver us from Your Majesty's hand. But even if he does not, we want you to know, Your Majesty, that we will not serve your gods or worship the image of gold you have set up."*

These three Hebrew captives were already administrators over the province of Babylon at the recommendation of Daniel (Dan. 2:49). But, the end result of this fiery trial was recorded in Dan. 3:28-30, *"Then Nebuchadnezzar spake, and said, Blessed be the God of Shadrach, Meshach, and Abednego,* *who hath sent his angel, and delivered his servants that trusted in him, and have changed the king's word, and yielded their bodies, that they might not serve nor worship any god, except their own God. Therefore I make a decree, That every people, nation, and language, which speak anything amiss against the God of Shadrach, Meshach, and Abednego, shall be cut in pieces, and their houses shall be made a dunghill: because there is no other God that can deliver after this sort. Then **the king promoted** Shadrach, Meshach and Abednego in the province of Babylon"* (author's emphasis).

Likewise, Joseph had to survive and pass several life and death tests before being promoted. Gen. 39:7-9 says, *"It came about after these events that his master's wife looked with desire at Joseph, and she said, "Lie with me." But he refused and said to his master's wife, "Behold, with me here, my master does not concern himself with anything in the house, and he has put all that he owns in my charge. There is no one greater in this house than I, and he has withheld nothing from me except you, because you are his wife. How then could I do this great evil and **sin against God**?"* (author's emphasis). Every great spiritual leader sees temptation and sin not as abstract or distant or impersonal, but as a sin against God. Notice that Joseph did not say, 'How can I do this great evil and sin against my master, Potiphar, or against you, his wife, or against my own self.' He properly and correctly understood that all sin is ultimately against God, and that sin separates us from God, and invites negative consequences and ultimately death.

Joseph could be trusted with influence and authority, so he was promoted by God. David endured years of testing, similar to Joseph, before His promotion to the kingship and inheriting his promises from God. He had to wait 13 years from the time of Samuel's prophecy of his kingship (1 Sam.

16:13) to become king of Judah, and another 7 years (20 total) to become king over a united Israel.

Elisha had to pass several tests from Elijah before he could receive Elijah's mantle and inherit a double portion anointing or blessing from him. Elijah tested him several times to see how faithful he was and how ready he was to pay the price required. Elisha demonstrated his commitment and resolve to stay with Elijah at all costs, and in turn received his mantle and a double portion when Elijah was taken to heaven in a fiery chariot.

And even Jesus, the only begotten Son of God, had to fulfill his mission and die as a righteous sacrifice for sin, be resurrected and ascend to heaven before being promoted or exalted to the right hand of God. *"Since, then, you have been raised with Christ, set your hearts on things above, where Christ is seated at the right hand of God"* (Col. 3:1). *"And being found in appearance as a man, he humbled himself and became obedient to death—even death on a cross! Therefore God exalted him to the highest place and gave him the name that is above every name, that at the name of Jesus every knee should bow, in heaven and on earth and under the earth, and every tongue confess that Jesus Christ is Lord, to the glory of God the Father"* (Phil. 2:8-11). *"But we see Jesus, who was made a little lower than the angels, now crowned with glory and honor because he suffered death, so that by the grace of God he might taste death for everyone"* (Heb. 2:9).

So, regardless of what men may say or do to you, God is still able to promote you in due season. God is still in the promotion business today, and He is looking for faithful stewards. Scripture says His eyes roam to and fro in the earth, seeing if there are any who fear the Lord. God is not mocked; whatsoever a man sows, he shall also reap. God is

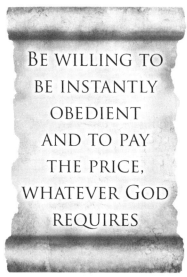

BE WILLING TO
BE INSTANTLY
OBEDIENT
AND TO PAY
THE PRICE,
WHATEVER GOD
REQUIRES

an equal opportunity employer and does not discriminate, but He does honor faith and obedience. I often tell people, If you want to be promoted by God, learn to die to yourself faster and more often. Be willing to be instantly obedient and to pay the price, whatever God requires. It will be worth it, and it will cause you to bear fruit both in this life (on earth) and in the life to come (eternity). This is what you will learn and experience for yourself during your times on the 8th Mountain, as you commune with the God of Promotion; this is the way of the Lord when it comes to your future promotions from Him!

The 8th Mountain's leaders have been elevated to their positions because they have embraced death, and have paid the price for promotion. This provides tremendous credibility as they mentor the leaders of the 7 Mountains of Culture, each of whom desires promotion and greater impact. Now we turn our attention to the topic of glory in Chapter 16.

SIXTEEN

GLORY: GOD'S CREATIVE PURPOSE FOR MANKIND

"The Word became flesh and made his dwelling among us. We have seen his glory, the glory of the one and only Son, who came from the Father, full of grace and truth."
(John 1:14, NIV)

"For the earth will be filled with the knowledge of the glory of the LORD, as the waters cover the sea."
(Hab. 2:14, NIV, NKJV)

It's all about the glory! It's about the intimacy and revelation that comes from daily walks in the garden with the God of Glory. It's about us as His kings on this earth bringing the Kingdom of God and the will of God as it is being done, in the Mountain of the Lord in heaven, to the Seven Mountains of Culture on earth. This is the glory that is the atmosphere on the 8th Mountain which we are honored and privileged to soak, bask, saturate and linger in, whenever we spend time with the Lord on the 8th Mountain!

Glory is the supreme perfection of the manifested nature and presence of God. The Father is called *The God of Glory* in Acts 7:2. Jesus is called *The King of Glory* in Psa. 24:7 and the Holy Spirit is called *The Spirit of Glory* in 1 Pet. 4:14. The Trinity (Godhead) is full of glory; in fact, glory is rooted, coded and embedded in their very essence, nature, identity and design!

Man was made in the image and glory of God (1 Cor. 11:7). The Lord created Adam and put him in the Garden He had planted East of Eden that contained every tree that is pleasant to the sight and good for food to tend and keep it (Gen. 2:15). Then, He made Eve out of one of Adam's ribs and brought her to Adam. As His new creations, they were clothed in the glory of God, yet in the natural they were naked and not ashamed (Gen. 2:25). The Father of Glory walked in intimate fellowship with His new creations, those who were made in His image and glory.

We read how God would come down in the cool of the day to walk in the garden with Adam and Eve (Gen. 3:8). This time in the garden was apparently a time of intense loving intimacy between the Father of Glory and His new creations. It was the loving intimacy that had been the heart of the Father from eternity past and for which He had created man and woman.

Regrettably, Adam and Eve sinned and fell short of the glory of God (Rom. 3:23). Their covering of glory was gone, their natural eyes were opened, and they knew that they were naked; in a futile attempt, they tried to cover themselves with fig leaves. In shame, they tried to hide themselves behind a bush when they heard God coming for a walk with them in the glory. So, men and women will never be all that they were created to be until their glory has been restored. In God's great love for mankind – those who were created for His glory – He sent His Son, "The King of Glory", as their Substitute Redeemer. Through death, He paid the penalty of their sin and thereby, according to the wisdom of God, He could restore mankind to the glory for which they were originally created.

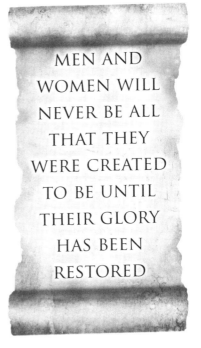

MEN AND WOMEN WILL NEVER BE ALL THAT THEY WERE CREATED TO BE UNTIL THEIR GLORY HAS BEEN RESTORED

Paul the Apostle wrote to the Corinthians, *"But we speak the wisdom of God in a mystery, the hidden wisdom which God ordained before the ages for our glory, which none of the rulers of this age knew; for had they known, they would not have crucified the Lord of glory"* (1 Cor. 2:7-8). Because of God's great wisdom, once again we will be able to say with the angel mentioned in Revelation, chapter eleven, *"The Kingdoms*

IT IS ALL
ABOUT GOD'S
KINGDOM IN
HEAVEN BEING
MANIFESTED
ON EARTH

of this world have become the kingdoms of our Lord and of His Christ, and He shall reign forever and ever." The "kingdoms of our Lord and of His Christ" speaks of what has been called "The 8th Mountain" or The Mountain of the Lord (Mic. 4:1 and Isa. 2:2). Mountains in Scripture refer to kingdoms, authority, rule and dominion. It is all about God's kingdom in heaven being manifested on earth. It is for this, Jesus taught us to say when we pray, *"Your kingdom come. Your will be done On earth as it is in heaven"* (Luke 11:2).

"The Mountain of the Lord," The Kingdom of God, is to rule over and exert influence on each of the Seven Mountains of Culture on this earth (Arts & Entertainment, Business & Economy, Education, Family, Government & Law, Media, and Religion). When we pray as Jesus taught us how to pray, we are actively bringing the will of God, the Kingdom of God, or the Mountain of the Lord, from heaven to earth. Jesus is "The King of kings." We as God's new creations on earth, are to operate according to God's creative purpose for Adam and Eve who were given "dominion over this earth and all that is in it."

In Gen. 1:26-28 we find these words, *Then God said, "Let Us make man in Our image, according to Our likeness: let them have dominion over the fish of the sea, over the birds of the air, and over the cattle, over all the earth and over every creeping thing that creeps on the earth." So God created man in His own image; in the image of God He created him; male and female He created them. Then God blessed them, and God said to them, "Be fruitful and multiply; fill the earth and subdue it: have dominion over the fish of the sea, over the birds of the air, and over every living thing that moves on the earth."*

God's creative purpose for mankind, His new creations which were created in His image and His glory, was that by using their God-given dominion and authority on earth, they were to bring His Kingdom from heaven into every area of culture, in all Seven Mountains on earth. As we do, we, who were created for His glory, are bringing God's glory from heaven, the Mountain of the Lord, into every culture where God has given us influence on earth.

If there is any word that can best describe the move of God that we are coming into today, it is the word "Glory!" God's awesome glory is being restored to His disciples, His Ekklesia, today. By the cloud of glory, God led the children of Israel from the bondage of Egypt into the abundance of the land of Promise. When the glory cloud stopped moving, they stopped and pitched their tents. When the glory cloud moved, they were to move with it.

I have seen many moves of God in the many years of my lifetime. With each move, I have had to be willing to move on as He led me from glory to glory. Many have been left behind because they have found themselves comfortable where a past move of God has led them. They have soon found themselves in a very dry place as the Children of Israel would have if they had not moved with the glory cloud.

When Moses was on the mountain with God for 40 days and nights, the children of Israel sinned by convincing Aaron to create a golden calf for them to worship. God stated he could not continue to go with them because of their sin. In Exodus 32, Moses interceded intensely for them. *"Yet now, if You will forgive their sin – but if not, I pray, blot me out of Your book which You have written."*

And God replied, *"Now therefore, go, lead the people to the place of which I have spoken to you. Behold, My Angel shall go before you."* In the next chapter, Exodus 33, He continued, *"Depart and go up from here ..., I will send My Angel before you... Go up to a land flowing with milk and honey; for I will not go up in your midst, lest I consume you on the way, for you are a stiff-necked people."*

Moses took his tent and pitched it outside the camp, far from the camp, and called it the tabernacle of meeting... Then the glory, the presence, of God could still come down and commune with him.

As we study the many moves of God, we find that each of the major revivals, the new moves of God, started "outside the camp." They started in small places like the Bonnie Brae House or the crude Azusa Street Mission instead of in the big religious buildings of their day.

Then Moses entreated, *"If Your Presence does not go with us, do not bring us up from here."*

And after God saw the heart and insistence of Moses, He answered, *"My Presence will go with you, and I will give you rest."*

Moses was not willing to go on without God's presence. To be in the presence of God is to be in the place of His glory. Just a few verses later, Moses cried out, *"Please, show me Your glory."*

Many today are no longer satisfied with religion or having church as usual. They are crying out with Moses, *"Please, show me Your glory."* We are coming into a day that Habakkuk spoke about in Chapter 2 and verse 14, *"For the earth will be filled with the knowledge of the glory of the Lord, as waters cover the seas."* Take time to think about this. In this coming day, there will be no place in the whole earth, including anywhere in the 7 Mountains of Culture, where God's glory is not being manifested as we as God's kings on this earth bring God's Kingdom from heaven to earth. Each of these mountains will come under the influence of the "Mountain of the Lord" in heaven.

Isaiah had a "Throne Room" experience. We read in Isaiah 6:1-3, *"…I saw the Lord sitting on a throne, high and lifted up, and the train of His robe filled the temple. Above it stood seraphim; each one had six wings: with two he covered his face, with two he covered his feet, and with two he flew. And one cried to another and said: "Holly, holy, holy is the LORD of host; the whole earth is full of His glory!"* It is interesting to note that these "seraphim" were in the awesome glory of the very throne room of the God of Glory, and yet they were singing about a glory they saw on earth – a glory that was so great, they were rejoicing, *"the whole earth will be filled with His glory!"*

There are three biblical words for glory, and each has a distinctive meaning. The Greek word *doxa* means "a most glorious condition, a perfect state of blessedness."

In Hebrew there are two words used for the word glory. There is the word *shekinah* which means, "The bright cloud of God's Presence." It was seen on the face of Moses when He came off the Mountain of the Lord. His face was so radiant, with the bright shining of the glory of the Lord, that they couldn't look upon his face. A veil had to be put over his face before they could even look on his countenance. It is the glory by which all heaven is illumined. It is the glory that Isaiah wrote about, *"Arise, shine; For your light has come! and the glory of the LORD is risen upon you"* (Isa. 60:1).

There is also the Hebrew word *kabod* which refers to "the weight of glory" or "to be heavy." This was the manifestation that the priest experienced when they brought in the Ark of the Covenant representing the presence of God on the day when they were dedicating Solomon's Temple. Now when Solomon had finished praying, fire came down from heaven and consumed the burnt offering and the sacrifices; and the glory of the LORD filled the temple. And the priest could not enter the house of the Lord, because the glory of the LORD had filled the Lord's house (2 Chron. 5:14).

Many have experienced the *kabod* glory when they have experienced what has been called "being slain in the Spirit." Ezekiel wrote about one of these *kabod* glory experiences, *"Behold, the glory of the Lord filled the house and I fell on my face"* (Ezek. 44:4).

We were created by God, like Adam and Eve, for the intimate experiences of taking our daily walks in the garden with Him. To be in the garden, is like being within the veil of the tabernacle just as the High Priest did on the Day of Atonement. However, this is no longer a once a year event. It can be a daily experience in our lives. The veil of the temple has been removed. We can now come boldly into a place of intimacy with the God of Glory. To be within the veil, we, just as Adam and Eve in their original condition, can have the same intimacy with God as they experienced. We can abide under the shadow of the Almighty. It is here, in the awesome glory of His presence, that we are changed from glory to glory.

We can experience the overwhelming, life-changing experience of having an intimate relationship and fellowship with the Father of Glory, the King of Glory and the Spirit of Glory. The glory realm is a place of intense worship. We, like Abraham, can be "friends of God."

IN THE AWESOME GLORY OF HIS PRESENCE, WE ARE CHANGED FROM GLORY TO GLORY

Everywhere Abraham went, he built altars and worshipped God. Numerous times, right after we read of Abraham's worship experiences, we read that angels, or God Himself, appeared and spoke to Abraham. One of those places we know as Bethel. In Genesis 28, we read of the time Abraham's grandson, Jacob, came back to Bethel where his grandfather had built an altar and worshipped God. When Jacob arrived there, he was tired and took "a stone" and put his head on it and went to sleep. Perhaps, that "stone" was actually part of the altar that his grandfather Abraham had built to worship God. Perhaps, he was in the exact place where Abraham had chosen to worship God. We know it was a place of "open heaven", and a place of great angelic activity.

Then he dreamed, and behold a ladder was set up on the earth, and its top reached to heaven; and there the angels of God were ascending and descending on it. And behold, the Lord stood above it and said, "I am the Lord God of Abraham your father and the

God of Isaac; the land on which you lie I will give to you and your descendants…" (Gen. 28:13).

Then Jacob awoke from his sleep and said, *"Surely the LORD is in this place, and I did not know it." And he was afraid and said, "How awesome is this place. This is none other than the house of God, and this is the gate of heaven"* (Vs. 16-17)!

There was something different about this place where Abraham had built an altar and worshiped God. Jacob described it as "an awesome place" and even as "the gate to heaven!"

David, as a shepherd boy, watched over his father's sheep in the field outside the town of Bethlehem. Day after day, he would take his harp and worship God. It appears that David had opened the heavens by his worship in this shepherd's field, for it was here in this field, where the angels appeared on the night Jesus was born.

And suddenly there was with the angel a multitude of the heavenly host praising God and saying, "Glory to God in the highest, and on earth peace, goodwill toward men!" (Luke 2:13-14, NKJV).

David mentioned the power of opening up the gates of heaven through praise and worship. In Psa. 24:7-10 (NKJV), he wrote, *"Lift up your heads O you gates! And be, lifted up, you everlasting door! And the King of glory shall come in. Who is this King of Glory? The Lord strong and mighty, The LORD mighty in battle, Lift up your heads, O you gates! Lift up, you everlasting doors! And the King of glory shall come in. Who is this King of Glory? The LORD of host, He is the King of glory."*

Places we have set aside to worship God are places where we, like Abraham and David, have opened up the gates of heaven so the King of Glory can come in. They are awesome places. They are places of open heaven. They are places where it is easy to hear from God. They are places like those represented by one or more of those Seven Mountains of influence on this earth where God has given us influence and where God will speak to us from the Mountain of the Lord revealing His wisdom, divine ideas, connections, wisdom, favor, witty inventions and His plans for us to bring the Kingdom of God and the will of God from heaven to earth.

Let's keep taking those "walks in the garden" with the Father of Glory. Let's continue to open the heavens through high praise and intimate worship that we might live under an open heaven where it is so easy to hear from God. Let's, like Abraham and David, be passionate worshipers of God.

Let's be like David's son, King Solomon, who sought and received the wisdom of God from the Mountain of the Lord above all else. Then, we will be kings on this earth like King Solomon and like those described in the 60th chapter of Isaiah (NKJV), *"Arise, shine; For your light has come! And the glory of the LORD is risen upon you. For behold, the darkness shall cover the earth, And deep darkness the people; But the LORD will arise over you, And His glory will be seen upon you.*

"The Gentiles shall come to your light, And kings to the brightness of your rising. Lift up your eyes all around, and see, They all gather together, they come to you; Your sons shall come from afar, And your daughters shall be nursed at your side. Then you shall see and become radiant, And your heart shall swell with joy; Because the abundance of the sea shall be turned to you, The wealth of the Gentiles shall come to you. The multitude of camels shall cover your land, The dromedaries of Midian and Ephah; All

those from Sheba shall come; They shall bring gold and incense. And they shall proclaim the praises of the LORD. ...I will glorify the house of My glory. ... The ships of Tarshish will come first, To bring your sons from afar, Their silver and their gold with them, To the name of the LORD your God, And to the Holy One of Israel, Because He has glorified you.

"Therefore your gates shall be open continually; They shall not be shut day of night, That men may bring to you the wealth of the Gentiles, And their kings in procession. For the nation and kingdom which will not serve you shall perish, And those nations shall be utterly ruined. The glory of Lebanon shall come to you ...And I will make the place of My feet glorious. Also the sons of those who afflicted you Shall come bowing to you, And all those who despised you shall fall prostrate at the soles of your feet... Instead of bronze I will bring gold... But the LORD will be to you an everlasting light, And your God your glory. A little one shall become a thousand, And a small one a strong nation. I, the LORD, will hasten it in its time."

We were created for those daily walks in the glory of His presence as Adam and Eve did in the beginning in the awesome garden. God's daily walks in the garden with Adam and Eve reveal His desire for daily walks of intimacy with us today while bringing His mountain – the 8th Mountain, the Mountain of the Lord – to take its rightful place through us, His kings over the 7 Mountains of Culture on earth today. Jesus taught His disciples, to pray, *"Lord, Your Kingdom come, Your will be done, on earth as it is in heaven!"* As we do this, we will experience what was prophesied by Habakkuk the prophet, *"For the earth will be filled with the knowledge of the glory of the LORD, as the waters cover the sea"* (Hab. 2:14, NKJV).

It's all about those daily times with the Father of Glory where we receive intimate secrets fresh from the Mountain of the Lord, and where we will experience what was prophesied by Haggai the prophet when he declared, *"The glory of this latter temple shall be greater than the former..."* (Hag. 2:9, NKJV). Next, we turn our attention to sonship, inheritance and identity in Chapter 17.

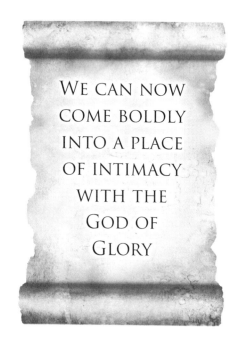

WE CAN NOW
COME BOLDLY
INTO A PLACE
OF INTIMACY
WITH THE
GOD OF
GLORY

SEVENTEEN

SONSHIP, INHERITANCE AND IDENTITY

"When the angel of the Lord appeared to Gideon, he said, 'The Lord is with you, mighty warrior.'"
(Judg. 6:12, NIV)

"And because you are sons, God has sent forth the Spirit of His Son into your hearts, crying out, "Abba, Father!" Therefore you are no longer a slave but a son, and if a son, then an heir of God through Christ."
(Gal. 4:6-7, NIV)

B efore you were born, there was a book written that contains the framework of your identity, purpose for being, and eternal destination. Every human being starts at the same place — as a thought or idea in the heart of

God. We then start out life from our mother's womb as an untold story. The glare of the lights and the transition from a warm place, dramatically welcome us into an unknown world. There is only one place of safety and that is upon our mother's breast. We begin the journey of life.

Obviously, not every child is so fortunate, and in some cases the child never experiences the warmth and comfort of a loving mother's arms, sweet kisses and gentle touch. Regardless of what those first few seconds of life outside the womb may look like, you are an untold story. The forces that come to bear upon the newborn, and child as it grows, are enormous – its family of origin, its culture, language, ethics, morality, education, economics, faith position or tradition, and geographic location.

In addition, you are exposed to authority figures, teachers, police, ministers, little league coaches, doctors, dentists, etc. Each one leaves an imprint of who to believe, what to believe, how to conduct yourself and what not to believe. And, through it all, you are trying to make sense of what is happening around you, to you, and for you. What you see, hear, taste, touch and smell is all working to build a perception of what is real.

In the heart of God, He was already dreaming of your potential. He imagined a beautiful life for you free of all failure and with every possible gift to assist you in fulfilling the purpose why you were born. A heavenly library was opened up in your name. In that library, He placed one key book, your book of God's thoughts and plans for you, that is written in heaven. You could easily say that book is His will for you, and your purpose or destiny.

Psa. 139:13-18 (NASB) says, *"For You formed my inward parts; You wove me in my mother's womb. I will give thanks to You, for I am fearfully and wonderfully made; Wonderful are Your works, And my soul knows it very well. My frame was not hidden from You, When I was made in secret, And skillfully wrought in the depths of the earth; Your eyes have seen my unformed substance;* **And in Your book were all written The days that were ordained for me**, *When as yet there was not one of them. How precious also are Your thoughts to me, O God! How vast is the sum of them! If I should count them, they would outnumber the sand. When I awake, I am still with You"* (author's emphasis).

Are you curious as to what is written in that book? Psalm 56:8 (MSG) says, *"You've kept track of my every toss and turn through the sleepless nights, Each tear entered in your ledger, each ache written in your book."* From the time we are born and we begin our journey in life, two things are forming our belief systems, filters, lenses, grid, and analysis capabilities. First, there is what we are taught. Knowledge forms the first piece of convictions. Second, are the experiences we have to validate our knowledge. If you were told, "Don't touch the hot stove!", that is knowledge. If you then touched the hot stove, you just formed more than knowledge; you formed a conviction. If you are told that all products of a certain company are inferior or of poor quality, and then are shown some example(s) of that, together, these form a conviction. You know it and then you experience it. The same process could be applied to races, nations, people groups, genders, and other groupings.

The challenge is that now all knowledge inside of you is actually not true, and not every feeling or emotion has a basis in truth. So, from the time we are born, we are taught what life is all about, and how to survive and thrive, as well

GOD HAS A BOOK WRITTEN ABOUT YOU THAT IS BEAUTIFUL AND FILLED WITH LOVE, HOPE AND LIMITLESS POSSIBILITIES

as how to cope and get by. And, we begin to have experiences that validate that knowledge, whether right or wrong.

Life comes at us on its own terms and we know God has a book written about each of us that is beautiful and filled with love, hope and limitless possibilities. So, what went wrong with this picture? If we are born as a clean slate (*tabula rasa*), a blank canvas and endless potential, what happened to you and me? With all that is good and wonderful in the world, there is also evil coming from four main places: 1) the world, with its greed, corruption and lies; 2) the flesh, with its lust and self-centered pride; 3) other people who may be broken, wounded, confused or simply motivated to prevent you from ever learning, much less living in, truth; and 4), a very real enemy of our souls who is out to kill, steal and destroy, all that we gain or aspire to achieve, accomplish or acquire materially, morally, intellectually, psychologically or spiritually.

The one powerful arbitrator from the beginning was and always will be the power of choice. Your free will is the one thing that determines what all of these forces at play will accomplish in your life. You have the power to choose and ultimately, most of us will do what we really want to do deep inside. Prov. 4:23 says, *"Keep your heart with all diligence, For out of it spring the issues of life."*

What is common and predictable in this life is to either never reach the heights and glory of what is written in our books, or to reach some of it, and even maybe reach its fullest possibility. You can be like the man who took the one talent entrusted to him and buried it, and therefore had a zero percentage increase (he actually lost money when we factor in inflation and opportunity cost). Or, maybe you are a 30 percenter, or maybe a 60 percenter, or are you bold enough to dream of the 100 percent level of attainment? (Matt. 13:8, 25:18; Mark 4:20).

So, continuing, life on earth began for you at birth and you began this grand adventure. Quickly, you probably learned that you had the capacity to be very good, sort of good, and not good at all. To the degree that pride was allowed to germinate in your soul, fueled by people with confused intent, the world system with its politics, bigotry, pain and suffering, all began to bear upon your thoughts, words and actions. All of this was fueled by the enemy of our souls, that devil of old, Satan, who is working to undermine, sabotage and prevent you from ever arriving at the truth of what was written in your Book in Heaven by God.

Add to this, that inside of you, there has always been an intuitive pressure to be more, reach higher, and accomplish grand feats of glory. And, there is within you a constant call of what is written in your book, which is always asking you to stop and read what is written there. Over this noise or chaos, the Holy Spirit has always been brooding over you as He did over the earth at the Creation. There has always been, somewhere in your ears, or heart, the call of your Heavenly Father calling your name, much like He did for Adam and Eve in the Garden of Eden. "Where are you?"

What you believe, what you do, and what you say, reveals your character. Every life situation, without exception, will reveal who you really are. Every single person, opportunity, circumstance and life encounter, works as a mirror to show you who you have become. What you have done with the knowledge and experiences of life, has all come together with your agreement to form your convictions and the basis for all your decisions.

At some point, we are all presented with an ideal of human perfection. We are shown the illusion shattering truth that breaks through all the distortions. We are confronted with truth that is based on knowledge outside of our knowing and our experiences. The Lord Jesus Christ is presented to us and we are broken. We see clearly that outside our worldview, there is a higher plain of reality that we could not have imagined. For many of us, we have spent much of our lives looking backward at Adam and seeing reality upside down. Only by turning completely around and looking at Jesus Christ, is reality turned right side up. Only by looking and thinking with His mind, do we then see what our natural eyes, ears, fingers, tongues and nose could never perceive.

We are confronted with a choice, and that is to hold to the familiar visual world around us or to let go and like a jumper out of an airplane, free fall with nothing but faith for a parachute. If He is who He says He is, then you can trust Him completely without reservation. If He says He will catch you, then you must believe Him and choose to jump.

After taking a leap of faith, the demand for the highest level of discipline comes to bear as you choose to not go back. You burn the emotional bridge to the past behind you and lean into the gift of the Holy Spirit to lead you in this new life, this born-again life, the life you were created for. Now, what is written in your Book in Heaven, begins to unfold before your very eyes.

Once you make the decision to turn around and repent, a whole new process begins. I call it regeneration. You are born again and now in so many ways, you must unlearn the lies and deception that have been a part of you. You must allow the strongholds of pride, vanity and arrogance to be dismantled and removed, along with any other areas of darkness in your life. So often, this is a difficult time as the process will only go as deep as you are willing to let it go. It will usually take time, like peeling the layers of an onion, to see these old mindsets and habits broken and replaced with healthy ones, as our minds are renewed and transformed. But, some people are delivered and set free instantly by the power of God. This is an example of a miracle.

ONCE YOU MAKE THE DECISION TO TURN AROUND AND REPENT, A WHOLE NEW PROCESS BEGINS

Our walk with Jesus begins at the point of salvation, when we enter the kingdom and are born again. In discipleship, we begin the process of sanctification, which involves submitting to the Lordship of Jesus in every area and giving Him the preeminence in our lives. The sooner we do that, the faster we can grow and mature spiritually. Then, after we are discipled and have a firm foundation and are rooted and grounded in Christ and have been weaned from spiritual milk and have graduated to spiritual meat, we are ready for sonship. Spiritual sonship is gender neutral and applies equally to males and females, sons and daughters.

GOD'S PLAN IS TO HAVE MANY SONS AND DAUGHTERS

God's plan from the beginning has been to have a large spiritual family with many adopted sons and daughters, including you and me. Eph. 1:3-10 (NIV) tells us, *"Praise be to the God and Father of our Lord Jesus Christ, who has blessed us in the heavenly realms with every spiritual blessing in Christ. For he chose us in him before the creation of the world to be holy and blameless in his sight. In love* **he predestined us for adoption to sonship through Jesus Christ***, in accordance with his pleasure and will — to the praise of his glorious grace, which he has freely given us in the One he loves.*

"In him we have redemption through his blood, the forgiveness of sins, in accordance with the riches of God's grace that he lavished on us. With all wisdom and understanding, he made known to us the mystery of his will according to his good pleasure, which he purposed in Christ, to be put into effect when the times reach their fulfillment—to bring unity to all things in heaven and on earth under Christ" (author's emphasis).

As part of God's divine master plan, all those who freely accept His son Jesus as their Lord and Savior, and receive the gift of salvation through grace, are adopted into God's family through the blood of Jesus and the Holy Spirit.

Thereby, we can know God in an intimate way and call Him "Abba, Father!" Gal. 4:4-7 (NIV) says, *"But when the set time had fully come, God sent his Son, born of a woman, born under the law, to redeem those under the law,* **that we might receive adoption to sonship**. *Because you are his sons, God sent the Spirit of his Son into our hearts, the Spirit who calls out, 'Abba, Father.'* **So you are no longer a slave, but God's child**; *and since you are his child,* **God has made you also an heir"** (author's emphasis).

This adoption process involves a change of identity as well. We are no longer slaves to the flesh, or slaves to our sinful desires and carnal nature, and no longer slaves to the evil practices and corruption in the world. Col. 2:6-10 says, *"The mind governed by the flesh is death, but the mind governed by the Spirit is life and peace. The mind governed by the flesh is hostile to God; it does not submit to God's law, nor can it do so. Those who are in the realm of the flesh cannot please God. You, however, are not in the realm of the flesh but are in the realm of the Spirit, if indeed the Spirit of God lives in you. And if anyone does not have the Spirit of Christ, they do not belong to Christ. But if Christ is in you, then even though your body is subject to death because of sin, the Spirit gives life because of righteousness."*

We must also give up and renounce an orphan spirit – the spirit of being abandoned, unloved, unwanted, rejected, and/or alone – as well as the spirit of performance — the lie that my value and worth as a person is based either solely or primarily on what I do, and not on who I am. For those with a victim mentality or spirit, that must go, too. Receiving your godly identity in Christ is often a healing, liberating, and pleasantly surprising experience, which opens up new vistas and doors, and resets your internal self-image, and the way you perceive and respond to God, other people, opportunities and situations. Then and only then are we ready to receive the full rights and responsibilities of sonship.

WE HAVE AN INCORRUPTABLE INHERITANCE

Inheritance is reserved for mature sons. The inheritance is available but not yet released while we are being tutored and discipled because we are not yet ready for it, and could not properly handle or steward it prematurely. Even after we become sons, God will choose to refine us and may even reinvent us, through tests, discipline, promotion, or identity upgrades. God sees the end from the beginning, and so He sees us as a finished work, a perfected saint. He invests

GOD SEES THE END FROM THE BEGINNING, AND SO HE SEES US AS A FINISHED WORK

heavily in our development and expects a return on His investment (ROI). He is patient and longsuffering, not willing that any should perish, but that all should come to repentance (2 Pet. 3:9). All sons and daughters of God are citizens of His Kingdom (Eph. 2:19; Phil. 3:20) and also have spiritual citizenship. That is one reason the assembly or gathering of saints, the called-out ones, is named the *ekklesia* in Greek.

"Ekklesia" is a Greek word literally meaning "assembly," and is often used in Scripture for "church" to refer to a local church, the global church, or the church in a city. In Greek culture, it was the group of citizens who voted, debated and decided civic matters and public policy. Other common meanings or uses of *ekklesia*, which is also variantly spelled *ecclesia*, are "called out" and "called forth." Ekklesia is used in the New Testament 114 times, according to Wikipedia, and also was used historically to refer to either a synagogue or congregation. Some streams of Christianity view *ekklesia* as a visible structure, while others see it as an invisible reality. At any rate, being called forth, set apart, sanctified, and connected with other parts of the body, are vitally important to living the Christian life and being a Kingdom citizen.

Rom. 8:14-17 (NIV) says, *"For those who are led by the Spirit of God are the children of God. The Spirit you received does not make you slaves, so that you live in fear again; rather, the Spirit you received brought about* **your adoption to sonship**. *And by him we cry, "Abba, Father." The Spirit himself testifies with our spirit that we are God's children. Now if we are children, then* **we are heirs**—*heirs of God and co-heirs with Christ, if indeed we share in his sufferings in order that we may also share in his glory"* (author's emphasis).

As co-heirs, we have much to enjoy and to look forward to. Even the gift and indwelling of the Holy Spirit is called the "firstfruits" of our inheritance as we wait to have our physical bodies redeemed and to be clothed with immortality (Rom. 8:23), and as all of creation waits eagerly for the revealing of the sons of God. Rom. 8:19-22 (NIV) says, *"For the creation waits in eager expectation for the children of God to be revealed. For the creation was subjected to frustration, not by its own choice, but by the will of the one who subjected it, in hope that the creation itself will be liberated from its bondage to decay and brought into the freedom and glory of the children of God. We know that the whole creation has been groaning as in the pains of childbirth right up to the present time."*

SONSHIP IS A PART OF GOD'S MASTER PLAN

Spiritual sonship is a big deal, and not only for us, but for all of creation, and as part of God's master plan for planet Earth and the universe, and the body of Christ becoming the bride of Christ, and preparing for Armageddon, the Great Tribulation, the Rapture and 2nd coming of Jesus, the Son of God, to planet Earth, and His triumphal return and reign during the Millennial Kingdom. Rom. 8:29-30 (NIV) says, *"For those God foreknew he also predestined to be conformed to the image of his Son, that he might be the firstborn among many brothers and sisters. And those he predestined, he also called; those he called, he also justified; those he justified, he also glorified."*

Sonship also conveys and carries with it several associated concepts such as stewardship, leadership, and rulership. We are to steward resources and relationships, exercise leadership (influence, wisdom, vision, strategy, persuasion, diplomacy, and teamwork), and rule and govern the earth in our spheres or metrons of influence and authority. God uses human families, clans and tribes and the Trinity (Godhead) itself to teach and illustrate headship, and then finally the apostles, through their calling and commissioning to apostleship, appointed elders in every city (Acts 14:23) and also gave instruction to appoint elders in every church (Paul's instruction to Titus in Tit. 1:5), and so the eldership which we also see in the church at Jerusalem (Acts 15:23, 16:4), continues to this day in the Church (1 Tim. 3:1-7).

Of course, deacons were also appointed by the apostles, and later by elders or bishops, so it can also be said there is a deaconship as well in the Church today (Acts 6:1-7; Rom. 16:1; 1 Tim. 3:8-13). Finally, we should all aspire to friendship with God. A few people in the Bible such as Abraham and Enoch were called friends of God, and David was called a man after God's own heart. This requires a high level of faith, obedience, intimacy, sacrifice, worship, humility, honor and trust with God.

Most people run from the crucibles of life, the fire of purification and process of removing faulty thinking, pride, vanity, arrogance and wrong motives. Others learn to romance the flame and embrace the desert times, wilderness times, and the pressure that comes to bear to extrude your very soul into a true identity, form and shape. This is nothing less than the image of Christ. It takes an adult to become fully grown and fully alive. However, a true son or daughter knows that afterward, all the pressure produces the peaceable fruit of righteousness.

WE SHOULD ALL ASPIRE TO FRIENDSHIP WITH GOD

I know that my Redeemer lives and I have proved that by diligently seeking Him, His word, His Spirit, His nature, His ways, His glory, and His people. I have found His smile, His approval, His love, His acceptance, His affirmation, His protection, His covering, His provision, and all my security. I choose to let go and hold nothing from Him. I am living what was written in my Book in Heaven. I pray it every day by praying in the Spirit. I know I am a son of God! You can, too!

As we spend time with the Lord on the 8th Mountain on a regular basis, He will shape our identity and lead us into new dimensions of sonship and inheritance that will enable us to fulfill what is written in our Book in Heaven! Eph. 1:11 (NLT) says, *"Furthermore, because we are united with Christ, we have received an inheritance from God, for he chose us in advance, and he makes everything work out according to his plan."* While the many benefits of the 8th Mountain are available to everyone alive on the earth, being a son in a healthy, powerful, royal family is vastly superior to any other non-family role in the Kingdom. Modeling the life of a lavishly-loved son or daughter will provoke the leaders of the 7 Mountains of Culture to inquire about becoming adopted into the royal family, and receiving their inheritance. Now we turn our attention to the topic of angels in Chapter 18.

EIGHTEEN

ANGELS

*"The angel of the Lord encamps around
the righteous, to save him."*
(Psa. 34:7, NKJV)

*"For he will command his angels concerning
you to guard you in all your ways; they will
lift you up in their hands, so that you will
not strike your foot against a stone."*
(Psa. 91:11-12, NIV)

*"Praise the LORD, you angels, you mighty ones
who carry out his plans, listening for each of his
commands. Yes, praise the LORD, you armies of
angels who serve him and do his will! Praise the
LORD, everything he has created, everything in all
his kingdom. Let all that I am praise the LORD."*
(Psa. 103:20-22, NLT)

Angels are a special class of spirit beings created by God (Psa. 148:2-5; Col. 1:16) sometime prior to the existence of man (Job 38:7). They are beautiful, wise, powerful, large in stature, and radiant, and that is why Paul the Apostle warned that we are not to worship them (Col. 2:18). In fact, John the Apostle was so moved and overcome by what he saw and heard in heaven that he fell down at the feet of an angel to worship him, but was told twice by the angel not to worship him. The angel said, *"Do not do it! I am a fellow servant with you and with your brothers..."* (Rev. 19:10, 22:8-9).

Joshua also fell facedown on the ground in reverence when an angel stood before him (Josh. 5:14), as did Daniel when Gabriel was sent to him (Dan. 10:8-11), and the two women who went to the tomb on Sunday after Passover with spices to anoint Jesus' body and saw two angels wearing "clothes that gleamed like lightning" (Luke 24:1-8) — most likely these two women were Mary Magdalene and Mary the mother of James, although Salome is also mentioned in Mark's account and only Mary Magdalene is mentioned in John's account— (Matt. 28:1-8; Mark 16:1-8; John 20:1-18).

The Greek word *aggelos* or *angelos* means "messenger," and the Hebrew word *malak* has the same meaning. The most important role for angels in addition to being messengers and helping people, is apparently praising and glorifying God. One of God's many names is God-of-the-angel-armies (Psa. 46:1-3; Mal. 1:11). Angels also guide, protect, strengthen, encourage us, and fight for us, serve as witnesses, foretell future events, and help interpret dreams and revelation, among other things. Angels have also brought plagues and death to God's enemies (Egypt during the time of Moses; one angel destroyed 185,000 soldiers of the Assyrian army in one night – Isa. 37:36), and executed divine judgments on entire cities (Sodom and Gomorrah during the time of Abraham).

Types of heavenly angels include angels, cherubim, seraphim, and archangels. Angels in Scripture always appear as full grown adults, and not as children, and are almost always male, except for one case in Zech. 5:9 where Zechariah was speaking with an angel and saw two winged women lifting up a basket between heaven and earth. The angels in heaven do not marry, reproduce, or die (Luke 20:35-36; Jude 6); and, since they are immortal, if they do choose to sin, they cannot repent and be forgiven; they are banished (more on this later).

Angels are spirit beings and as such, have their own celestial bodies and are usually invisible to humans, but often take on human form and appearance while on earth, and on occasion appear to humans in their spirit form. Heb. 13:2 adds, *"Do not forget to show hospitality to strangers, for by so doing some people have shown hospitality to angels without knowing it."* Several translations of this verse use the phrase *"for by so doing some people have entertained angels unawares."* Indeed, this was the premise and story line of the popular television series *Touched By An Angel*, as well as several feature-length movies.

Ironically, God made man a little lower than the angels, but created angels to serve man as well as God. Psa. 8:3-8 (NIV) says, *"When I consider your heavens, the work of your fingers, the moon and the stars, which you have set in place, what is mankind that you are mindful of them, human beings that you care for them? You have made them a little lower than the angels and crowned them with glory and honor. You made them rulers over the works of your hands; you put everything under their feet:*

all flocks and herds, and the animals of the wild, the birds in the sky, and the fish in the sea, all that swim the paths of the seas."

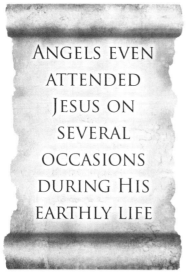

ANGELS EVEN ATTENDED JESUS ON SEVERAL OCCASIONS DURING HIS EARTHLY LIFE

In fact, even Jesus, the Son of God, the Christ, Emmanuel, Prince of Peace, the King of kings and Lord of lords, was temporarily made lower than the angels for the 33+ years he was on the earth in human form. *"But we see Jesus, who was made a little lower than the angels, now crowned with glory and honor because He suffered death, so that by the grace of God He might taste death for everyone"* (Heb. 2:9, NIV). Angels even attended Jesus on several occasions during His earthly life and ministry (Matt. 4:11, 28:1-7; Mark 4:12-13, 16:5; Luke 22:43, 24:4; John 20:10-12). However, after His resurrection, angels were once again in submission to Him (1 Pet. 3:21-22).

In fact, Jesus could have called or summoned more than 12 legions of angels to come to His defense in the Garden of Gethsemane (a Roman legion was at least 6,000 soldiers and could be larger). Matt. 26:53-54 (NIV) says, *"Do you think I cannot call on my Father, and he will at once put at my disposal more than twelve legions of angels? But how then would the Scriptures be fulfilled that say it must happen in this way?"* Jesus basically told His disciples in a straightforward manner without boasting, that the Roman Empire (including its famed army), was no match for Him, and there was no force on earth strong enough to take Him against His will, and against the vast resources of heaven. He could only be taken if He voluntarily allowed it and surrendered! He later made this point again when He told Pilate, *"You would have no authority over Me at all if it had not been given to you from above"* (John 19:11, AMP). Rick Renner has written an insightful article on these verses titled "Twelve Legions of Angels" (www.renner.org/problems/twelve-legions-of-angels/).

And, like Jesus, all saints of the Most High God have angels assigned to them to help them fulfill their purposes, assignments and destinies here on earth. For example, Matt. 18:10 (MSG) says: *"Watch that you don't treat a single one of these childlike believers arrogantly. You realize, don't you, that **their personal angels** are constantly in touch with my Father in heaven?"* (author's emphasis). The Amplified translation says, *"See that you do not despise or think less of one of these little ones, for I say to you that **their angels in heaven** [are in the presence of and] continually look upon the face of My Father who is in heaven"* (author's emphasis).

Many Christians, unfortunately, have no grid for this nor experience in seeing or hearing their angels, nor in learning how to communicate or interact with them. Heb. 1:14 (NIV) says, *"Are not all angels ministering spirits sent to serve those who will inherit salvation?"* The Amplified translation says, *"Are not all the angels ministering spirits sent out [by God] to serve (accompany, protect) those who will inherit salvation? [Of course they are!]"* The Greek word for service here is *diakonian,* from the root *diakonia,* meaning: waiting at table, service, ministration (Strong's G1248). Angels of God can travel swiftly and cover great distances. *Regarding the angels, he says, "He sends his angels like the winds, his servants like flames of fire"* (Heb. 1:7, NLT).

Those who are sensitive to the Spirit can often discern the presence of angels in a room or meeting. I have seen and heard them several times while recording, mixing and mastering worship CDs, and also during intercession and other ministry times. Once when I was attending a ministry meeting, the minister released an impartation from an angel assigned to him named Breakthrough. I was the first person in line to be prayed for, and I was thrown back about six feet when the minister touched me. As I was lying on the floor, I opened my eyes and saw a very large, muscular angel that looked gigantic and enormous, perhaps 60 feet tall, in the room.

On another occasion, I was on assignment praying at an international airport in a major metropolitan city in the US, and as I prayed with the prophet who was accompanying me, I saw a very large angel appear in the distance. He was several hundred feet high and very broad in diameter and was muscular in build. He took both his hands and effortlessly pushed the sky apart like a curtain over the airport, and placed an invisible, divine dome of protection over it.

I have also seen angels in heaven on numerous occasions, and several times financial or Treasury angels have given me guided tours of vaults, warehouses and/or treasuries in heaven. I have also seen angels in a trading room or trading floor in heaven, in a key room, in several different court rooms, and in other heavenly rooms. During our time with the Lord on the 8th Mountain, we may receive new assignments from Him. Depending on the nature of those new assignments, the Lord may also assign angels to help us fulfill those assignments!

Our proper posture in prayer is to invite and summon angels, rather than to command them, and to recognize and honor them when present, and to seek to engage and interact with them as appropriate in ministry, family, business and governmental contexts. One thing is certain: Angels are mission critical to God's people, God's plans and God's purposes on the earth. We ignore them at our own peril as Balaam learned the hard way (Num. 22:21-39).

When I pray for saints about their angels, I usually pray this simple prayer: "Lord, please assign and send the full allotment and the full assortment of the angelic host to help your sons and daughters, and give them eyes to see and ears to hear their angels so they can be more effective in their assignments and destinies. Amen."

ONE THING IS CERTAIN: ANGELS ARE MISSION CRITICAL TO GOD'S PEOPLE

Angels loyal to God are described as elect (1 Tim. 5:21) and holy (Matt. 25:31; Mark 8:38). The total number of angels is said to be "innumerable" (Heb. 12:22) and is estimated to be in the millions or billions. *"Then I looked, and I heard the voice of many angels around the throne, the living creatures, and the elders; and the number of them was ten thousand times ten thousand, and thousands of thousands"* (Rev. 5:11). Angels as spirits apparently have their own spirit language (1 Cor. 13:1), but also have the ability to speak the language(s) of any person or people group they are serving, or delivering a message to.

All angels were originally holy and lived in heaven, but Satan (aka Lucifer) grew prideful and led a rebellion against God along with one-third of the angels and they were defeated and expelled ("hurled down") from heaven to the earth (Ezek. 28:12-19; Isa. 14:12-14; Matt. 25:41; Luke 10:18; Jude 6; 2 Pet. 2:4; Rev. 12:3-9). These evil angels are usually called demons or fallen angels, and are included in *"the spiritual forces of evil in the heavenly realms"* (Eph. 6:12). They are grotesque and hideous in appearance, as their form and nature has been corrupted and perverted by their sin of rebellion and pride. These evil angels are loyal to and serve Satan, whose mission is to "steal, kill and destroy" (John 10:10), and who walks around "like a roaring lion, seeking whom he may devour" (1 Pet. 5:8-9). Satan is also called "the accuser of our brethren" (Rev. 12:10). God even cursed Satan because he had deceived Eve (Gen. 3:14-15).

THESE EVIL ANGELS ARE LOYAL TO AND SERVE SATAN, WHOSE MISSION IS TO "STEAL, KILL AND DESTROY"

According to Dr. Barbie Breathitt, "Angels of darkness can appear as people and transform into snakes, bats, crows, owls, dogs and cats, as well as other creatures of darkness from the animal kingdom" (*Angels*, 2017, p. 180).

Paul the Apostle noted, *"And no wonder, for Satan himself masquerades as an angel of light. It is not surprising, then, if his servants masquerade as servants of righteousness..."* (2 Cor. 11:14-15, NIV). The Greek word used here for masquerades is *metaschēmatizetai,* from the root *metaschématizó,* which means to change the outward appearance, transfigure, adapt (Strong's G3345). Other Bible translations use synonyms such as disguises and transforms instead of masquerades; all involve deception.

This is one of the reasons why Paul the Apostle said, *"But even if we, or an angel from heaven, preach any other gospel to you than what we have preached to you, let him be accursed"* (Gal. 1:8, NKJV). Demons or evil angels can also take the form of disembodied spirits, which inhabit people. Luke 11:24-26 (AMP) says: *"When the unclean spirit comes out of a person, it roams through waterless places in search [of a place] of rest; and not finding any, it says, 'I will go back to my house (person) from which I came.' And when it comes, it finds the place swept and put in order. Then it goes and brings seven other spirits more evil than itself, and they go in [the person] and live there; and the last state of that person becomes worse than the first."* See also a parallel account of this in Matt. 12:43-45.

Scripture says that Jesus cast seven demons out of Mary Magdalene, and also that there were "other women who had been cured of evil spirits and diseases", including Joanna, Susanna, and many others (Luke 8:2-3). Jesus also cast at least 6,000 demons or evil spirits out of a wild man in the region of the Gerasenes, whom no one had been able to subdue. The strongman demon spirit reported its name to Jesus as "Legion, for we are many" (Mark 5:1-20; Luke 8:26-39). The evil spirits asked Jesus for permission to go into a nearby herd of swine.

"A large herd of pigs was feeding on the nearby hillside. The demons begged Jesus, 'Send us among the pigs; allow us to go into them.' He gave them permission, and the impure spirits came out and went into the pigs. The herd, about two thousand in number, rushed down the steep bank into the lake and were drowned."

Scripture also teaches that we must first bind the strong man in order to plunder his goods and possessions (Matt 12:29; Mark 3:27; Luke 11:21-22). Jesus said, in Luke 11:20-22 (NLT), *"But if I am casting out demons by the power of God, then the Kingdom of God has arrived among you. For when a strong man is fully armed and guards his palace, his possessions are safe — until someone even stronger attacks and overpowers him, strips him of his weapons, and carries off his belongings."* Jesus has given (delegated to) you and me the same authority that He had while on the earth, and greater works are available for us to do. John 14:12 (NIV) says, *"I tell you the truth, anyone who has faith in me will do what I have been doing. He will do even greater things than these, because I am going to the Father."*

The good news is that we are not alone. We have the Holy Spirit, we have access to Jesus and to Abba Father, and we have the body of Christ – the Church, the Ekklesia – and we have access to angels, just as Jesus did. All we have to do is pray, and learn to open our eyes and ears to the spiritual realm and the heavenly dimension, while we are here on earth. We may not need angelic assistance when we're in heaven, and clothed with immortality. The angels are available to help us now, in this lifetime on earth, so we should learn to recognize and appreciate that, and take every advantage available to us.

In closing this chapter, Dr. Barbie Breathitt has listed a typology of angels in her latest book (*Angels*, 2017, pp 36-37), which I share with her permission here:

- Healing Angels bring healing virtue
- Miracles, Signs, and Wonders Angels
- Angels of Promise and Breakthrough
- Breaker Angels remove stumbling blocks; (Matthew 18:7, Romans 14:13)
- Messenger Angels
- Angels of Joy and Laughter
- Angels of Fire
- Harvest Angels brings in souls
- Evangelism Angels help us advance God's Kingdom
- Entrepreneur Angels bring creative ideas and inventions to create wealth that finances kingdom advancement
- Scribe Angels give people the ability to write anointed books
- Revelation Angels interpret dreams, visions and spiritual encounters
- Prophetic Angels bring enlightenment, spiritual insights and God's end time mandates
- Gathering Angels (Matthew 13:37,41; 24)
- Guardian Angels protect people
- Glory angels produce, transport, impart and guard God's glory

- Intercession and Prayer angels hold the sensors in heaven full of incense
- Praise and Worship Angels glorify God around His throne night and day
- Rain Angels bring rain, snow, and weather patterns
- Deliverance Angels (Acts 12:7, Daniel 6:22, Psalm 34:7)
- Financial Angels bring in money, investment opportunities, and prosperity
- Diminish Darkness Angels brings in light
- Spiritual Warfare Angels defeat evil and darkness
- Revival Angels bring in anointed leaders to awaken people to true spirituality
- Renewal and Awakening Angels

Angels have no testimony of their own. Angels can only share in the rewards of what we invite them to do through inviting them to minister alongside of us.

Finally, angels have a wide variety of functions, and Dr. Breathitt has also compiled the following list of angelic functions which are listed below (*Angels*, 2017, pp. 24-25).

- Judge evil
- Bless the Lord
- Excel in strength
- Do God's pleasure
- Continually worship
- Warn of coming dangers

- Relieve hunger and thirst
- Minister on God's behalf
- Are agents of destruction
- Heed God's voice and Word
- Guard the way to the Tree of Life
- Protect and care for God's people
- Engage in the service of the saints
- Escort our souls to heaven at our death
- Delight in praising the name of the Lord
- Give Divine strength and life to the weary
- Provide protection, skill and spiritual insight
- Remain at God's side to do His every command
- Release anointings for salvation, healing and deliverance (John 5)
- Are mediums of revelation to the prophets, seers, and God's people
- Guide through answered prayers, dreams, visions, trances, and visitations
- Interested in and announced the birth of Jesus the Messiah, the prophets, Samson and John the Baptist.

Obviously, it's wonderful to have God's holy angels available to help us in time of need! I hope to see you on the 8th Mountain – The Mountain of the Lord! The 7 Mountains of Culture will never be the same once you arrive on the scene in your transformed and empowered state of being! Now we turn our attention to stewardship and rest in Chapter 19.

IT'S
WONDERFUL
TO HAVE
GOD'S HOLY
ANGELS
AVAILABLE TO
HELP US IN
TIME OF NEED!

NINETEEN

STEWARDSHIP AND REST

"Are you tired? Worn out? Burned out on religion? Come to me. Get away with me and you'll recover your life. I'll show you how to take a real rest. Walk with me and work with me — watch how I do it. Learn the unforced rhythms of grace. I won't lay anything heavy or ill-fitting on you. Keep company with me and you'll learn to live freely and lightly."
(Matt. 11:28-30, MSG)

"As each one has received a gift, minister it to one another, as good stewards of the manifold grace of God."
(1 Pet. 4:10, NKJV)

"Let us labor to enter into His rest."
(Heb. 4:11)

REST

Jehovah God, Elohim, El Shaddai, Yahweh, is a God of rest. He rested on the 7th day of creation, and He instituted a day of rest for His people known as the Sabbath. He even created the earth to rest through the seasons, and instituted a year of rest every seven years for the land that His people farmed, tended and stewarded. Gen. 2:2-3 (NIV) says, *"By the seventh day God had finished the work he had been doing; so on the seventh day he rested from all his work. And God blessed the seventh day and made it holy, because on it he rested from all the work of creating that he had done."* Rest is a promise, privilege and blessing from God for His children, and for the creation.

It is important to note here that godly rest is not laziness or slothfulness. God's rest is for recharging, re-energizing, and refreshing our bodies, minds and spirits. We are diligent, and productive, but we work from the place of being in God's rest, and not from our own strength or wisdom. Instead, we are able to access all of the resources of the 8th Mountain to help us.

Too many people get caught up in the "rat race" of daily existence and survival, and are functioning in striving mode to achieve or accomplish or earn or become something, or are chasing things. When we chase things, we are operating from "push" mode, where we are constantly pushing, trying to open doors and make things happen, and our thought process is, "If it is to be, it is up to me." Or you may be thinking, "It all depends on me." Or, "I have to make it happen."

Clearly, we each have our part to play in our areas of responsibility and assignments, but we can also access God's help and support, strength and wisdom, at any time when we need it. We are never alone, and we are never overwhelmed, even though we may feel that way at times, especially when we try to take on burdens that we are not able to carry and were never intended or designed to pick up (Matt. 11:28-30). It is true that at times we may

WE CAN ACCESS GOD'S HELP AND SUPPORT, STRENGTH AND WISDOM, AT ANY TIME WHEN WE NEED IT

be called upon to make sacrifices, for the good of others, and exert strenuous and even "superhuman" effort to go above and beyond the call of duty in special situations, or to meet project deadlines, or mission objectives, or in times of natural disaster, national security, or terrorist threats or attacks. However, most people don't live that way all the time, or have jobs that require that level of exertion on a continuous basis, or have to deal with life and death situations every day.

We are certainly thankful and grateful for those who do, such as first responders, policemen, firemen, paramedics, military personnel, medical professionals and staff, intelligence services, and law enforcement agencies. But, even for those who are specially trained and equipped, and/or gifted, God has rest available as well.

God created us to operate from "pull" mode where we have the mindset that we already have everything that is needed for or pertains to life and godliness through Christ Jesus, and that rivers of living water flow from within us.

1 Pet. 1:3 (NLT) says, *"By his divine power, God has given us everything we need for living a godly life. We have received all of this by coming to know him, the one who called us to himself by means of his marvelous glory and excellence."* John 7:38 (NIV) says, *"Whoever believes in me, as the Scripture has said, streams of living water will flow from within him."* As the living water

WHEN WE FEEL PHYSICALLY OVERWHELMED, OUR CARNAL NATURE CAN SURFACE

and Spirit of God flow out of our mouths, hearts and bellies, other people will be attracted or "pulled" to us. We don't have to chase them; they will begin to chase us.

There is a place of rest in the spirit realm reserved for us as we abide in Christ. When we clear our minds of distraction and clutter, we can come into sync with the resonant frequency of the Holy Spirit. When we're in sync with Him, we can perceive and access the spirit realm with the calm center of Christ.

When we avoid rest, it's easy to become exhausted, and our thoughts and emotions can get out of kilter, and our reflexes slow down. When we feel physically overwhelmed, our carnal nature can surface as we allow our minds to entertain ungodly grief, anger, bitterness, fear, and envy. Out of fatigue, we fall more easily into agreement with the enemy. It's easier to believe lies about ourselves and others, and we can feel discouraged.

Rushing with constant busyness creates toxic emotions and leads to irregular heart rhythms and stress. Stress is a major cause and contributing factor to various diseases and premature death. Lack of rest makes us less effective thinkers and evaluators and analyzers and planners. The result is lessened or lowered performance at work, and an inability to evaluate the need for adequate rest, and set proper boundaries for ourselves and others. We may get swept up into cycles of work and activity that set us up for burnout or exhaustion.

Conversely, good things happen in our brains when we rest. We are refreshed and renewed. We have energy to complete our Kingdom assignments. Rest gives our bodies a chance to relax. Our heart rates slow. Our minds clear. We can breathe easier. We can sense the Lord's love deeply.

Deep sleep produces peace in our emotions. Peace fosters grace and forgiveness. When we forgive those who've hurt us, we're more likely to take a more lighthearted view to govern how we think and speak to ourselves and others.

"But when you go over the Jordan and live in the land that the LORD your God is giving you to inherit . . . he gives you rest from all your enemies around, so that you live in safety" (Deut. 12:10-11, ESV).

On the 8th Mountain are fields of open land where God gives us rest from the enemy, and in this rest, we find safety. When we rest, the peace that surpasses understanding guards our hearts and our minds. We have a mind governed by the life and peace of the Holy Spirit.

"Those who live in accordance with the Spirit have their minds set on what the Spirit desires. The mind governed by the flesh is death, but the mind governed by the Spirit is life and peace" (Rom. 8:5–6).

Events like meetings, conferences, prayer meetings and worship services can tend to fill up our calendars. With the constancy of collective demands on our time, we sometimes lack the mindfulness to take care of our body's simple needs like eating. The 1st Century apostles were familiar with that experience when they were overwhelmed by big crowds at times.

"The apostles gathered around Jesus and reported to him all they had done and taught. Then, because so many people were coming and going that they did not even have a chance to eat, he said to them, 'Come with me by yourselves to a quiet place and get some rest.' So they went away by themselves in a boat to a solitary place" (Mark 6: 30-32).

Rest is the wisdom of margin. Rest is a blank space for God to write on. Rest is a posture of receiving. Here we wait restfully on God until He speaks. When we rest, we focus on the fact that God has been faithful to us in the past and that He'll speak to us again in His time.

Rest can come in the form of meditation. When we meditate, we have a focused, godly awareness of the nature of Christ and His Word. Meditating on a specific verse or passage of Scripture relaxes us as it recalibrates our souls to come into sync and rhythm with Him.

Research studies show that meditating produces more folds in the cortex of the brain. These extra folds allow the brain to process information faster, make decisions quicker, and improve memory. This helps us to integrate thinking, emotions, and self-regulation. Our working memory and monitoring of thoughts and feelings also improve dramatically. Neuroscience has proven that moments of creativity happen when our minds are at rest. Networks of neurons that typically don't communicate, such as a stray thought, a random memory, and an unrelated image, combine in unique ways to create novel ideas. Relaxing makes us more creative.

The natural flow of prayer that follows rest is filled with God's presence. God said, *"My presence will go with you, and I will give you rest"* (Exo. 33:14, ESV).

Jesus listens as we spend time with Him. We listen to Him as well. Practicing His presence brings restorative healing. How? The more time we spend in prayer, the greater His awakening of our senses to His vibrant life within us. In the quiet presence of Christ's transforming power, His finest miracles emerge. That is why the writer of Hebrews exhorts us, *"Let us labor to enter into His rest"* (Heb. 4:11). The labor comes in dying to self, and resisting the lure of the world to suck up all of our time. This modern craze for workaholism and scheduling every moment has engendered several books on the topic of "Margin," and has spawned time management as an area of coaching emphasis, focus and specialization. One of my friends, Dr. Joseph Peck, describes himself as the Time Doctor, and coaches others to free up and manage their time to optimize their potential and bring glory to God.

One rule of thumb I use for decisions and time management, is that for every one thing I say 'yes' to, I know I will usually need to say 'no' to at least 10 other things, in order to do the one thing with excellence. We need to evaluate every opportunity and invitation to see if it is in God's will for us, and if it aligns with our assignments and destiny. If we allow Him, God will direct and lead us on paths of peace, and connect us to those with interlocking assignments.

A deep, relational place with God the Father, the Source of renewed vision, is not a temporary resting place. Heb. 4:9-11 (NKJV) says, *"There remains therefore a rest for the people of God. For he who has entered His rest has himself also ceased from his works as God did from His. Let us therefore be diligent to enter that rest..."* We are called to live there — and to embrace the process that He uses to renew our minds and hearts as we shed layers of perceived limits. There we can boldly take our expression of His glory to the next level.

STEWARDSHIP

The 8th Mountain displays the glory of God when we recognize that *"Every good and perfect gift is from above, coming down from the Father of the heavenly lights, who does not change like shifting shadows"* (Jas. 1:17). If every gift is from our heavenly Father, then they belong to Him, and we are simply stewards, or managers, of all He has created.

Among those gifts are His love, hospitality, and encouragement. *"And above all things have fervent love for one another, for 'love will cover a multitude of sins.' Be hospitable to one another without grumbling. As each one has received a gift, minister it to one another, as **good stewards** of the manifold grace of God"* (1 Pet. 4:8-10, NKJV, author's emphasis).

In verse 10 above, the Greek word for "steward" is *oikonomos*, which comes from *oikos*, ("house") and *nemo* ("to arrange"). This word referred to the manager of a household or estate and later came to mean its steward. In 1 Peter 4:10, stewards use their gifts to build up and encourage others.

Psa. 24:1 (NIV) says, *"The earth is the LORD's, and everything in it."* The KJV translation notes, *"The earth is the Lord's, and the fullness thereof, the world, and everything that dwells therein."* We are stewards of all God has created. We're administrators of all He gives, including what He pours into us out of His wealth and abundance.

God has blessed us with resources of time, talent, and treasure, as well as wisdom, work and wealth. He calls us to manage them with godly authority, wisdom, prudence, humility, integrity, discernment and obedience.

WE ARE WISE STEWARDS WHEN WE MANAGE OUR TIME WITH INTENTIONALITY

We are responsible and effective stewards of His time when we obediently and diligently obey the commands He gives us. The fruit of the Spirit will grow best when we couple times of activity with times of rest and meditation. Our times are in God's hands (Psa. 31:15). We can trust that our earthly (chronos) time unfolds with ripe windows of opportune and strategic (kairos) times ordained in heaven. We are wise stewards when we manage our time with intentionality, while recognizing God's sovereignty and wisdom in causing or allowing events to transpire, and allowing our schedules to be interrupted by God.

God has given each of us divine gifts so that we can live them out with alacrity. He calls us to be good stewards of

His mysteries. *"Let a man so consider us, as servants of Christ and stewards of the mysteries of God. Moreover **it is required in stewards that one be found faithful**"* (1 Cor. 4:1-2, NKJV, author's emphasis). Faithful here means integrous, honest, diligent, prudent.

A steward is not the owner, but rather the overseer or manager of resources with the best interests and practices of the owner in mind. 1 Tim. 6:7 says, *"For we brought nothing into the world, and we can take nothing out of it."* Whatever we accumulate on earth, remains on earth, but we can store up treasure in heaven. Matt. 6:19-21 says, *"Do not lay up for yourselves treasures on earth, where moth and rust destroy and where thieves break in and steal; but lay up for yourselves treasures in heaven, where neither moth nor rust destroys and where thieves do not break in and steal. For where your treasure is, there your heart will be also."* Jesus said that faithful and wise stewards are known by their obedience (Luke 12:43-44). A good steward *"is faithful in what is least"* and *"is faithful also in much"* (Luke 16:10).

God rewards us when we invest Kingdom gold — our treasures — wisely. In Matthew 25, Jesus told the parable of the talents. A man going on a journey entrusted his wealth to three servants. He gave each of them gold to invest or trade: one servant received five bags, one received two, and one received a single bag of gold. After a long time, the master returned and asked each what they had done with the gold they were given to manage. The servants with five bags and two bags doubled what they had been given. But, the servant with only one bag hid his gold in the ground.

In the parable, the master gave the single bag to the servant who had ten. Christ said, *"For whoever has will be given more, and they will have an abundance. Whoever does not have, even what they have will be taken from them*" (Matt. 25:29). The Lord honors our faithfulness to invest His gifts with the intent of increase. 8th Mountain stewardship never buries Kingdom gold. When it is invested wisely, a regenerative spirit and multiplication are released for the Body.

A good steward believes that the sovereign Lord is about to shift things in his or her favor. A good steward fills his or her mind and self-talk with hope from heaven about the future. *"Therefore I tell you, whatever you ask in prayer, believe that you have received it, and it will be yours"* (Mark 11:24, ESV). Doubt might temporarily distract us from Christ-certainties, but Jesus is our primary focus. He is always good; sometimes, like a radar using radio waves to detect aircraft, we need to make "sweeps" for His goodness and favor. We are likely to come across His wide, long, high, and deep love along the way.

A godly steward manages Holy Spirit lenses by asking questions to gain His perspective. "Holy Spirit, what's going on? How must I shift my thinking to see what You see?" Then, with His upward lift to new elevations on the 8th Mountain, we can reach forward and refocus or reprioritize from a whole new vantage point.

Kingdom and 8th Mountain stewards are unselfish and other-centric, keeping others in mind and looking after their needs. Phil. 2:4 (ESV) states, *"Let each of you look not only to his own interests, but also to the interests of others."* James 1:27 adds, *"Pure and undefiled religion before God and the Father is this: to visit orphans and widows in their affliction, to keep oneself unspotted from the world."* 2 Cor. 9:8 (NIV) says, *"And God is able to make all grace abound to you, so that in all things at all times, having all that you need, you will abound in every good work."* All grace is a lot of grace, and every good work is a lot of works.

Kingdom stewards are also diligent, both in natural resources and things of the Spirit. Prov. 10:4 says, *"A slack hand causes poverty, but the hand of the diligent makes rich."* Prov. 12:24 adds, *"The hand of the diligent will rule, while the slothful will be put to forced labor."* Prov. 13:4 states, *"The soul of the sluggard craves and gets nothing, But the soul of the diligent is made fat (or richly supplied)."* Prov. 21:5 notes, *"The plans of the diligent lead surely to abundance, but everyone who is hasty comes to poverty."*

Deut. 4:9 records, *"Only give heed to yourself and keep your soul diligently, so that you do not forget the things which your eyes have seen and they do not depart from your heart all the days of your life; but make them known to your sons and your grandsons."* Heb. 6:11 says, *"And we desire that each one of you show the same diligence so as to realize the full assurance of hope until the end."* And 2 Peter 3:14 states, *"Therefore, beloved, since you look for these things, be diligent to be found by Him in peace, spotless and blameless."*

When we are stewards of Christ-possibilities, we see that God redeems our past and releases expansive, explosive possibilities for our futures. Those of us on the 8th Mountain who activate possibilities with hope-filled expectation are called "possibilitarians." Possibilitarians see opportunities in everything. Jesus was the ultimate Possibilitarian. When we understand God's multi-dimensional nature, we can accept the past, because ribbons of redemptive, crisscrossing possibilities intersect in us and our circumstances. Next, we turn our attention to Chapter 20 and prospering in health, wealth and hope.

TWENTY

PROSPERING IN HEALTH, WEALTH AND HOPE

"Beloved, I pray that in all respects you may prosper and be in good health, just as your soul prospers."
(3 John 2, NASB)

"But remember the Lord your God, for it is he who gives you the ability to produce wealth, and so confirms his covenant, which he swore to your forefathers, as it is today."
(Deut. 8:18, NIV)

"I pray that God, the source of hope, will fill you completely with joy and peace because you trust in him. Then you will overflow with confident hope through the power of the Holy Spirit."
(Rom. 15:13, NLT)

The benefits of coming to the Mountain of the Lord in this age include hope, health and wealth. These are not temporal or even transitional attributes. Rather, they foreshadow the very essence of the features of the new Jerusalem described in Revelation chapters 20-22, a permanent, even eternal dwelling for the saints of God. The streets are paved with gold, no artificial lighting is needed, and the 12 gates are made of pearls – each gate from a single pearl! A beautiful tree – the Tree of Life – grows beside the water, the river of God, on both sides of the river, and bears fruit each month in perpetuity, and its leaves are for the healing of the nations. No illness, sickness or disease are present. There are also vaults, treasuries, and vast resources in abundance. No one is depressed or distressed, and there is no anxiety, fear, worry or hopelessness in heaven.

"Then the angel showed me a river of the water of life, clear as crystal, flowing from the throne of God and of the Lamb (Christ), in the middle of its street. On either side of the river was the tree of life, bearing twelve kinds of fruit, yielding its fruit every month; and the leaves of the tree were for the healing of the nations" (Rev. 22:1-2, AMP).

On earth the sons and daughters of God have every reason to be healthy, wealthy, and hopeful, but they have not always fared as well as might be expected. Some have, but many others have not. There are many reasons for this, of course – man's inhumanity to fellow man; sin; greed; bribes; corruption; theft; war; communism; socialism; totalitarianism; dictatorships; economic models and systems that do not acknowledge, honor, or factor in God's nature and values; tax policy; trade policy; labor laws; unions; economic incentives; education or the lack thereof; personal character; our personal relationship with God or lack thereof; disobedience; lack of faith; doubt; fear;

unbelief; skills, gifting and abilities; work ethic; degree of self-motivation; love; honor; faith; anointing; favor; rest; stewardship; prayer and intercession or the lack thereof; spiritual warfare; family of origin; nation of origin; and generational cycles of systemic poverty in some families, neighborhoods, cities, regions and nations. In light of that, we will start this chapter by focusing on hope before exploring health and wealth.

HOPE IS A STRONG AND TRUSTWORTHY ANCHOR FOR OUR SOULS

First of all, God is the source of hope for all humanity, including His children. Rom. 15:13 (NLT) says, *"I pray that **God, the source of hope**, will fill you completely with joy and peace because you trust in him. Then you will overflow with confident hope through the power of the Holy Spirit"* (author's emphasis). God wants us to be filled to capacity with hope and to overflow in hope as we trust Him. Heb. 10:23 (NLT) adds, *"Let us hold tightly without wavering to the hope we affirm, for **God can be trusted to keep his promise**"* (author's emphasis). We must get a firm grip mentally, spiritually and emotionally on hope in God and never let it go. God keeps His promises. The rainbow in the heavens is one such reminder. Num. 23:19 (NLT) says, *"God is not a man, so he does not lie. He is not human, so he does not change his mind. Has he ever spoken and failed to act? Has he ever promised and not carried it through?"*

Heb. 6:17-19 (NLT) also states, *"Because God wanted to make the unchanging nature of his purpose very clear to the heirs of what was promised, he confirmed it with an oath. **So God has*** *given both his promise and his oath*. *These two things are unchangeable because it is impossible for God to lie*. *Therefore, we who have fled to him for refuge can have great confidence as we hold to the hope that lies before us*. **This hope is a strong and trustworthy anchor for our souls**. *It leads us through the curtain into God's inner sanctuary*" (author's emphasis). The poet Emily Dickinson once wrote:

> Hope is the thing with feathers
> That perches in the soul,
> And sings the tune without the words,
> And never stops at all.
> And sweetest in the gale is heard;
> And sore must be the storm
> That could abash the little bird
> That kept so many warm.

Hope helps us to be joyful, and is tied to joy and peace and trust (Rom. 15:13). Rom. 12:12 (NIV) notes, *"Be joyful in hope, patient in affliction, faithful in prayer."*

Hope is also connected to our salvation. Rom. 8:24-25 (NIV) says, *"For in this hope we were saved. But hope that is seen is no hope at all. Who hopes for what they already have? But if we hope for what we do not yet have, we wait for it patiently."* Hope is also part of a process that involves tribulation (great trouble or suffering), perseverance and character. Rom. 5:1-5 (NKJV) records, *"Therefore, having been justified by faith, we have peace with God through our Lord Jesus Christ, through whom also we have access by faith into this grace in which we stand, and rejoice in hope of the glory of God. And not only that, but we also glory in tribulations, knowing that tribulation produces perseverance; and perseverance, character; and character, hope. Now hope does not disappoint, because the love of God has been poured out in our hearts by the Holy Spirit who was given to us."*

Psa. 31:24 says, *"Be strong and take heart, all you who hope in the Lord."* Numerous Scriptures mention putting our hope in the Lord God, or in His Word (see Psa. 3:2-6; Psa. 25:5; Psa. 33:22; Psa. 42:11; Psa. 71:5; Psa. 119:14; Psa. 130:5; Psa. 147:11; Lam. 3:24; Isa. 40:31; Micah 7:7). He is our refuge, our hiding place, our shield and defender, and our high tower. Other references to hope include Col. 1:27, *"Christ in you, the hope of glory"*; 1 Pet. 1:3-6, *"a living hope"*; 1 Pet. 3:15, *"be ready to give an answer to every man [anyone] who asks you a reason for the hope within you"*; Eph. 4:4, *"you were called to one hope"*; and Heb. 11:1 (NIV), *"Now faith is confidence in what we hope for and assurance about what we do not see."*

Then there are other Scriptures that talk about being "without hope," or having no hope, such as Ruth 1:12; 1 Chron. 29:15; and Job 5:16, 6:8, 6:11, 11:18-19, and 17:15. Job first asked (6:11, NIV), *"What strength do I have, that I should still hope? What prospects, that I should be patient?"* Then he poignantly and prophetically asked later (17:15, NIV), *"[W]here then is my hope — who can see any hope for me?"* The ESV says, *"[W]here then is my hope? Who will see my hope?"* You and I are called to see and speak hope for and to others, and there are countless millions on the earth today with little or no hope, so the task is enormous, and laborers are needed for the harvest in the 7 Mountains. Some may even be hopeless and in despair or depression due to their circumstances and/or their identity or their past. That's where you and I come in. We are called to be bearers and bringers of hope. And, as we overflow with

WE ARE ALL CALLED TO BE BEARERS AND BRINGERS OF HOPE

hope from the 8ᵗʰ Mountain, we will have plenty of hope to share and an abundant supply to steward and release, and invest or deposit in others.

In closing this section, one of the best known verses on hope is Prov. 13:12 (NIV): *"Hope deferred makes the heart sick, but a longing fulfilled is a tree of life."* This verse, of course, is speaking of natural hope, or of hope in the world, and not our hope of eternal life, or our trust in God, and all of His promises, which are yes and amen in Christ Jesus (2 Cor. 1:20). Our natural longings and desires may or may not be fulfilled, depending on our motives, and God's will (Jas. 4:1-5), but, as we grow and mature in Christ, our desires and His desires become closer and closer together, until they are one and the same. Psa. 37:4-5 says, *"Take delight in the LORD, and he will give you the desires of your heart. Commit your way to the LORD; trust in him and he will do this."* We first have to align our heart with His, delight ourselves in Him, commit our ways to Him, trust in Him so we can have a strong hope, and have the same foundation for our lives as His throne in heaven (see chapter 2). Then, godly desires take care of themselves, since our Abba Father is an extravagant giver, and knows how to give good gifts (see Chapter 6).

PROSPERING IN WEALTH IS AVAILABLE TO GOD'S PEOPLE —WHOSOEVER WILL

In this same vein of delighting ourselves in the Lord first, Matt. 6:33 (ESV) says, *"Therefore do not be anxious, saying, 'What shall we eat?' or 'What shall we drink?' or 'What shall we wear?' For the Gentiles seek after all these things, and your heavenly Father knows that you need them all. But seek first the kingdom of God and his righteousness, and all these things will be added to you."* The NLT version reads, *"So don't worry about these things, saying, 'What will we eat? What will we drink? What will we wear?' These things dominate the thoughts of unbelievers, but your heavenly Father already knows all your needs. Seek the Kingdom of God above all else, and live righteously, and he will give you everything you need."* The first step for saints in prospering financially is to get your priorities and affections aligned with and centered on God, and to seek first the kingdom of God in all that you do. Then, God promises to bless you!

In fact, financial blessing and prosperity were a conditional part of God's old covenant instituted by Moses with the Israelites, or Jewish nation. *"But remember the Lord your God, for it is he who gives you the ability to produce wealth, and so confirms his covenant, which he swore to your forefathers, as it is today"* (Deut. 8:18, NIV). Some translations say, *"...for it is he who gives you the power to get wealth."* Today, we have similar promises under the new covenant instituted by Jesus. *"God is able to provide you with every blessing in abundance, so that you may always have enough of everything and may provide in abundance for every good work... He who supplies seed to the sower and bread for food will supply and multiply your resources, and increase the harvest of your righteousness"* (2 Cor. 9:8-10).

Money is simply a tool, and as such, it is neither good nor evil – but it is necessary. Solomon wrote, *"Money answereth all things"* (Eccl. 10:19). He also wrote, *"Whoever loves money never has money enough; whoever loves wealth is never satisfied with his income"* (Eccl. 5:10). Paul later echoed Solomon in the New Testament: *"For the love of money is a root of all kinds of evil"* (1 Tim. 6:10). When asked by a reporter how much money was enough, John D. Rockefeller is reported to have said, "Just a little bit more." That kind of thinking or mentality demonstrates an insatiable appetite, and a poverty spirit, despite being a philanthropic patriarch, and captain of industry. It does not demonstrate godly contentment. Some historians consider Rockefeller, founder of Standard Oil Co., to have been the first American billionaire.

One of the names of God is Jehovah Jireh, The Lord is Our Provider. Psa. 35:7 (NKJV) says, *"Let them shout for joy and be glad, Who favor my righteous cause; And let them say continually, "Let the Lord be magnified, Who has pleasure in the prosperity of His servant."* The word prosperity is also translated well-being. God desires that we prosper in all areas of our life, including financially. And, the good news is that God is not a respecter of persons, and does not show favoritism among His children (Rom. 2:11, Acts 10:34). He is an equal opportunity employer and Father.

This means we each have the same access to God and the same opportunity to receive blessings from God, no matter what our background, education level, age, race, gender, nationality, or economic status is, and no matter what our current situation is like. Many of the earlier chapters have touched on the character traits required, and the processes involved, and the intimacy needed, in receiving divine favor, promotion and inheritance from the Lord. Unfortunately, not everyone is willing to pay the price involved. So, our faith in and obedience to God play a large role in identifying for Him who are true disciples, committed to the Lordship of Christ, and those who are along for the ride – who received salvation but are either still on spiritual milk, or may be resisting sanctification or discipleship, and are window shoppers, fence sitters, comfort seekers, fans, spectators, visitors, tourists, pew warmers, and/or Christians in name only.

So, it should come as no surprise then, that riches and wealth are usually distributed unequally in society, and in the kingdom of God as well. God seems to reward effort, diligence, perseverance, competence, skill, gifting, intimacy, love, mercy, forgiveness, grace, knowledge, wisdom, understanding, revelation, prayer, prudence, counsel, discernment, honor, humility, integrity, excellence and stewardship, and He seems not to reward laziness, slothfulness, prayerlessness, incompetence, nonperformance, mediocrity, ignorance, stupidity, pride, arrogance, unforgiveness, bitterness, lack of grace, lack of honor, lack of discernment, lack of wisdom, lack of mercy, lack of intimacy, lack of love, lack of effort, lack of integrity, dishonesty, fraud, theft, corruption, etc. And, He expects His children to

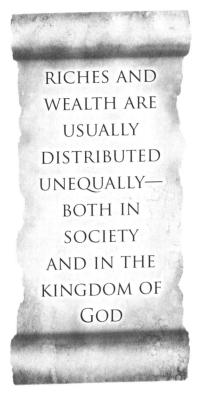

RICHES AND WEALTH ARE USUALLY DISTRIBUTED UNEQUALLY— BOTH IN SOCIETY AND IN THE KINGDOM OF GOD

work and to be involved in His Family Business, Almighty & Sons Unlimited, which has many branches and divisions globally. Since we also are beneficiaries and partakers of a New Covenant or Testament, put into effect and force by the blood and death of Jesus, God expects us to keep, honor and fulfill our side of the covenant, just as He does His side.

God has shared basic principles of increase, multiplication, and stewardship throughout His word. We covered some of this previously in Chapter 19 on Stewardship. Gal. 6:7

(KJV) says, *"Be not deceived; God is not mocked: for whatsoever a man soweth, that shall he also reap."* 2 Thess. 3:10 says, *For even when we were with you, we gave you this rule: "The one who is unwilling to work shall not eat."* 1 Tim. 5:8 (NIV) adds, *"Anyone who does not provide for their relatives, and especially for their own household, has denied the faith and is worse than an unbeliever."* And, Luke 16:10-11 says, *"He that is faithful in that which is least is faithful also in much: and he that is unjust in the least is unjust also in much. If therefore you have not been faithful in the unrighteous mammon, who will commit to your trust the true riches?"*

The Parable of the Talents provides a good indication and clear picture of God's heart toward stewardship. Those who looked after their Master's money and prospered were given more to steward, and the one who buried his talent in the ground, was rebuked and the talent was taken away from him and given to another. Similarly, Jesus said that some saints would prosper 30-fold, some 60-fold, and some 100-fold in this life. Matt. 13:8 (NLT) states, *"Still other seeds fell on fertile soil, and they produced a crop that was thirty, sixty, and even a hundred times as much as had been planted!"* Mark 4:20 (ESV) notes, *"But those that were sown on the good soil are the ones who hear the word and accept it and bear fruit, thirtyfold and sixtyfold and a hundredfold."* Isaac demonstrated the hundredfold return when he planted in faith at God's word in a foreign country during a famine in his own land, and reaped a hundredfold in the same year because of the Lord's blessing (Gen. 26:12). Prov. 10:22 (NKJV) adds, *"The blessing of the Lord makes one rich, And He adds no sorrow with it."*

STEWARDSHIP IS THE KINGDOM MODEL OF FINANCE AND ECONOMICS

Historically, extremes have been the norm in terms of finance and economics in the Church and kingdom of God on earth. At one extreme has been the Gospel of Poverty, sometimes referred to as "pious poverty," in much of the Orthodox Church and Catholic Church, which have viewed and taught poverty as both a virtue and a vow for nearly 1,700 years. At the other extreme, more recently over the last 50 years or so, has been The Gospel of Prosperity, sometimes referred to as name it/claim it or blab it/grab it. This gospel espouses and teaches faith without factoring in the character of individuals or the timing of God. Both of these schools of teaching and practice have been unbalanced and out of step with the full counsel of God as found in Scripture, in my opinion.

In recent years, a third line of teaching has emerged, which I call the Gospel of Stewardship. This is the message of the Bible and what Jesus and the early church apostles taught, and is what I believe to be an accurate and biblically-sound view of the Scriptures. This view teaches that God owns everything (the cattle on a thousand hills; all the gold and silver are his, etc.) and that we are stewards of what belongs to God, and we are to steward His resources, including time, talent and treasure as well as work, wisdom and wealth, and our relationships. It is important to have an accurate understanding of the basic theme of the roughly 2,200 Scriptures which discuss money or finance in some way, and that is Stewardship. Eccl. 2:26 (NIV) says, *"To the man who pleases him, God gives wisdom, knowledge and happiness, but to the sinner he gives the task of gathering and storing up wealth to hand it over to the one who pleases God."* So again, pleasing God and delighting ourselves in Him, pay rich dividends. Solomon said that the task of sinners is to gather and store up wealth so that it can be handed over, conveyed and/or transferred to those individuals who please God. That is you and me, and other disciples of the Most High God. God's ways are often mysterious, past finding out, and higher than ours. He is full of surprises.

TWO ECONOMIC SYSTEMS CO-EXIST

There are two economic systems which co-exist on planet Earth – the World Financial System, which is usually referred to as Babylon, and the Kingdom of God. They differ significantly and in many respects. The world system runs on and revolves around buying and selling, which equates to trade and exchange, production and consumption. God's financial system operates on sowing and reaping, giving and receiving. The world system is temporal and God's kingdom is eternal. The world system is based on scarcity and self-preservation; God's financial system is based on abundance – "more than enough" – and self-sacrifice. The world economic system is based on win-lose and one party dominating or prevailing; God's economy is based on win-win-win, and all parties benefiting, as well as the kingdom community. The world system is based on debt; God's economy is based on profit, savings and investment.

The world system is based on transaction; God's economy is based on covenant. There can be transactions within the covenant, but the covenant is more important than any single transaction. The world financial system is based on immediate gratification, quarterly profits where "cash is king" and "earnings are exalted", slash and burn tactics, plunder & pillage strategies and maneuvers; God's economy is based on generational wealth accumulation and transfer to families or partners. The world system is based on slavery; God's economy is based on freedom. The world system teaches and breeds entitlement; God teaches empowerment. The world system is based on competition; God's economy is based on collaboration and completion. We have to be wise as serpents but innocent as doves (Matt. 10:16) to walk this tightrope and not compromise our convictions and ethics in the marketplace.

THREE TYPES OF EXCHANGE

The world's economic and financial system recognizes and revolves around Economic Exchange and Social Exchange, from which originate the basic theories underlying, governing, and controlling economics, finance, banking, governments, business, and the nonprofit sector (NGOs, charities, foundations and philanthropy). Economic Exchange is monetary exchange and underpins governments and corporations. Social Exchange is an exchange involving social good or social value, where the exchange is not fully captured in money or goods, but spills over into society; this theory underpins the nonprofit sector. Neither of these two theories factor in or consider the Spirit of God, which is ironic since economics as a field of study and academic discipline originated as Moral Philosophy in universities (see Tomas Sedlacek, *The Economics of Good and Evil*, Oxford University Press, 2013).

Therefore, these two current theories of exchange are fundamentally flawed since they are incomplete and inadequate to explain or predict human behavior fully without factoring in the spiritual dimension. Spiritual Exchange is a third type which is currently unnoticed and unrecognized, and includes such things as worship, prayer, mercy, self-sacrifice, forgiveness, and love, just to name a few. These are all examples of spiritual exchanges which cannot be measured, analyzed or predicted by current exchange theories. I suggest that a Theory of Spiritual Exchange be developed, and presented to the academic and scientific community. I am working on that but would welcome collaboration from other scholars or a research university. Such a theory could have significant implications for a number of different areas of policy.

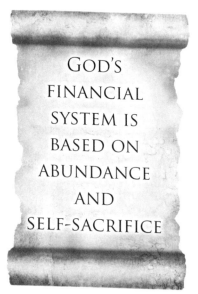

GOD'S FINANCIAL SYSTEM IS BASED ON ABUNDANCE AND SELF-SACRIFICE

Finally, it is no surprise that we run across our foundational value coordinates of righteousness and justice in this discussion. With Wisdom narrating, Prov. 8:17-21 says, *"I love those who love me, and those who seek me find me.* **With me are riches and honor, enduring wealth and prosperity.** *My fruit is better than fine gold; what I yield surpasses choice silver.* **I walk in the way of righteousness, along the paths of justice, bestowing wealth on those who love me and making their treasuries full"** (author's emphasis). Several of the earlier chapters converge here in this verse – specifically, 2, 3, and 7. That is no accident as God is intentionally making a point and emphasizing those things in this Scripture to show their correlation.

WEALTH AND RICHES CLARIFIED AND CONTRASTED

We close out this section by noting and clarifying the difference between riches and wealth in Scripture, and then take a quick look at risk and reward. Why is this important to us? Because it is important to God, who has made different declarations for wealth and for riches. In 2 Chron. 1:12, God promised Solomon both riches and wealth. Riches (*osher*) are normally used for liquid assets used as a money-equivalent means of exchange, or barter. Wealth (*nekec, hon, or chayil*) is an asset that may multiply in value with wise stewardship, or quickly plummet in value through foolishness or neglect.

Psa. 112:3 declares, *"wealth and riches are in his house…"*

In Deut. 8.18, the covenant people are reminded, *"It is the Lord who gives you the power to get wealth, that he might fulfill his covenant with you…"* If you read further, the "Promised Land" had little in the way of cash, minted metals, or gemstones (riches). But, it was abundant in land, water, crops, houses, animals, and mineral wealth.

This "wealth" required faithfulness. Without wise stewardship, animals die of disease and starvation and predators. Land becomes overtaken with weeds, streams become clogged with algae, and houses become leaky and bug infested.

With wisdom, land increases in fertility and harvests multiply. Animals breed and guard their healthy young, and minerals are safely extracted from the earth without poisoning the environment.

Jesus warned about accumulating grain in bins without replanting it, and scolded the rich young ruler, but was friends with wealthy men including Joseph of Aramathea, Zaccheus, and Nicodemus. Paul declared, "I know how to abound" but warned against the love of riches.

So, what is wealth transfer, and what are some ways that it may come about?

The Hebrew word most often translated "wealth" is *chayil*, which is an idiom that is translated in many ways, as seen in the list below:

- army (56x),
- man of valour (37x),
- host (29x),
- forces (14x),
- valiant (13x),
- strength (12x),
- riches (11x),
- wealth (10x),
- power (9x),
- substance (8x),
- might (6x),
- strong (5x),

Much of the "wealth" described above is character. Will you be known as more valiant, of greater courage, stronger resolve, and rugged determination than the sinners around you? Will you have a more powerful group of loyal followers willing to exercise their skill and resolve to accomplish your assignment? David's "mighty men" were only 30 men strong, but were undefeated by humans, giants, and even lions! You cannot buy loyalty like this!

Riches are temporal and often fleeting — includes money, stocks, bonds, securities, possessions, investments, lands, houses, material things, patents, copyrights, royalties, and inheritance. Wealth is usually generational and encompasses family, friends, reputation, influence, character, wisdom, health, honor, awards, integrity, values, titles, ideas, creativity, gifts, callings, mantles, identity, destiny, stewardship, and philanthropy. They are different.

NO RISK, NO REWARD

Sir Richard Branson sold his successful, 20-year-old music label Virgin Records in 1992 to Thorn EMI for $1B USD so he could use the proceeds to fund and build Virgin Atlantic (acquired by Alaska Airlines in 2016 for $4B USD). He wept that day. Countless other entrepreneurs and CEOs have made similar tough decisions in their careers. Such decisions are not always easy, and involve risk, but are necessary for future growth and expansion.

As disciples of Christ, our tears are tears of joy because we have found a priceless treasure in the field, and this treasure has benefits both for this life, and the life to come (eternity). Matt. 13:44 says, *"The kingdom of heaven is like a treasure hidden in a field. When a man found it, he hid it again and then in his joy went and sold all he had and bought that field."* Isa. 33:5-6 says, *"The Lord is exalted, for He dwells on high; He has filled Zion with justice and righteousness. And He will be the security and stability of your times, A treasure of salvation, wisdom and knowledge; The fear of the Lord is your treasure."* Therefore, of our own volition, we willingly and voluntarily pay the price required to buy the field so that we might gain this treasure.

As we count the cost and willingly pay the price required to be a disciple of Christ, we gain access to all the treasures of God hidden in Christ. Col. 2:3 says, *"All the treasures of wisdom and knowledge are hidden in Him."* The Greek word used for treasures here *thesauroi* is the same root word as in Matt. 13:44, which is *thesauro* (Strong's Greek 2344), which means a treasury or storehouse.

Sometimes it is necessary for us to let go of what we have, and the just enough, or the not enough, in order to receive the more than enough, the abundance of God through Christ, who promises us "the riches of his glorious inheritance in the saints, and his incomparably great power for us who believe", and a "more than we can ask or imagine" portion (Eph. 1:18-19, 3:20). *"Now to him who is able to do immeasurably more than all we ask or imagine, according to his power that is at work within us, to him be glory in the church and in Christ Jesus throughout all generations, for ever and ever! Amen."*

That is what faith is all about, and taking the leap of faith, by taking a calculated risk. We can be at peace knowing that His incomparably great power is at work within us, and His immeasurably more portion is available to us by faith, and that His divine wisdom, grace, favor, love, and protection are ours as well. So, go ahead: buy the field and gain the treasure that God shows you, and if necessary, sell all you have in order to do so after you have first counted the cost and discerned and determined God's will for you. God has called us to be stewards of His resources, and since He owns the cattle on a thousand hills, and all the gold and silver are His, He is not poor, and His kingdom is not broke. There is a better way, life abundantly through Christ, and it includes financial blessing and prosperity as well as spiritual blessing, salvation, sanctification and eternal life (Gen. 1:26-28; Deut. 8:18; John 10:10; 2 Cor. 9:8; 3 John 2).

In closing, learn to accept and embrace risk, as long as it is calculated, and God is part of the calculation. Risk is the way of life, and the way of the kingdom of Heaven. No risk, no reward. Risk and reward are part of life. Seek wise counsel and use wisdom, discernment and prudence in your decision-making process, and realize that different types and levels of risk may be more appropriate at different stages of life, and different levels of income.

RISK AND REWARD ARE PART OF LIFE IN THE KINGDOM

Pray through your decision thoroughly, count the cost, seek discernment and confirmation of the Lord's will and timing, find the inner witness of peace, and then be bold and courageous to act accordingly. And, don't be afraid of pursuing and receiving a reward. Fear is not from God (2 Tim. 1:7; 1 John 4:18). Heb. 11:6 says, *"But without faith it is impossible to please Him, for he who comes to God must believe that He is, and that He is a rewarder of those who diligently seek Him."* Now we look at healing and health.

HEALTH AND HEALING ARE AVAILABLE ON THE 8TH MOUNTAIN ALSO

Our last section in this chapter is Health & Healing. Since we discussed inner healing in an earlier chapter, we will focus our brief comments on physical healing. There is a German saying: "Man es was man ess." Man is what man eats. This means for the body and the soul and the spirit. Make sure you're eating the word of God; meditate on it day and night. Listen to positive worship music. Create a positive atmosphere in your home as a sanctuary and place of peace, joy, laughter, love, worship, prayer and rest.

Fellowship with light, not darkness. Be careful with what goes in your eyes and ears. Also, be careful with what comes out of your mouth. Think and speak wholesome, healthy words. Phil. 4:8 (AMP) says, *"Finally, believers, whatever is true, whatever is honorable and worthy of respect, whatever is right and confirmed by God's word, whatever is pure and wholesome, whatever is lovely and brings peace, whatever is admirable and of good repute; if there is any excellence, if there is anything worthy of praise, think continually on these things [center your mind on them, and implant them in your heart]."*

The tongue has the power of life and death. Prov. 12:18 states, *"There is one who speaks like the piercings of a sword, But the tongue of the wise promotes health."* Prov. 15:30 adds, *"The light of the eyes rejoices the heart, And a good report makes the bones healthy."* Prov. 16:24 says, *"Pleasant words are like a honeycomb, Sweetness to the soul and health to the bones."*

Sin often brings sickness, and begins a process of spiritual death (Jas. 1:13-15). Psa. 38:3 says, *"There is no soundness in my flesh Because of Your anger, Nor any health in my bones Because of my sin."* Disease can also be caused by heredity and genetic predisposition, germs, viruses, bacteria, insect bites, rodents, and other ways. Honoring the Lord brings health to our bones. Living a holy, righteous life supports health. Prov. 3:7-9 (NKJV) says, *"Do not be wise in your own eyes; Fear the LORD and depart from evil. It will be health to your flesh, And strength to your bones."* We need health for body, soul, and spirit; the body alone isn't enough. Psa. 34:18 notes, *"The LORD is near to those who have a broken heart, And saves such as have a contrite spirit."*

Psa. 28:7 says, *"The Lord is my strength and shield. I trust him with all my heart. He helps me, and my heart is filled with joy. I burst out in songs of thanksgiving."* Neh. 8:10 says, *"Don't be dejected and sad, for the joy of the Lord is your strength!"* When you're feeling down and have no strength, tap into God's joy. Prov. 17:22 (ESV) says, *"A joyful heart is good medicine, but a crushed spirit dries up the bones."* The King James version adds, *"A merry heart doeth good like a medicine: but a broken spirit drieth the bones."* The NET Bible states, *"A cheerful heart brings good healing, but a crushed spirit dries up the bones."* Psa. 126:2 declares, *Then our mouths were filled with laughter; our tongues sang for joy. Then it was said among the nations, "The Lord had done great things for them."* Laughter is a sign of victory and confidence.

Psa. 30:5 (NLT) says, *"For his anger lasts only a moment, but his favor lasts a lifetime! Weeping may last through the night, but joy comes with the morning."* Sorrow is temporary, and transient, but we have access to joy anytime, and should have deep reserves and wells of joy to draw from in our spirit.

Jesus, for the joy set before Him, endured the cross. We are why He endured the cross. We are His joy and He is our joy. His yoke is easy and burden is light. Lay down your problems, burdens and troubles and take up His easy yoke. Labor to enter into His rest. In Matt. 11:30 (NLT) Jesus said, *"For my yoke is easy to bear, and the burden I give you is light."* Don't worry about tomorrow. Let God who set the stars and sun and moon in place, take care of your tomorrow. Rest in Him. He takes care of sparrows; he can handle you.

Matt. 8:17 says Jesus fulfilled that which was spoken by Isaiah the prophet, saying: *"He Himself took our infirmities And bore our sicknesses."* Jesus took our infirmities and sicknesses to the cross and beforehand he was beaten by the Roman soldiers and mocked, and received 39 stripes, which symbolically represents all known major diseases, and the fullness of man's cruelty, violence and judgment into his own body.

Matt. 10:1 adds, *"And when He had called His twelve disciples to Him, He gave them power over unclean spirits, to cast them out, and to heal all kinds of sickness and all kinds of disease."* His same power that Jesus gave to the Twelve, is available to you and me today through the Holy Spirit and by faith, since God is no respecter of persons, and does not play favorites. Gifts of healing is also specifically listed in 1 Cor. 12:9, 30. Pray and ask the Holy Spirit to receive that gift.

Jas. 5:14-16 adds, *"Is anyone among you sick? Let him call for the elders of the church, and let them pray over him, anointing him with oil in the name of the Lord. And the prayer of faith will save the sick, and the Lord will raise him up. And if he has committed sins, he will be forgiven. Confess your trespasses to one another, and pray for one another, that you may be healed. The effective, fervent prayer of a righteous man avails much."* As an elder and apostle, I have prayed for many people over the years and have seen several instantaneous healings of people, including cancers, tumors, blindness and COPD. It is always a joy to see Jesus touch and heal someone through you. Step out in faith and exercise your healing gifts by faith today. Give God someone to work through. All that is required is the simple faith of a child. "Healing is the children's bread." Of course, utilizing the services of gifted doctors, nurses and healthcare professionals can also be beneficial at times. God can move in healing in various ways.

Decree the word of God over yourself as a healing remedy. Psa. 103:1-5 says, *"Bless the Lord, o my soul, and all that is within me bless his holy name."* Stand on the promises of God. Many have gotten healing through reading and meditating on healing Scriptures and not backing down or shying away from the promises of God. Decree God's word over your life. This concludes Chapter 20. Now we turn our attention to destiny and legacy in Chapter 21.

WE HAVE
ACCESS TO JOY
ANYTIME, AND
SHOULD HAVE
DEEP RESERVES
AND WELLS OF
JOY TO DRAW
FROM IN OUR
SPIRIT

TWENTY ONE

DESTINY AND LEGACY

"Now the rest of the acts of Jehu and all that he did and all his might, are they not written in the Book of the Chronicles of the Kings of Israel?"
(2 Kings 10:34, NASB)

"For I know the plans I have for you," declares the Lord, "plans to prosper you and not to harm you, plans to give you hope and a future."
(Jer. 29:11, NIV)

"For if you remain silent at this time, relief and deliverance for the Jews will arise from another place, but you and your father's family will perish. And who knows but that you have come to your royal position for such a time as this?"
(Est. 4:14, NIV)

Only about one third of leaders finish well, according to the writings of several leaders I trust and respect, such as John Maxwell, Os Hillman and the late Dr. C. Peter Wagner and Kent Humphries. God wants us to finish well, and by His grace and divine guidance, we can and will.

Destiny is what God gives to us, and legacy is what we give to God, to our family and friends, and the world. For example, I had a spiritual encounter with Jesus in Jan. 1995. He offered me a choice between a career and a destiny. (These are not always mutually exclusive). I chose a destiny, and He told me that my destiny from Him is to be a bridge builder and connector of His people, and a financier of His kingdom. Within that purpose and destiny, I have had many assignments. Favor is given to our assignments when we are obedient to God.

Legacy acts are defining moments, deeds we are remembered by and for. Moses leading the Israelites safely across the Red Sea and the pursuing Egyptian army being drowned by God, was a turning point for the nation, a memorable event passed down to future generations. David killing Goliath was a legacy act. Joseph interpreting Pharaoh's dream was a legacy act. Daniel receiving 11th hour, just in time help from God and interpreting King Nebuchadnezzar's dream, was a legacy deed. Samson pushing the pillars apart and killing his enemies, the Philistines, in the temple of Dagon, was a legacy act. Jehu having Jezebel thrown out an upper story window to her death was a legacy act. Jael driving a tent peg through the head of Sisera was a legacy deed. Esther standing before King Xerxes uninvited was a legacy act. Elijah facing off with, defeating and killing 850 false prophets of Baal and Asherah on Mount Carmel, was a defining moment. These things forever marked the trajectory and course of their lives, and their nations, and how they were perceived and remembered by others and by history.

Mary, the virgin Jewish teenager from Nazareth saying yes to God and the angel Gabriel, and her willingness to carry in her womb, birth and raise the Christ child, was a legacy moment. A different Mary (variously known as Mary of Bethany or Mary Magdalene), anointing the feet of Jesus with expensive spikenard perfume, was a legacy act. Judas betraying Jesus for 30 pieces of silver and kissing him in the Garden of Gethsemane, was a legacy act. Stephen being the first Christian martyr and being stoned to death by the Jews in Jerusalem because of his testimony and faith in Jesus, was a legacy act. Ananias and Sapphira lying to Peter and the Holy Spirit, was a legacy act that cost them their lives. Jesus being sacrificed (crucified) for our sins and dying on the cross was a legacy act, as well as His resurrection from the dead, and these mighty deeds forever altered the course of history, and the fate of mankind.

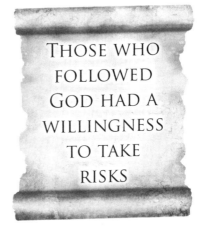

THOSE WHO FOLLOWED GOD HAD A WILLINGNESS TO TAKE RISKS

God's heart for each of us is that we would know the good plans He has for us, know that He has a destiny planned and scripted for our lives, a destiny that will bring us joy and fulfillment, success and satisfaction. He is with us, guiding us and caring for us each and every step of the way. Provisions have been established for us along the road, ready and waiting for us to arrive at each place where

He's provided everything we need for the next season in our lives. His love for us leads the way.

The Bible is filled with stories of men and women, families and nations who lived and died pursuing either God's path or their own way. Each left a legacy recorded in Scripture, some good, some bad. Those who followed God had a willingness to risk and an understanding that God had a plan for them. Throughout the Old and New Testament, there are numerous examples of people who stepped out in faith to do what God was leading them to do.

Many of these people built family dynasties, including good ones and bad ones. Let's take a look at several of these as we process what it means in this day and age to have a divine destiny, and to leave a legacy of what we accomplished, what we stood for and believed, how we lived our lives, and who we discipled and raised up as mature sons and daughters, and as our successor(s).

Hebrews Chapter 11 is known as the Hall of Fame of Faith in the Bible. Listed are a number of men and women who stepped out of the usual, ordinary and expected dimension, and stepped into their destiny through their choice to trust in God. We're going to look at several examples from Hebrews 11. Some were elite and wealthy, some were seemingly nobodies, but all chose to walk with God and they left a legacy of faith. We're going to start with the first recorded instance of a family by looking at Adam and Eve.

ADAM AND EVE

In Genesis chapters 1 and 2, Adam and Eve began well, living their lives as a model of the good life. God gave them a very clear purpose and destiny: have dominion or rulership over all the earth, tend the Garden of Eden, be fruitful and multiply. God planted this garden paradise full of plentiful herbs and plants for food and a mist would come up and water everything in the garden for them. Adam was assigned the job of naming all the animals, speaking and imparting destiny into their lives by virtue of their names, and exhibiting wisdom and understanding. Even more, Adam and Eve walked with the Lord. In a very real way, they were family with God the Father who created them, communing and fellowshipping with each other. Life was good!

One of the things of note in this Genesis record is that Adam and Eve were naked and not ashamed. They were transparent in who they were and how they lived their lives. They had no sin or shame to hide from each other. They lived a beautiful life...until...sin entered the garden through their disobedience. Destiny was shattered, their lives were forever changed, and death entered the earth.

Now, their legacy was one of sweat and toil in the earth and increased pain in childbirth, not only for themselves, but for all who came after them...as well as a legacy of walking with God. Both are realities – one not so pleasant, in fact, painful, and the other, extremely pleasant. Because we sin or fall down and mess up, does not erase the good we do. It may hinder or tarnish or undermine some of it, but it doesn't erase it. Peter walked on water, then started to sink. That he lapsed doesn't take away from the fact that he got out of the boat and walked. He also denied the Lord three times in one night, but Jesus forgave and restored him. Together Adam and Eve birthed all of mankind. They are our father and mother, genealogically speaking, and though they fell, we need to honor their memory just as we honor our own father and mother.

In God's grace and mercy, God gives a destiny of the seed of the woman crushing the head of the serpent, fulfilled in Jesus, our Lord. *"And I will put enmity Between you and the woman, And between your seed and her Seed; He shall bruise your head, And you shall bruise His heel"* (Gen. 3:15, NKJV).

We battle sin because Adam and Eve disobeyed God and their legacy and generational inheritance of sin carried forward. To destroy the death that held mankind captive, Jesus had to redeem us through His perfect life; in context, he was the second and final Adam, and through His death and resurrection, we have the promise of eternal life – *"For as in Adam all die, so in Christ all will be made alive"* (1 Cor. 15:22, NIV). Later in that same chapter we read, *So it is written: "The first man Adam became a living being"; the last Adam, a life-giving spirit"* (1 Cor. 15:45 NIV).

ABRAHAM AND SARAH, ISAAC, AND JACOB

Abraham had an amazing relationship with God and he was blessed beyond imagination. God spoke to him and told him to leave his home and go to a new place that God would show him and Abraham got up and went.

"When Abram was ninety-nine years old, the Lord appeared to Abram and said to him, "I am Almighty God; walk before Me and be blameless. And I will make My covenant between Me and you, and will multiply you exceedingly." Then Abram fell on his face, and God talked with him, saying: "As for Me, behold, My covenant is with you, and you shall be a father of many nations.

No longer shall your name be called Abram, but your name shall be Abraham; for I have made you a father of many nations. I will make you exceedingly fruitful; and I will make nations of you, and kings shall come from you. And I will establish My covenant between Me and you and your descendants after you in their generations, for an everlasting covenant, to be God to you and your descendants after you. Also I give to you and your descendants after you the land in which you are a stranger, all the land of Canaan, as an everlasting possession; and I will be their God" (Gen. 17:1-8, NKJV).

Sarah also walked in faith conceiving Isaac at the age of 90. Read Gen. chapters 11-23 through the eyes of Sarah and you'll be surprised at what this woman went through and how she hung on through faith and bore her son, Isaac. Heb. 11:11 (NKJV) records, *"By faith Sarah herself also received strength to conceive seed, and she bore a child when she was past the age, because she judged Him faithful who had promised."*

We looked at Gen. 22:16-18 in Chapter 14 where God told Abraham that because of his obedience, *"I will surely bless you and make your descendants as numerous as the stars in the sky and as the sand on the seashore. Your descendants will take possession of the cities of their enemies, and through your offspring all nations on earth will be blessed, because you have obeyed me."*

Abraham was blessed with immense wealth. He had servants and people enough that he was able to battle three kings of three nations at one time and win! His son, Isaac, who continued the family business, increased so much that potential wars flared up over water rights for his flocks. Jacob served his Uncle Laban to secure Laban's daughters as his wives and God prospered him so much that eventually he had more livestock than his uncle. God preserved him and pursued him until Jacob, whose name was changed to Israel, became the father of the 12 tribes of Israel.

They each walked out a huge destiny. They each left a legacy of walking with God, of receiving promises and

THEY EACH LEFT A LEGACY OF WALKING WITH GOD

blessings of a magnitude that is difficult to understand in this day and age. They each left a legacy of the promises of God passed on to their children and great wealth as an inheritance.

Abraham, Isaac, and Jacob are mentioned together 33 times in the Bible (NKJV). Abraham, Isaac and Israel are mentioned 7 times for a total of 40 times in the Bible. It was to the God of Abraham, Isaac, and Israel that Elijah identified with and prayed to in front of all of Israel and 850 enemy prophets with Jezebel. God answered with fire from Heaven, consuming the offering and turning Israel back to God (1 Kings 18:36-39). This family – Abraham, Sarah, Isaac, and Jacob – birthed a nation that worshipped God. Abraham's legacy continues today as we who are Christians are counted into his family and seed through faith in Jesus Christ.

ELIJAH

Elijah challenged and rebuked the people of Israel in 1 Kings 18:21 (NIV). *Elijah went before the people and said, "How long will you waver between two opinions? If the Lord is God, follow him; but if Baal is God, follow him." But the people said nothing.* The MSG version says, *Elijah challenged the people:*

"How long are you going to sit on the fence? If God is the real God, follow him; if it's Baal, follow him. Make up your minds!" Nobody said a word; nobody made a move. So, Elijah arranged for a public demonstration of God's power and sovereignty to turn the people's hearts back to God.

And it came to pass, at the time of the offering of the evening sacrifice, that Elijah the prophet came near and said, "Lord God of Abraham, Isaac, and Israel, let it be known this day that You are God in Israel and I am Your servant, and that I have done all these things at Your word. Hear me, O Lord, hear me, that this people may know that You are the Lord God, and that You have turned their hearts back to You again. Then the fire of the Lord fell and consumed the burnt sacrifice, and the wood and the stones and the dust, and it licked up the water that was in the trench. Now when all the people saw it, they fell on their faces; and they said, "The Lord, He is God! The Lord, He is God!" (1 Kings 18:36-39, NKJV).

Then Elijah slew (put to death) the 850 false prophets of Baal and Asherah who served at Jezebel's table, with help from the people. Elijah's servant Elisha later received his mantle as he was taken into heaven, and went on to do twice as many miracles as Elijah during his lifetime.

RAHAB

Clearly, God is no respecter of persons. Heb. 11:30-31 (NIV) says, *"By faith the walls of Jericho fell, after the army had marched around them for seven days. By faith the prostitute Rahab, because she welcomed the spies, was not killed with those who were disobedient."*

Joshua sent two spies into Jericho and they found lodging with Rahab the prostitute. The King of Jericho found out that the spies were staying with her and ordered Rahab to give them up. That's a pretty scary situation to have the King find out you're harboring enemy spies. She knew the risk she was taking and she did it anyway. By doing so, she served God by helping in the taking of Jericho and she saved her whole family and earned her spot in Hebrews 11.

RUTH

The Book of Ruth is one of my favorite stories in the Bible. When I need encouragement, I tuck myself into the book of Ruth and read about this woman of Moab who was widowed and how she and her mother-in-law Naomi made their way to Naomi's old home in Bethlehem. The trip would have been quite risky, two women alone, but they made it. They had nothing left and Ruth took the risk of going out into the fields to forage for grain. The Lord led her to the field of a wealthy landowner named Boaz where she picked up fallen grain in the corners of the field and brought home enough food for her and Naomi. She was a foreigner in the land and things could have gone very bad, very quickly. But, this sweet woman had favor with God who gave her favor with Boaz and she soon found herself with more than enough grain for her and Naomi plus protection in the fields where she gathered grain. The story progressed and in time, Boaz married Ruth and together they had a son, Obed, who became the grandfather of King David.

Seemingly a nobody, Ruth was poor, a foreigner, and widowed, but she loved her mother-in-law and wouldn't leave her. She took risk after risk and became the great grandmother of King David. There's no way she could have known this was her destiny or that she would have the legacy of her kindness and goodness and faithfulness as a book in the Bible. All she did was love and continue to love as she cared for her mother-in-law Naomi and followed the path laid out for her by the Lord.

KING DAVID

King David's life is one of the best known in the Bible for good reason. David went from being a shepherd watching sheep to King of all Israel and Judah, subduing every nation around them. His son, King Solomon, was the wealthiest and wisest man ever. And, from David's offspring, came Jesus, son of David.

The Lord anointed David to be King of Israel as a young man but it was 20 years before he would see that come to pass fully – 13 years for one kingdom, and another 7 years for a united Israel. He was diligent in doing the thing in front of him whether it was tending sheep or slaying giants. Over time and a lot of battles, David became King and David earnestly desired to build the temple of God, but it wasn't to be. So, what did he do? He gathered all of the materials – the wood, stone, gold, silver, brass, gemstones, and everything that would be needed to build and furnish the temple – and stored it up for his son, Solomon. That's a pretty

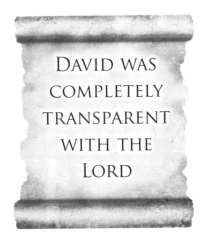

DAVID WAS COMPLETELY TRANSPARENT WITH THE LORD

good inheritance along with all the wealth that David had accrued along the way.

One of the most quoted legacies of David is that he was known as "a man after God's own heart." David loved God with every fiber of his being. You can see his heart in the psalms he wrote. He laid everything before the Lord – praises and laments, despair and trust, joy and weeping; David held nothing back. In a sense, David was completely transparent with the Lord, much like Adam and Ever before the fall.

"[Prayer and Thanksgiving for the Lord's Righteous Judgments] [To the Chief Musician. To the tune of "Death of the Son." A Psalm of David.] *I will praise You, O Lord, with my whole heart; I will tell of all Your marvelous works*" (Psa. 9:1, NKJV).

"[God the Sovereign Savior] [To the Chief Musician. A Psalm of David the servant of the Lord, who spoke to the Lord the words of this song on the day that the Lord delivered him from the hand of all his enemies and from the hand of Saul. And he said:] *I will love You, O Lord, my strength*" (Psa. 18:1, NKJV).

GOD'S GOOD PLANS

In the Book of Jeremiah, we see that the nation of Judah had wandered away from the Lord, bit by bit getting farther away from their covenant and deeper into idol worship, and forsaking God's commandments. Babylon invaded and conquered them and they were taken away as captives and slaves. Jer. 29:11 is set in the middle of a description of the woes that Israel is experiencing and is a ray of hope in a very dark situation. *"For I know the plans I have for you,"* declares the Lord, *"plans to prosper you and not to harm you, plans to give you hope and a future"* (NIV).

The Lord told the people to settle in where they were and to plant vineyards and build their families, let their children get married, live their lives in Babylon, and in 70 years He would return them to their homeland. For God had good plans for them. Sure enough, 70 years later, they were able to return to their homeland.

These same words apply to us today. God has a plan for our lives, a good plan to prosper us, and not to harm us, to give us hope and a future. We have so many promises from God throughout the Bible. We may be in a dungeon, like Joseph, or we may be in captivity to circumstances that surround us, but Joseph, great grandson of Abraham, was promoted to the palace in a single day. God has a plan for our lives, a purpose for our lives, and hope for our future. He has written destiny in our Book of Heaven before we were even born. Job wisely commented, *"I know that You can do everything, and that no purpose of Yours can be withheld from You"* (Job 42:2, NKJV).

Rom. 8:28 (NKJV) says, *"And we know that all things work together for good to those who love God, to those who are the called according to His purpose."* There's no one better than our God at accomplishing His purposes in our lives. He is the Master Architect, Designer, Engineer and Planner all in one. If we will trust Him and follow His way instead of our own, He will bring and/or lead us into His good and perfect plan for our lives.

JESUS

Jesus inherited from his Heavenly Father a world that was sick and dying – a world that needed him desperately, yet rejected him and turned their backs on him. He came to a people who had earnestly looked for Him, expecting Him for centuries, and somehow missed Him when He came. And yet, His destiny was to live a life of kindness, forgiveness, and determination to spend His life on the very ones who rejected Him, paying the ultimate price of death on the cross in order to be raised up, conquering death and securing our destiny in Himself.

John 3:17 (NASB) says, *"For God did not send the Son into the world to judge the world, but that the world might be saved through Him."* In salvation, we are now the children of God, brought into His family through faith. We are heirs of God and co-heirs with Jesus Christ. We have an inheritance of love and life everlasting, of a kingdom without end. There is no way to measure how great this is in our lives. It is infinite.

God chose to birth Jesus through a young woman of the lineage of David. David's legacy would continue on through Jesus, son of David. *Then the multitudes who went before and those who followed cried out, saying: "Hosanna to the Son of David! 'Blessed is He who comes in the name of the Lord!' Hosanna in the highest!"* (Matt. 21:9, NKJV).

Jesus, in turn, left us with the greatest legacy of all, complete and utter redemption of our lives, his life for ours, paid forward to all who will believe on His name. In His life, we find examples of how to live our lives in righteousness and truth. In His love and mercy, we find forgiveness of sins. In His grace and goodness, we find the power, the ability, to be more than conquerors in this life because He is in us, working in us and with us to reach our full potential and achieve our destiny. Only through Jesus and the Holy Spirit can we find our true purpose in life and live it to the fullest. Rom. 8:37 (NKJV) says, *"Yet in all these things we are more than conquerors through Him who loved us."*

In Jesus, we have a great destiny and legacy available to us. We have an inheritance from Abraham through faith in Jesus, Hebrews 11. We have the legacy of the early church and what they accomplished. We have a call, a destiny, that is both corporate to the Church and individual to saints based on the callings and gifts we've received from God. We have an unimaginable inheritance of life everlasting with God.

WHO WE ARE

Eph. 4:15-16 (NASB) says, *"But speaking the truth in love, we are to grow up in all aspects into Him who is the head, even Christ, from whom the whole body, being fitted and held together by what every joint supplies, according to the proper working of each individual part, causes the growth of the body for the building up of itself in love."*

For the human body to function at peak performance, every part has to be present, and functional, doing its part and doing it well. We are all part of the body of Christ. We have a function, a job, and it's important. Every part depends on every other part.

"But now indeed there are many members, yet one body. And the eye cannot say to the hand, "I have no need of you"; nor again

the head to the feet, "I have no need of you" (1 Cor. 12:20-21, NKJV).

No part is more important than another. Each is necessary for the proper working of the body and God gives honor to all parts, regardless of the placement in the body.

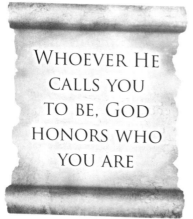

WHOEVER HE CALLS YOU TO BE, GOD HONORS WHO YOU ARE

Whoever He called you to be, God honors who you are and is proud of you, His child, the one He created in love, adoring you as a doting parent. Receive this, His love and His purpose for you into your heart, into your being.

You have a purpose for your life, a destiny; you're needed and you're wanted by God and by your family in Christ Jesus. It doesn't matter how big or how small, everyone is needed and every part is necessary.

And, you don't have to be a mom or dad to fulfill your destiny! There are many examples in the Bible of single people and childless people who have great destinies and legacies, including a number of prophets, like the prophetess Anna who waited for the day Jesus was presented in the Temple; many are called out in the New Testament for their service and devotion to Jesus. Mary and Martha were single women who loved and served Jesus.

"Sing, barren woman, you who never bore a child; burst into song, shout for joy, you who were never in labor; because more are the children of the desolate woman than of her who has a husband," says the Lord. "Enlarge the place of your tent, stretch

your tent curtains wide, do not hold back; lengthen your cords, strengthen your stakes. For you will spread out to the right and to the left; your descendants will dispossess nations and settle in their desolate cities" (Isa. 54:1-3, NIV).

There are many single saints today who have devoted themselves in this same way and have many spiritual sons and daughters who they've discipled and raised up in the Lord, who then go on to live lives of faith, work and destiny, and eventually leave their own legacy.

YOU ARE COMMISSIONED

Matt. 28:18-20 (NIV) states, *Then Jesus came to them and said, "All authority in heaven and on earth has been given to me. Therefore go and make disciples of all nations, baptizing them in the name of the Father and of the Son and of the Holy Spirit, and teaching them to obey everything I have commanded you. And surely I am with you always, to the very end of the age."*

This is the global commissioning Jesus leaves with us – go disciple nations. He gives us new life, a calling, authority, purpose and power to do all that He directs us to do. He leaves us with everything we need (and more than we know what to do with at times!)

Your destiny today is to fulfill the call of God on your life, and to be faithful and excellent in your assignments, and honorable, humble, peaceful and loving in your relationships. Then you will have a legacy for this life, and for eternity. This is the most exciting time ever in creation and now is the time to live in boldness, faith, zeal and confidence in our God.

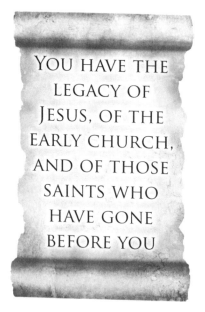

YOU HAVE THE LEGACY OF JESUS, OF THE EARLY CHURCH, AND OF THOSE SAINTS WHO HAVE GONE BEFORE YOU

You have the legacy of Jesus, the legacy of the early church, the legacy of the saints who have gone before you. And, through Jesus, you have a Father in Heaven who sees you, knows you, loves you, and has plans for you in the Family Kingdom Business. You have a place in His Business and it's important or you wouldn't be here, now, in this time and season. Your job, your life's work, is to fulfill the call of God on your life.

Who you are and where you are right now is your gateway into the new thing that God is doing here on earth. Step in. Step into the place He's planned and ordained for you. Trust Him to lead you in His path of truth and righteousness for your life. This mountain before you looks steep when you begin but as you go, He will lift you up onto the high places and bring you into the new heights He designed for you before your life began. He will teach you to fly!

Trust God. Invest your very life in Him. He is faithful and He will finish the good work that He has begun in you. You will live your destiny to the fullest as an 8th Mountain climber and summiteer – part of a growing global community. *"Being confident of this very thing, that He who has begun a good work in you will complete it until the day of Jesus Christ"* (Phil. 1:6, NKJV). You will also leave a powerful and dynamic legacy to your family and friends, associates and colleagues, the next generation and the world!

EPILOGUE

The 8th Mountain is calling your name. You've read about what awaits you, and what lies ahead on this trek to the spiritual summit. You can think of this book as your mountaineering school curriculum and training manual for the 8th Mountain, to educate, train and prepare you for climbing, and reaching the summit, of the highest peak in the universe. It teaches you survival skills, how to thrive and be successful, how to work as a team, how to ascend and descend, how to avoid or minimize danger, what gear and supplies to take, how to monitor changing weather conditions, and how to save your life and protect yourself and those around you in the harsh climate, adverse conditions, and unforgiving environment of the 7 Mountains of Culture.

God wants to meet with you, and is available now. He is Omniscient, Omnipotent, and Omnipresent – which means, All Knowing, All Powerful, and All Present. God can be many places at once, or everywhere at once. He can have multiple conversations with different people at the same time. And, He's interested in you. In fact, He's wildly, passionately, hopelessly in love with you, and thinks you're really cool, awesome and amazing. He actually thinks you're powerful and anointed and special and uniquely gifted and qualified. He also thinks you're fun and He would like to hang out with you and spend time together, and have you get to know Him as well as He knows you.

And, He sees a bright future and hope for you, no matter what your present circumstance or situation looks like.

He's right, of course. And, we at 8thMountain.com happen to agree with Him. We invite you to join us on a journey, and help us build a global community of 8th Mountain climbers and summiteers, who we call IdeaLeaders, to invade and transform the 7 Mountains of Culture. We would love to meet you, hear your story, get to know you, and find out your assignment and destiny, and the God-inspired ideas you are stewarding, and the innovation and distinction and glory you are bringing to the world in your sphere of influence, and in your Mountain(s) of Culture. Come visit and connect with us at https://8thMountain.com. And, if you have any feedback on this book, or want to contact the author, you can reach him via email at brucecook77@gmail.com.

Just as Mount Everest is the highest point on earth, the 8th Mountain – the Mountain of the Lord – is the highest point in the universe, and is heaven itself. The old saying, "It's lonely at the top" doesn't apply here. There's no reason to be lonely on the 8th Mountain, and lots of reasons to be fulfilled and satisfied – full of joy and peace and love – and there's a whole community of fellow climbers for you to meet and get to know. Some are more experienced than others, and are at different levels of skill and knowledge and physical and spiritual conditioning, but we're all still learning and growing, and are on a journey that will last for a lifetime, and an eternity. We hope that you will join us, and we invite you to do so.

For those of you who may not yet know Christ Jesus as your Lord and Savior, and would like to, it's really simple.

Rom. 10:9-10 (NKJV) says, *"That if you confess with your mouth the Lord Jesus and believe in your heart that God has raised Him from the dead, you will be saved. For with the heart one believes unto righteousness, and with the mouth confession is made unto salvation."* Ask Jesus to come into your heart now, repent of your sins, ask him to forgive you and to fill you with His Holy Spirit, and confess His name as your Lord and Savior.

For those who prayed that prayer of faith, welcome to the kingdom and the family of God.

ABOUT THE AUTHOR

Bruce Cook, Ph.D., is an ordained minister and a commissioned apostle and prophet and has significant experience in business consulting, fundraising, private equity investments, business development, marketing, corporate communications, branding, media relations, advertising, and higher education and is considered a leading authority on private equity, fundraising, publishing, corporate finance, marketplace ministry and philanthropy. He is a frequent speaker for conferences, seminars and workshops, resides in the Seattle, Washington area, and is married with two grown sons and two granddaughters.

He is the Chairman & CEO of VentureAdvisers.com Inc., Kingdom House Publishing, and Kingdom Congressional International Alliance (KCIA). In addition, he is a director or trustee of WorkLife, The Glory House Ministries, Indigenous People's Foundation, Family Church of Gig Harbor, and Kingdom Economic Yearly Summit (KEYS). In 2015 he received the Distinguished Leadership Award from I Change Nations and was designated an Honorary Ambassador by Golden Rule International.

Earlier in his career Cook was Research Coordinator for the University of Texas Investment Management Company (UTIMCO), where he was a member of the Private Markets team responsible for alternative asset investments totaling over $500 million per year, and in aggregate, several billion dollars. Prior to that he was Assistant Manager of the largest bank in Arkansas, Worthen Bank, now owned by

Bank of America, and was responsible for $10M daily in transactions.

Dr. Cook is an author, ordained minister, and contemporary Christian songwriter and producer. His CDs include *Songs in the Night* (2003), *Daddy's in the House* (2004) and *Wealth of the Kingdom* (co-producer, 2008); *Seven Mountain Symphony: Transforming the 7 Mountains of Culture* was a two-disc set released in 2009 (co-producer).

He is the author of *Partnering with the Prophetic* (2011, 2014) and also completed a five-volume apostolic anthology titled *Aligning with the Apostolic: An Anthology of Apostleship* (2013), for which he served as General Editor and wrote Volume One. Several other books are currently in process dealing with finance, economics, and business.

To contact him:

- brucecook77@gmail.com
- www.kcialliance.org
- office@kcialliance.org